George Eliot

A BIOGRAPHY

Also by Rosemary Sprague

BIOGRAPHY

Forever in Joy:
The Life of Robert Browning

NOVELS

Red Lion and Gold Dragon
The Jade Pagoda
Fife and Fandango
Dance for a Diamond Star
Conquerors of Time
Heir of Kiloran
Heroes of the White Shield
A Kingdom to Win
Northward to Albion

Poems of Robert Browning (Edited)

George Eliot

A BIOGRAPHY BY

ROSEMARY SPRAGUE

CHILTON BOOK COMPANY

Philadelphia   New York   London

FOR John Francis Marion

ACKNOWLEDGMENTS

I would like to thank the Yale University Press for permission to quote from *George Eliot and John Chapman* by Gordon Haight and also for permission to quote from *The George Eliot Letters.* I am also grateful to The Macmillan Company for permission to quote from *George Eliot* by Walter Allen and to John Day Company, Inc., for permission to quote from *George Lewes and George Eliot* by Anna T. Kitchel.

I would also like to thank Charles Scribner's Sons for permission to quote from *Notes on Novelists* by Henry

James and Columbia University Press to quote from *Nineteenth Century Studies* by Basil Willey.

In Great Britain I wish to thank Chatto & Windus, Ltd., for permission to quote from *Nineteenth Century Studies* by Basil Willey and from *The Great Tradition* by F. R. Leavis, and the Manchester University Press for permission to quote from *The Early Life of George Eliot* by Mary Deakin.

INTRODUCTION

A biographer of George Eliot, searching for source materials, is at first glance confronted by an *embarras de richesses*. In addition to the selections from her letters and journals, published in 1885 by her husband, John Walter Cross, the recent seven-volume edition of her letters, magnificently edited by Gordon S. Haight is also available besides several additional studies covering specific periods of her life. And there is the constantly increasing number of critical works devoted to examining the various phases of her writing career. Such amplitude should, seemingly, make the biographer's task a comparatively simple one.

But a thorough examination of these sources quickly dispels such easy assumptions. They are reminiscent of the comment made by an after-dinner speaker in humorous rebuttal to a criticism of an earlier speech, to the effect that the criticism reminded him equally of the Mother Hubbard style of dress which covered everything and touched nothing, and of the present-day style of feminine attire which touched everything and covered nothing!

It is a documented fact that George Eliot did not want her biography to be written. She resolutely refused all requests during her lifetime, and took every possible precaution against any posthumous work being written. When, because of the enormous popularity of her works and the concomitant interest they aroused in her life, John Walter Cross finally was persuaded to do a biographical study, he followed her wishes as he understood them by including only those facets of her life which he felt she would not mind having made public; and he was also, admittedly, handicapped by her having destroyed almost all the letters she had received, and by the reticence of her friends in those years immediately following her death. In consequence, his biography—and, to an extent, even the seven volumes of letters—suffer from one-sidedness, though the latter has had the benefit of Chapman, Lewes, and Blackwood material of which Cross knew practically nothing. Nevertheless, the sources are quite as remarkable for what they do *not* tell us about George Eliot as for what they do, and for some areas of her life there simply are no facts, as the present computer age defines them. In this biography, therefore, I have followed the procedure of using primary sources to the fullest extent possible, and such secondary sources as have received the warrant of sound scholarship, or genuine knowledge, or both; but I have not denied myself the privilege of a few surmises and suggestions, based on those sources, plainly labeled as such.

As far as criticism is concerned, no one working in the field of Victorian literature can be unaware of the plethora of books and articles about George Eliot. "Keeping up with scholarship" is a *sine qua non* of life in academe. But critical debate and difference of opinion which may enliven a scholarly meeting, or permit adversaries to cross pens in the Learned Journals, can often generate more heat than light and consequently confuse the issue. Besides, George Eliot wrote her novels to be read, not to be used as specimens for dissection in an age where even the elementary-school child is encouraged to favor an author with his own ideas of the kind of book which he (the author) should have written. So I have deliberately avoided all published critical opinion in this biography, with the exception of Dr. F. R. Leavis's brilliant paragraph about *Middlemarch,* without which no analysis of that novel could be complete. All other critical comment herein is my own, set down after a careful study—and a joyous rediscovery—of George Eliot, with the hope that this approach may send new readers to her books, through which she also gave to the world her biography.

ROSEMARY SPRAGUE

November 22, 1967

George Eliot

A BIOGRAPHY

I

In the year 1819, in the aftermath of disillusion following England's spectacular victory over Napoleon Bonaparte at Waterloo, two special children were born, both little girls. Beyond her own immediate family circle, neither occasioned any special excitement at the time. The first of them, Alexandrina Victoria, was born at Kensington Palace on May 24th, the niece of the then Prince Regent, who within a few months would ascend the throne as King George IV; and the second was Mary Ann Evans, whose arrival on November 22nd at South Farm, Arbury,

Warwickshire, at five in the morning, was carefully noted by her father in the pages of his diary. It is a matter of record that no one, in 1819, realized that the infant princess would one day reign over England as Her Majesty, Queen Victoria. And certainly no one in the Evans household remotely suspected that Mary Ann, asleep in the cradle beside her mother's bed, would ultimately exert as profound an influence upon her time as that of her sovereign, as the novelist "George Eliot."

It has been said that genius arises out of external conflicts with a tumultuous environment, but one looks in vain for this factor in the childhood of Mary Ann Evans. No place on earth could have seemed more peaceful than rural Warwickshire in the early nineteenth century. South Farm, part of the beautiful Arbury Estate for which Robert Evans was agent (or manager, to use the contemporary term) was not far from the King's Highway connecting the towns of Coventry and Nuneaton, but the only communication between these two towns was the stagecoach which ran twice a day, coming and going. There were no railroads, no telegraph wires, no telephones. Houses were remote from each other; an invitation to dinner, usually served around two in the afternoon, was interpreted by guests as an invitation to "come early and spend the day"—a custom reflected in the gathering of the Dodson family at Dorlcote Mill in *The Mill on the Floss.* Except for the new and not very popular threshing machines, farms were unmechanized. Trees were felled and sawed into boards by hand. Cows were milked and butter was churned by hand. Fruit was picked as it ripened in the summer, and the kitchens were filled with busy women "putting up" preserves and making wines and vinegars. Even children picked herbs and beans for drying. The land supported them, and when prices for crops were low for a particular year, or if a crop failed altogether, at least shelter and enough food could be provided until opportunity came with the spring to begin again. Families like the Evanses prided themselves on their ability to weather bad times. Financial failure, bankruptcy, was considered a disgrace to be avoided at all cost, whatever the sacrifice. Family pride demanded that a man work to his utmost, and in addition be thrifty and prudent; that his wife feel secure in his ability to provide for her; that his children be educated and married advantageously, if possible never below their station. Such a man had the respect of his neighbors, and need bow his head to no one except his king and his God.

Robert Evans, Mary Ann's father, was just such a man. He was of yeoman stock, the class commonly spoken of as "the backbone of England." As a boy he had been trained to carry on the family business of carpentering and building, which had been long established at Roston Common, Derbyshire, but he was not content with just carpentering. After his day's work, he attended night classes conducted at the village school in reading and mathematics, and by study and observation he also became an expert in forestry. It was said of him later that he could tell simply by looking at a tree how many board feet it would yield, and he was also one of the few men of his time who recognized the need for replenishing the forests as the trees were cut down. This led him to study other types of agriculture, and his ability and interest eventually attracted the notice of Francis Newdigate. At the age of twenty-six, he was made manager of the New-digate estate; in 1806, when Squire Newdigate inherited the Arbury estate and moved to Warwickshire, Robert Evans accompanied him. Here he soon became much relied upon for his judgment and for his never-failing fairness in business matters, and respected for his knowledge as well. Though he had come to Warwickshire as a stranger, and county society was notably inclined to be reserved toward anyone not born in its midst at least five generations back, he was well liked by his neighbors. He was orthodox in his religious beliefs, definitely "church" and not "chapel," and, quite as important, conservative in politics. It was in such an environment that the novelist George Eliot lived during what psychologists term the most impressionable years of her life. In her last book, *The Impressions of Theophrastus Such,* the hero, in speaking of his father, reflects her affection and admiration for her own:

> To my father's mind, the noisy teachers of revolutionary doctrine were, to speak it mildly, a variable mixture of the fool and scoundrel; the welfare of the nation lay in a strong Government which could maintain order; and I was accustomed to hear him utter the word "Government" in a tone that charged it with awe, and made it part of my effective religion, in contrast with the word "rebel" which seemed to carry the stamp of evil in its syllables, and, lit by the fact that Satan was the first rebel, made an argument dispensing with more detailed inquiry.

In the year 1819, a man in Robert Evans's position would have found any other political affiliation quite impossible. He had accomplished all he had by hard work. He had been a boy of sixteen when revolution brought France to chaos, and as a young man he had witnessed the rise and fall of Napoleon Bonaparte. The victory at Waterloo had been won only three years before Mary Ann's birth. He was firmly convinced that the revolution had not been a spontaneous uprising of the French peasants, but had been deliberately engineered and maneuvered, if not originally contrived, by a small group of power-hungry individuals, far worse intentioned in their cruelty and avidity than the Bourbon monarchs had been. As for Napoleon—Robert Evans could have been one of the tens of thousands who at first had praised the Little Corporal for restoring order to France, but for the dictator who had plunged an entire continent into war, and had forced England to send her own men to die in France and Spain, he had nothing but contempt.

Events in his own country, too, were causing him no little concern, for the same kind of agitators who had aroused the French mobs had been at work in England since 1815; there had been constant upheavals in both agricultural and manufacturing districts. Wealthy landowners, because of the war, had increased their crops; when peace came, there was too much corn and wheat on the market, and prices plummeted disastrously. In protest against allowing the grain to be sold at low prices, the farm workers marched into the fields with torches and set the grain afire, at the same time wrecking the threshing machines. The estate owners, faced with enormously high taxes, often lost their holdings entirely, for, because of the resultant financial crisis, the banks had no money to lend. At the same time, the mill owners suffered, for English sheep could not supply enough wool to meet their needs, and the mill owners could not pay the high tariffs on imported wool and cotton lobbied through Parliament by the landowners.

Workers, thrown out of their jobs, marched on the factories and destroyed the machines; owners, unable to pay taxes and replace their equipment, lost their mills. To make matters worse, thousands of soldiers arriving home from the wars increased the ranks of the unemployed. There were processions and demonstrations, and mass meetings where fiery orators like Henry Hunt in-

5

cited audiences to force acceptance of their demands, by violence, if necessary. Arbury Farm had not been too affected by the general unrest, though in July 1819 there had been a meeting at Birmingham, roughly twenty miles away, which twenty-five thousand people had attended to demand universal male suffrage and extended land reforms; and on August 16th, nearly fifty thousand had gathered at St. Peter's Fields in Manchester to listen to another inflammatory speech by Henry Hunt. There had been persistent rumors for weeks that secret military exercises were being conducted in the fields by night; it was generally understood that a mob in London had ransacked the gunsmiths' shops for weapons and had even tried to take possession of the armory at the Tower. The Government sent a company of hussars to Manchester to maintain order; the result was appalling violence. Before order finally was restored, eleven men had died and over two hundred had been wounded. The "Peterloo Massacre"—so called in ironic parody of Waterloo—only raised the anger of mobs throughout England to fever pitch, forcing the Government to apply against all public assemblies the most stringent and coercive measures ever known in that country's history.

All this upheaval, however, still seemed far and remote at Arbury Farm, for Robert Evans, as was customary at that time, seldom voiced his concern over matters outside his home. Home was not only his castle; it was also a sanctuary where wife and children were to be protected as much as possible from the wickedness and evil in the outside world. Not that Mrs. Robert Evans would have been averse to expressing an opinion on such political "goings on," had one occurred to her. Like Mrs. Poyser of *Adam Bede,* she would have been loath to deny any receptive ear the benefit of her notably sensible observations on

6

any subject whatsoever. She had been born Christiana Pearson, and she was Robert Evans's second wife. Her family had stayed on the land instead of "going into trade," as had the Evans family, so her social position at the time of her marriage was considered a little higher than that of her husband, especially since her three sisters, who all lived in the neighborhood, had married substantial business men. Undoubtedly, the Pearson family served as a model for the Dodson family in *The Mill on the Floss*. As a child, Mary Ann must have heard quite as much about the Pearson claim to superiority as did Maggie Tulliver about the Dodson. Not that Christiana Evans could be considered a snob—family pride was considered a virtue in those days, and family accomplishments were held up as examples and standards if they were of that caliber, or duly castigated if they fell short. She was a shrewd, practical woman, an excellent wife, a devoted mother to her own three children—Christiana, Isaac, and Mary Ann—and to Robert and Frances Lucy, the children of her husband's first marriage. Like Robert, she wanted the best for them all, and if, in the process of their upbringing, she resorted frequently to reproof and chastisement, this was done only as her "plain duty." Certainly, all five children loved her dearly.

It may have been Christiana Evans who managed the family move from South Farm to Griff House, a large red brick residence on the Arbury estate. If, indeed, there was "a considerable dash of the Mrs. Poyser vein in her," [1] it is not difficult to imagine her reminding her husband that his position had advanced considerably— he was now manager of four other estates besides Arbury —and pointing out that he therefore deserved a more imposing home than South Farm, comfortable though that might be. Also, she really had not recovered her health

7

as rapidly as might be wished after Mary Ann's birth, and Griff House was actually on the King's Highway, easier for a doctor to reach. Too, Isaac, three years older than his baby sister, would soon be ready to begin his education, and there was a good Dame's School directly across the road. These, and doubtless other equally practical reasons, made Robert Evans decide to move to Griff House when Mary Ann was about four months old. It was also at this time that he sent his eldest son, Robert, then seventeen, back to Kirk Hallam as agent for that property under his direction, and his eldest daughter, Frances Lucy, went with her brother to manage his house. That a boy of seventeen should have been responsible enough for such an undertaking may sound hardly believable to twentieth-century ears, but in 1819 seventeen was already man's estate, and Robert Evans had trained and prepared his son for this position with utmost care.

It was at Griff House that Mary Ann grew up, and it was Griff House and the surrounding countryside that so etched itself on her memory that, when she finally became George Eliot the novelist, she possessed the gift of total recall. The garden stretched into the open fields where she romped and played and tore her frocks; the canal, where lazy barges moved slowly from Coventry to Oxford and back again, flowed quietly at the bottom of the fields, a perfect place for a little girl to fish when her brother condescended to let her accompany him. From the distance she could see the oaks and the elms that had survived the general destruction of Shakespeare's Forest of Arden; there the gypsies camped, and once Mary Ann ran away to join them. They brought her back to Griff safely, much to her relief. On rainy days there was a long, low-raftered attic for her to play in; the attic was also her refuge where she hid her storms of tears after being punished. She had a wooden doll, on which she used to take out her rages by driving nails into its head—a picture of Jael and Sisera was the inspiration for this action —and then, when her temper was spent, she would hold the doll and sing to it, in recompense for having hurt it.

She was a tempestuous, passionate child, and she resisted to the uttermost all efforts to make a little lady out of her. Her light brown hair hung in ringlets over her shoulders like a pony's mane, and she was always losing her hair ribbons and handkerchiefs; tearing the lace on her petticoats; muddying her shoes in her rambles over the fields. She was the complete antithesis of her proper, well-behaved elder sister, Chrissey. Her mother frequently asked plaintively why she could not be more like Chrissey. Why, for instance, could she not watch the daily coach from her bedroom window, if she was so set upon seeing it, since her room overlooked the front lawn and the road beyond? But Mary Ann found it more exciting to run down to the gate with Isaac—and have a swing on it for good measure—while the heavy coach rattled by, almost near enough to touch, and to watch and then wait until the sound of the galloping horses with their jingling harness died away as they turned the bend in the road. Sometimes the coach would even stop with mail for Griff House; then Mary Ann would catch a glimpse of the passengers through the tiny windows— gentlemen with tall hats, and ladies in beautiful bonnets and, in the winter, soft fur collars and tippets. Isaac was always entrusted with the precious letters, and he would run up the long drive to the house, Mary Ann panting at his heels, while the coachman blew his horn, until she thought it sounded exactly like the description of the trumpet of the Last Judgment in the Bible.

Almost as soon as she could walk, her father used to

take her with him on his many and various errands. Sitting proudly in front of him on his enormous gray horse, Mary Ann would watch, fascinated, as he directed a group of surveyors laying out a new field, or listen to the ringing axes of the woodsmen as they felled the trees to be sold for lumber at Coventry. Sometimes, when she was a little older, he had business consultations with Squire Newdigate, and he would take her with him to Arbury Hall. If it was a very long visit, he would leave her with the housekeeper, who was very fond of her and enjoyed taking her on her rounds of the manor, which was one of the finest in Warwickshire. It had been built in Queen Elizabeth's time, though this fact did not interest Mary Ann as much as the prized portrait of the queen herself, considered one of the best likenesses ever painted. Mary Ann was still a little girl, but an unusual little girl, for she would stand before the portrait and study it for several minutes at a time. Perhaps it was this portrait of a woman who had ruled as the greatest queen the land had known that, in part, inspired her with the thought and the hope that she too would be great someday, even if she *was* a girl. She always enjoyed listening to her father discuss business and politics with the other men, much more even than passing the silver tray of cakes when her mother entertained ladies at tea. But she listened to them, too, while they spoke of shops and trips and gowns and gardens and sometimes of far-off lands. Unknown to herself, her quick, perceptive mind was absorbing the sights and the sounds of her own world, and she would occasionally startle her family by repeating some telling phrase she had heard or by making some astute observation of her own.

It was not only the immediate surroundings of the Arbury estate that absorbed her. Sometimes her father would have occasion to visit Bedworth, a village a few miles away, where the handloom weavers, whole families of them, continued to ply a craft which the mills had not yet completely abolished and could never duplicate in texture or beauty. In later visits to Bedworth, Mary Ann was struck more and more by the pale faces, especially those of the children who played in the muddy lanes in the worst weather, lest they interfere with the great looms set up in the cottages. Dirt and grime were everywhere, for coal had recently been discovered at Bedworth, and the great pits lay open to the skies, spreading a film of black dust over the entire landscape. There were no churches, only Dissenting Chapels, which seemed dingy and ugly compared with the beautiful medieval church at Chilvers Coton, where Mary Ann had been christened and which she attended every Sunday. Indeed, there were more alehouses at Bedworth than chapels. Sometimes she would see a crowd gathered in a field to listen to a Methodist preacher; and she would be reminded that her father's brother, her Uncle Samuel Evans, had become a Methodist—and that her Aunt Elizabeth Evans was that wonder of the world, a woman preacher, both much to her family's chagrin. Doubtless, her mother worried about these expeditions, from which Mary Ann always returned in a state of excitement, and her concern was not mitigated by her husband's indulgent, "Now, now, let the little wench be."

At the age of four, she had started going to Mrs. Moore's Dame School, where Isaac was already a pupil. She was supposed to learn reading, writing, and elementary ciphering, but at Dame's School she was not very quick to learn. Reading was difficult for her, not, as her brother later remarked, because she lacked intelligence, but because she liked to play games of her own imagination so much better. Each day, when she was released from the irksome stint of lessons, she would fly out of school at Isaac's heels, for, of all the family, she loved her brother best. He was her guide, mentor, and oracle:

I held him wise and when he talked to me
Of snakes and birds, and which God loved the best,
I thought his knowledge marked the boundary
Where men grew blind, though angels knew the rest.

she wrote many years later in "Brother and Sister Sonnets." Her devotion was blind; no demand he made upon her seemed too great:

If he said "Hush!" I tried to hold my breath;
Whenever he said, "Come!" I stepped in faith.

Isaac, for his part, reciprocated, though not so completely. His attitude was that of a fairly affectionate older brother, as long as Mary Ann did not bother him; he was proud of his little sister, but occasionally he lost his temper with her and scolded her severely. Then Mary Ann would retire to the attic, and Isaac would come after her, telling her not to be a silly, answering her avowals of affection with an embarrassed, "Of course I love you! Now for Heaven's sake come downstairs and have your tea." And for Mary Ann, the sun would come back into the sky. It was Isaac, too, when she had been sent to bed without supper, who would smuggle cakes or slices of bread and cheese into her room. When he went away to school at Coventry, she wept as though her heart would break. But she suffered an even greater anguish when he returned for his first holiday, and she discovered that he was no longer interested in running over the fields or fishing in the canal. This was her first experience of losing (for she felt Isaac's new separateness as a real bereavement) someone to whom she had given her complete trust and loyalty. Her affections ran deep, and she had lavished them on her brother; seemingly, he no longer needed her, but her need for him had not lessened. All her life she never forgot those precious years when she and her beloved brother

> . . . had the selfsame world enlarged for each
> By loving difference of a girl and boy.

until they were transmuted and metamorphosed by George Eliot into the beautifully, perceptively drawn relationship of Tom and Maggie Tulliver. For, though Mary Ann never ceased to love her brother with a special love, she also apparently recognized early that his nature was not like hers. When she loved, it was without reservations, but Isaac was chary in his bestowal of affection. He loved where his love would be exceedingly well reciprocated *and* where he felt it was deserved, a characteristic which led to the long, tragic estrangement between them. But, even then, Mary Ann clung to the memory of the old happiness and wrote wistfully,

> But were another childhood world my share,
> I would be born a little sister there.

However, her immediate sense of desolation was, on the surface at least, healed, for that same winter that Isaac went to Coventry, she herself was sent away to boarding school. Chrissey had already been a student for several years at Miss Latham's School at Attleboro, about ten miles away, and it was decided that Mary Ann should join her. The child was lonely at home without her brother and sister, and also, perhaps, her parents wanted to keep from her as long as possible the fact that her mother's health was in a precarious state, actually unequal to coping with an energetic five-year-old whose perceptive eyes saw and understood far more than was generally realized. Besides, Mary Ann was intellectually far advanced for her age; she had already learned to read, despite her reluctance to study. Her father had given her her first book when she was three, *The Linnet's Life,* which he read over and over to her aloud, until she had memorized it and so could "read it" for herself. About the time she went to Miss Latham's, she had discovered *Joe Miller's Jest Book* from which she would quote, in all innocence, to the startled amusement and amazement of her parents and their guests. She loved *Aesop's Fables,* especially the one about "Mercury and the Statue Seller," and Daniel Defoe's *History of the Devil* never failed to afford her the most delightful shudders. It was not exactly an approved reading list, but, despite its limitations, Mary Ann derived one great benefit from it—a feeling for words and what they could accomplish. And *Joe Miller's Jest Book* might even have had a share in sharpening her sense of point and repartee, which was to be one of her greatest assets as a novelist.

She was not unhappy at Miss Latham's. She was a quaint child, very much younger than the other students, and she immediately became everyone's special charge. The other girls petted and fussed over her, calling her "Little Mama" because she was so serious. She suffered greatly from the cold; later, she said that her chief memory was how hard it was to get near the fireplace. She was never really warm during her entire three years there. Also, for the first time in her life, she was afraid of the dark; she would lie shivering and trembling in her bed after the lamp was put out, not daring to call anyone to come to comfort her. She lived for those few Saturdays when her father would come up to Attleboro early in the morning to fetch her for a glorious day at home; still more eagerly she waited for the holidays at Christmas and summer. Even Isaac's withdrawal—he had his own pony, now, and so less time than ever for girls—could not dim her complete joy in simply being at home. Besides, by the end of her second year at Miss Latham's, she had really discovered books. Goldsmith's *The Vicar of Wakefield*, Samuel Johnson's *Rasselas*, Bunyan's *Pilgrim's Progress*, Charles Lamb's *Essays of Elia* had joined Aesop and Joe Miller. And it was about this time that a neighbor loaned a copy of Scott's *Waverley* to sister Chrissey. Mary Ann fell on it with gusto, and when the book had to be returned before she had finished it, she promptly proceeded to write the story from memory as far as she had gone. Then she embarked on her own conclusion to the novel, as she described it later with considerable humor, "In lines that thwart like portly spiders ran." [2] At this point, her astonished parents, discovering what she was doing, asked the neighbor to let Mary Ann have *Waverley* back again, and that Christmas Robert Evans gave her copies of all the novels written by Sir Walter Scott up to that moment. This was the beginning of her wholehearted admiration for the Waverley Novels, which were a constant source of pleasure to her all her life through.

Ordinarily, she would have remained at Miss Latham's school for several more years. But in the autumn of 1828, Chrissey, now fourteen, was ready for more advanced schooling, and had been entered at Mrs. Wallington's Academy at Nuneaton. Though Mary Ann had only just passed her ninth birthday, it was decided that she should accompany her sister. There is no record as to why this unusual decision was made, but certainly one factor taken into consideration must have been her devoted affection for Chrissey, who had in a sense replaced Isaac as mentor and confidante. The two girls were exact opposites in every way—Chrissey's placid disposition and gentle, pretty face contrasted sharply with Mary Ann's turbulent, enthusiastic temperament and more clearly cut, distinctive features. The bond between them, however, was very deep, though they could not really understand each other and did not try. "I had a very special feeling towards her, stronger than any third person would think likely," [3] Mary Ann wrote, shortly after Chrissey's death in 1859. But Mary Ann, though five years younger in age, was far in advance of her sister intellectually. She had never been comfortable with children her own age. There is at least one occasion on record when she was at a little children's birthday party, and, seeing her by herself, apart from the others, her hostess asked her if she was not enjoying herself. Soberly, almost tearfully, she replied, "No, I am not. I don't like to play with children. I like to talk to grown up people." [4] Obviously, she needed the challenge that a more advanced school would provide.

There seemed to be no immediate prospect that she would need to earn her own living, but, unlike Chrissey, neither did she seem destined to make an early marriage. Naturally, according to the conventions of the day, she would live at home if she did not marry, protected by her father for as long as he lived, and then by her brother. But political and economic conditions were far from stable, and even a gently raised girl might find herself forced to work. The only proper employment for a young lady in Mary Ann's position was teaching or being a governess, and for both these occupations a proper education was essential. So Mary Ann's trunk was packed and her pelisse carefully buttoned; and, doubtless with her mother's final injunction to mind her manners and to see to it that she always had *clean* gloves, along with a farewell kiss, she climbed into the family rig beside Chrissey as her father took up the reins. She must have been both excited and frightened. Now she was really going to be a student, instead of a petted "Little Mama." She was grown up, like Isaac and Chrissey, no longer the adored baby sister. But she was never one to shrink at the prospect of adventure. And she wanted to read everything the library had in it, and to learn—not just embroidery and French and music, but subjects like Latin and Greek and Algebra, that were supposed to be too hard for girls. Whatever thoughts actually were hers that day will never be known—but one thing is certain. She did not have the remotest idea of the tremendous influence this new experience would have in molding the character of George Eliot.

II

It was a dingy town, with a strong smell of tanning up one street and a great shaking of handlooms up another; and even in that focus of aristocracy, Friar's Gate, the houses would not have seemed very imposing to the hasty and superficial glance of a coach passenger . . . Certainly, in spite of the three assemblies and a charity ball in the winter, the occasional advent of a ventriloquist or a company of itinerant players, some of whom were highly thought of in London, and the annual three days' fair in June, Milby might be considered dull by people of a hypochondriacal temperament. . . .[1]

. . . Milby was nothing but dreary prose . . .[2]

In 1857, George Eliot so described Milby, the setting of "Janet's Repentance," the third story in *Scenes from Clerical Life*. In this, her first work of fiction, she re-created Nuneaton as she had thought of it in her school days, twenty-nine years before. Indeed, her first glimpse of the town, after the beauty and the serenity of Arbury Farm and Griff House, must have seemed unbearably drab and unattractive to Mary Ann Evans on that November day in 1828, for the once pleasant little market town, like so many others of its kind, was going through the full impact of the Industrial Revolution. A ribbon-making factory had already been established, and the factory had almost won the day over farming as a way of life, as the closely built rows of drab wooden houses —providing shelter and little else for the work force— testified. There was one really fine building: the Church of St. Nicholas, with its clipped yew hedge, which boasted some of the most remarkable examples of medieval stone-carving in England, and, at the opposite end of the town, stood the ruins of a Norman Abbey; but Nuneaton could boast little else of beauty or dignity. There were many Dissenting Chapels, indications of the splintered condition of religious life, which were easily outnumbered by the ale houses, the chief source of recreation and amusement for most of the town people—high and low, men and women. The theme of "Janet's Repentance" is a woman's redemption from drink—what the twentieth century would call "alcoholism"—and, when George Eliot wrote the story, she did not hesitate to lay at least part of the blame for her heroine's weakness on the dingy atmosphere of Nuneaton-Milby, where "many of the middle aged inhabitants often found it impossible to keep up their spirits without an abundant supply of stimulants." [3]

Mrs. Wallington's School stood in Church Lane, in the better part of town. Like most of the schools of the time, it was a good-sized building, large enough to accommodate thirty girls and four or five teachers. It was referred to as a "boarding school," which meant that the majority of the students lived there, though a few doubtless came in daily from Nuneaton as day students. No special mention is made of the grounds around it, but in an age when athletics for young ladies was unheard of, such accommodations would not have been needed. Probably there was some kind of formal garden at the rear, closed in by a wall made of stone carried from the Abbey ruins, where the girls might enjoy their supervised walks. The curriculum would not have been extensive, though what there was of it would have been thorough. Literature and composition, calligraphy, elementary arithmetic, and sewing were the usual subjects considered appropriate for "young females."

Mrs. Wallington, the headmistress, like many another widow of the time, probably had opened a school from sheer necessity of earning a living as genteelly as possible. Apparently she was not too well educated. But her principal teacher, Maria Lewis, was not only educated, but also dedicated, and, fortunately for the school, Miss Lewis was in charge of the entire academic program. Many years afterward, George Eliot wrote on the back of a calendar an idea for a possible story: "Widow supporting herself by keeping a school; imperfectly instructed; domineered over by her head teacher." [4] The story was never written, but the relationship between Mrs. Wallington and Miss Lewis was obviously in the novelist's mind. The later brief notation represented her more mature assessment of that relationship, because Miss Lewis's "domineering" was of the greatest possible benefit to the students, and especially to Mary Ann Evans, who, despite her youth, was placed immediately in the most advanced class.

The lot of a teacher in an early nineteenth-century girls' school was not always a happy one, and a student who was almost feverishly eager to learn was received with gratitude. From the beginning, Maria Lewis took a special interest in Mary Ann. Diction, vocabulary, and composition were her specialties, and, since the child was both eager and willing, she worked incessantly to rid Mary Ann's intonation of even the slightest tinge of Midlands accent. People meeting George Eliot the novelist in later years invariably commented upon her lovely, musical voice, certainly the result of those many hours of drill in pitch and expression. As for composition, under Miss Lewis's guidance Mary Ann soon led the entire school. She had come to Nuneaton already in love with books; now she was discovering the enchantment of hearing and learning beautiful words, and using them. It is possible to say that, even in those early days, there was an unusual and genuine friendship between pupil and teacher, for Mary Ann in many ways was advanced far beyond her years, and, intellectually, she was beginning to show signs of real brilliance. That she was devoted to Miss Lewis is evident from the letters she wrote to her long after leaving school; Miss Lewis was also a frequent visitor at Griff House and later at the Evans home in Coventry.

There was one other area in which Maria Lewis had a profound effect on her favorite pupil: that of religion. She was a devout member of the Church of England, but her faith was thoroughly imbued with Evangelicalism as taught by the Wesley brothers, popularly called "Methodism." By 1828, the Methodists had already formed a separate church (an action which the Wesleys during their lifetimes had never contemplated except with horror), but there were still many in the Established Church who, while adhering to the *Book of Common Prayer,* nevertheless concurred wholeheartedly in the Evangelical teaching that only the grace of God could redeem man from his own essential sinfulness—as expressed in one of their favorite hymns:

Not the labour of my hands
Can fulfill the law's demands:
Could my zeal no respite know,
Could my tears forever flow,
All for sin could not atone;
Thou must save, and Thou alone.

Nothing in my hand I bring,
Simply to Thy Cross I cling:
When I rise to worlds unknown,
See Thee at Thy Father's throne,
Rock of Ages, cleft for me,
Let me hide myself in Thee.

This fervent belief led to a concomitant conviction that every action, word, and thought must be directed to achieving that state of grace. Indeed, so strong was this conviction that, for the Evangelical minded, soul-searching became a major duty and occupation. They insisted on the relationship of cause to effect; the most innocent pleasure must be scrutinized lest it become the first step on the downward path to perdition. Rules governed every facet of life. In its extreme form, the Evangelical view echoed the gloomy Jansenism of seventeenth-century France, where God the Loving Father was superseded by God the Angry Judge; and it became the dour Pietism excluding all human consideration, which Ibsen used as the theme of his drama, *Brand*. Certainly, scrupulosity became an almost inevitable by-product of strict adherence to Evangelical beliefs.

Under Miss Lewis's scrupulosity, Mary Ann Evans renounced "worldly pleasures" to the extent of giving up novel reading and wearing an unbecoming bonnet to mortify her vanity. She began to study the Scriptures attentively, and to read historical works and sermons. One of the best and most important results of Evangelical zeal was the Sunday School, held on Sunday afternoons for the purpose of bringing the Gospel to the children of the poor. Since most of these children were illiterate, it was necessary to teach them to read, so that they could read the Bible for themselves. Mary Ann Evans was teaching a Sunday School class of children her own age and probably older before she was twelve. She avoided every kind of entertainment except instructive lectures; the question of whether or not she might attend a sacred oratorio became a matter for agonizing appraisal of her own motives: would it be a source of edification, or did she simply wish to hear the music for her own enjoyment? For she loved music. She had begun to take piano lessons, but they, seemingly, caused her no twinge of conscience whatever, perhaps because of the work involved in practicing. That she did not stop them is doubtless an early evidence of her characteristic later independence.

In every other respect, however, she schooled herself in the sober demeanor praised by her teacher; and while this way of life may seem unconscionably rigorous to us of the twentieth century, it evidently fulfilled some deep, conscientious demand of her own nature for discipline and self-sacrifice. She learned self-control and dedication from Maria Lewis, and, when she returned to Griff for vacations, her mother—and even the Pearson aunts—found little to criticize in her behavior. Now, paradoxically, her mother worried lest she become too much of a blue-stocking. Isaac constantly chaffed her about her religious qualms. His teasing caused her much anxiety, for she still longed to please her brother, even while she was trembling for his immortal soul and trying desperately to convert him to her way of thinking. Twenty years later, realizing how ridiculous and really priggish she had been, she remarked to a friend, "I used to go about like an owl, to the great disgust of my brother, and I would have denied to him what I now see to have been quite lawful amusements." [5] And there were occasions, even in the 1820's, when she was at home and away from the immediate influence of Maria Lewis, when her natural gaiety and high spirits overcame her carefully cultivated deportment, and she joined enthusiastically in charades and games, even willingly entertaining the family with "recitations." But it was generally acknowledged that she was growing up very quickly, even by contemporary standards, and could no longer be considered a child.

Three years passed. She had learned everything that Mrs. Wallington's School could teach her, and Chrissey was ready to complete her education at the Misses Franklin's School in Coventry. Once again, it was decided that Mary Ann should go with her sister, so, in the autumn of 1832, she found herself once again in new surroundings. The year 1832 was a tumultuous one for England; it was the year of the great debate on the Reform Bill which would widen the franchise that had been unaltered since the time of Queen Elizabeth I. Feeling for and against the bill ran high, and tempers frequently exploded into rioting. Mary Ann witnessed one such riot on December 21, 1832, while riding with her father through Nuneaton on the way to Griff for the Christmas holidays, but it was doubtful that she alluded to, or even thought very much about, the episode at the Misses Franklin's. Women were not supposed to interest themselves in politics; nevertheless, what Mary Ann Evans saw that day, George Eliot remembered and used in one of the most gripping scenes of her novel, *Felix Holt, The Radical*.

There is no doubt that schoolwork now kept Mary Ann fully occupied. Miss Mary and Miss Rebecca Franklin were two most exceptional women, who held quite advanced ideas about "female education." They were daughters of a Baptist minister, so, as might be expected, religious instruction was given a place of supreme importance in their curriculum; they concurred with the Reverend John Bennett, whose *Letters to a Young Lady* had made a significant contribution to educational theory and practice of the time, that religion must be one of a school's primary concerns, "that our daughters may be polished corners of the Temple." [6] The Misses Franklin made no attempt to proselytize their students. Mary Ann continued to attend the Church of England, but the Baptist view that baptism should be administered only when the individual had reached the age of reason and could, therefore, experience conversion, worried her intensely. That a twelve-year-old girl could actually go through such genuine spiritual anguish, and still be just a normal twelve-year-old girl, seems almost impossible, but it must be remembered that spiritual anguish was normal to that era. Tennyson's first volume, published in 1832, and Browning's *Pauline* in 1833, both freely explored and set down the religious doubts and difficulties of both poets; and Carlyle, in *Sartor Resartus*, also published in 1833, presented a thinly veiled account of his soul's tortured progression from doubt to faith. Mary Ann was quite definitely in tune with the times.

The emphasis on religious instruction, however, in no way lessened the importance placed on academic excellence. Again, the curriculum may seem limited, in comparison with that of the twentieth century: no mathematics beyond sufficient elementary arithmetic for household accounts; no science beyond a smattering of natural history and astronomy; no philosophy or metaphysics whatever, for these studies were considered too arduous for the female mind. But literature, composition (including the art of letter writing), and history were well and thoroughly taught, and in these Mary Ann excelled. Her essays were so remarkably good that Miss Rebecca Franklin used to read hers last, simply to enjoy them, since there was seldom much to correct. Instruction was available in both French and German, and Mary Ann studied both. She also continued with her music, and quickly became the pianist of the school; she was always the one summoned to the drawing room to play for important visitors. This she would do willingly enough, concealing her shyness and nervousness so well that only a few of her classmates ever knew that she invariably succumbed to tears, once she was safely in her room again. As an academic exercise, she translated one of Maria Edgeworth's stories into French; this was a first indication of her remarkable facility with languages which ultimately would lead her to earn her living as a translator.

But, despite these accomplishments and the honors she achieved, and the respect in which she was held, she was lonely. Her superior scholarship, combined with her youth and natural diffidence, were not the kind of surface attractiveness that intrigued people, and most people did not see easily beneath the surface. The students at the Misses Franklin's were quite a cosmopolitan little group —there was a girl from India, and one from America, and several from London—so the general attitude toward Mary Ann did not arise wholly from a limited provincial outlook. Her classmates were genuinely in awe of her; as said later by one of them, "They loved her as much as they could venture to love anyone so immeasurably superior to themselves." [7] However, this dubious admiration of her superiority—which she herself honestly did not feel—could not take the place of friendships; certainly not of confidences exchanged in whispers after the lamp was taken out of the dormitory where she slept. Before the world she preserved a mask of equanimity, but on at least one occasion she poured out her longing for sympathy and affection in a poem which one of her classmates found written on the flyleaf of her German dictionary. That great gift of friendship, which later was so characteristic of her, came with difficulty. She was shy and afraid. First, she had to find herself—a difficult task for any adolescent and especially difficult for one whose intellect was so beyond her age. At thirteen, Mary Ann possessed the mind of a mature adult, but in all other respects she was utterly unworldly. It was this combination of intellectual brilliance, emotional immaturity, and intense religiosity that was the source of her great confusion and frequent unhappiness.

Before she had completed her last term at the Misses Franklin's, in 1835, she had been forced to face the fact that changes inevitably would come, even within her own family circle which, up to now, had been the one stable, secure anchor in her life. Chrissey had already left school and was engaged to be married to Edward Clarke, a

27

young surgeon whose practice was at Meriden, quite some distance from Griff House. Her interests and loyalties would change, and Mary Ann dreaded that moment. But she was to sustain an earlier and even greater grief. In December 1835, when she went home for the Christmas holidays, she discovered that her mother was gravely ill. There was no hospital where she could be taken for the intensive care that she needed, and, at that time, only invalids without families to nurse them went to hospitals anyway. Doubtless the full extent of the gravity of her mother's condition had been kept from her as long as possible, but the moment Mary Ann saw her, there was no question in her mind as to where her duty lay. She did not return to school; she remained at Griff, and, together with Chrissey, nursed her mother through the last long weeks of painful illness. On February 3, 1836, Mrs. Evans died. Mary Ann was just sixteen. But there was no time to give way to sorrow—the work of the home must continue, the garden must be tended, the farm required supervision—above all, her father must be comforted. She found strength in her faith and in her daily tasks, putting aside her own anguish, restraining her tears lest she give more sorrow to others whose grief was as great as hers.

Then, on May 30, 1837, after the year of mourning had passed, Chrissey was married. Though Mary Ann was truly sincere in her wish for Chrissey's happiness, she knew that her sister's leaving meant yet another break in their closely knit family. She found an unexpected source of comfort in her brother; on the wedding day, after the bridal couple had gone, she and Isaac stood by a window and wept together, sharing a mutual emotion. They were no longer the little brother and sister who had gone fishing together or rushed to the gate to watch the stagecoach pass. Their father was growing older; he had been long in recovering from the severe renal infection which had attacked him that winter, during which his physician had tended him night and day. Isaac was already assuming many of his father's more arduous duties, and Mary Ann insisted that the responsibility for care of the household must be hers. Robert Evans half-heartedly offered to find a housekeeper, but neither Isaac nor Mary Ann wanted a stranger in their mother's place, and they knew instinctively that their father did not really wish it either. So, in the same year that another young girl, born in the same year as Mary Ann, was informed that she was now Queen of England, Mary Ann Evans also took hold of responsibility. She was only seventeen, but she had two things in common with her sovereign: she had been well trained for the role she was assuming, and she was determined to do her utmost to succeed in it.

III

Training and determination, however, are not the same thing as doing the actual work, as Mary Ann quickly discovered. True, there were servants at Griff, but they required direction, a time-consuming task in itself which demanded great tact and effort. Apparently she did a great deal of work herself, especially in the kitchen; and while she probably did not make butter (the story about her right hand being larger than her left because of butter-making is definitely apocryphal), she certainly saw to its making, for no one could have written the dairy scenes in *Adam Bede* in such detail without direct observation. Her letters that survive from this period, mostly to Maria Lewis, alternate between analyses of the state of her soul and descriptions of putting up jam and jelly. It did not take very long for her to learn that managing Griff by herself was very different from helping her mother, and housekeeping was additionally difficult for her because she not only lacked Chrissey's natural bent for domesticity, but also was a perfectionist to the *nth* degree. She discovered that it was a very rare servant indeed who possessed that artistic quality. "Pity the sorrows of a poor young housekeeper," she wrote ruefully to Martha Jackson, one of her schoolmates, "and determine to make the very best use of your present freedom *therefrom.*" [1] Her greatest difficulty was that she had little time now to read or study, occupations which were the breath of life to her.

Her responsibilities were indeed heavy, and her emotional state did nothing to lighten them. She missed Chrissey terribly. Even more, she was still in a state of shock from her mother's death. And, while she did not, of course, mention this in her letters, the rigid Victorian observance of mourning must have been an additional depressant. Funereal black clothes for at least a year, no social gatherings, a closed piano, yew wreathes and black crepe—these, combined with her present severe religious convictions which called for a life of "diligence and watchfulness, not for repose and amusement," [2] could very easily have brought a less balanced individual to the breaking point. Small wonder that she wrote to her father's sister—her Methodist aunt—"My soul seems for weeks completely benumbed!" [3] Yet, characteristically, she blamed herself for her emotional apathy, and censured herself severely for occasional rebellion. "If I were

31

truly spiritual minded, I should rather delight in an occasion of proving to myself the genuineness of my religious experience and of exercising a cheerful submission to the will of my Saviour," she wrote to Maria Lewis, "instead of acting as a bullock unaccustomed to the yoke, murmuring at the slightest opposition to my taste, the slightest mortification of my fleshly mind." [4] In a letter to her Aunt Elizabeth Evans, she flailed herself: "I feel that my besetting sin is . . . Ambition, a desire insatiable for the esteem of my fellow creatures. This seems the center whence all my actions proceed." [5]

In other words, despite her religious conviction that she should seek no approval of her efforts, even for those several extra ones that make a house a home, she was human enough to want praise, and she apparently received little or none from the two people in the world whose approbation she sorely needed: her father and Isaac. From their point of view, as long as they did not criticize or complain, that they should simply accept all she did without comment should be natural and sufficient. After all, she was doing "woman's work," no more arduous than thousands of other women were doing the length and breadth of England, and less arduous than many. Robert Evans was sixty-five years old, quite elderly for the 1830's; he had been seriously ill, and he had suffered an indescribable loss in his wife's death from which he never really recovered. His loneliness made him inarticulate, articulate as he might be on all other subjects. All he wanted was the peace and quiet, and routine to his liking, of a comfortable, well-managed home. According to his lights, in providing this, Mary Ann was only doing her Christian, filial duty. As for Isaac, he had been at swords' points for some time with his sister over their religious differences, and he was much preoccupied with his work.

Mary Ann tried to find comfort in her religious reading. Perhaps it was at this time she discovered St. Thomas a Kempis, whose teaching on renunciation so strongly appealed to Maggie Tulliver in *The Mill on the Floss*. But there was another, deeper reason for Mary Ann's restiveness and discontent, which she herself at that time did not entirely understand: managing a house, and permitting herself not one outside cultural or entertaining interest, simply was not enough for a young woman of her capacity and ability, and her yearning for affection, which up to now she had received from her mother and sister, was greater than she realized. Apart from a weekly lesson in Italian from Signor Brezzi, who rode over from Coventry, her mind remained unchallenged, and this lack of affection and mental stimulation was a very real, albeit subconscious, source of her rebellion. The Princess Halm-Eberstein's bitter words to Daniel Deronda—"You may try, but you can never imagine what it is to have a man's force of genius in you, and yet to suffer the slavery of being a girl"—probably represent George Eliot's mature interpretation of her own mood in the autumn of 1837.

Gradually, however, as she became more accustomed to the daily routine, and the regular tasks became less time consuming, she found various opportunities to occupy herself apart from complete domesticity. There was parish visiting to be done among the poor, for times were hard that winter and there was much unemployment among the Bedworth weavers. Her fine capacity for sympathetic understanding was now put to excellent use. She also began to read aloud to her father in the evenings;

they both enjoyed this diversion very much, especially the works of Sir Walter Scott, and, now that the year of mourning was over, she could play the piano again. Then, in the summer of 1838, Isaac took her up to London for a week's holiday.

This first visit to the city which was later to become her permanent home is chiefly notable for what she did *not* say about it. Evidently it was timed at the end of July or the beginning of August; she could not have been there on June 28th when Victoria was crowned Queen of England, or she surely would have commented on such an important occasion. Still, she must have at least noticed the "Coronation Fever" which had really gripped the city since early spring, for no sovereign had been crowned in the Abbey for over sixty years and London had been determined that the event would be marked with due pomp and ceremony. Throngs of visitors throughout England and all over the Continent had come for THE DAY. Ten thousand people had crowded into the Abbey for the actual ceremony; thousands more had stood in the streets for hours to watch the nineteen-year-old queen ride past in the gold coach, wearing her robes of state. And, for weeks afterward, excitement remained at fever pitch as an endless stream of visitors continued to pour into the city to see the sights, the decorations, and, hopefully, to even catch a glimpse of the young queen—who at that moment was universally adored—en route, magnificently gowned and jeweled, to a ball or to a state concert at Covent Garden.

But of all this Mary Ann Evans mentioned not one word. In a letter to Maria Lewis, written after her return to Griff, she said that she was "not at all delighted with the 'stir of the great Babel,' " [6] though she and Isaac "worked hard every day at sight-seeing." [7] Greenwich Hospital, the home for aged and disabled soldiers, impressed her most. She heard an interesting sermon preached by the Reverend Thomas Dale at St. Bride's, Fleet Street, on Sunday morning, and in the afternoon she attended Vespers at St. Paul's Cathedral, which pleased her not at all:

> . . . I grieve to say that my strongest feeling was that of indignation . . . towards the surpliced personages, chapters I think they are called, who performed the chanting, for it appears with them a mere performance, their behaviour being that of schoolboys, glad of an opportunity to titter unreproved.[8]

Her brother added, however, that she was deeply moved by the sonorous tone of St. Paul's great bell.[9] But he must have been a little exasperated when she refused adamantly to go to the theater with him, and spent the evenings by herself in her hotel room reading. Her one London purchase was a beautiful leather-bound set of Josephus's *History of the Jews,* which she had longed to own; Isaac, as might be expected, returned to Griff with a pair of hunting sketches bought at the same shop where Mary Ann had found her books. Isaac perhaps deserves praise, as well as sympathy, on the occasion of this visit. He had, with unwonted generosity, intended to give his sister a pleasant holiday, and she did not at all modify her ways to his holiday mood, so she could not have been the most delightful of traveling companions. For her part, Mary Ann was glad to return to the peace and serenity of Griff. She was essentially a country woman, and her first encounter with the city had left her bewildered and rather disappointed.

The next eighteen months passed quietly, at least on the surface; however, beneath the calm exterior of the devout young lady of the house, a new flame had been kindled that her father and brother never suspected. Mary Ann had found a new enthusiasm. Inspired by her great interest in the Oxford Movement, then at its height, she was immersed in the study of church history. The efforts of John Henry Newman and Henry Pusey to restore Catholic practices which the Church of England had abandoned at the Reformation had aroused heated controversy throughout the entire country. Part of the uproar was due to the insistence of certain of the Movement's adherents on continuing the symbolic externals of worship, such as vestments, incense, altar candles, holy water—which were considered "flagrant popery" by the solid middle-class upholders of the established order. But even more unsettling was Newman's unequivocal statement (he did not become a Roman Catholic until 1845) that the Thirty-Nine Articles, the rock and foundation of Anglican belief, could be so interpreted as to be in complete accord with Roman doctrine. To the average Englishman, who had firmly considered himself wholly Protestant, these words were nothing short of blasphemy. The "Tracts for the Times," leaflets regularly published by members of the Oxford Movement to disseminate their views, were read by the public and either praised or excoriated in public and in private, in sermons, in newspapers and magazines, in drawing rooms, in clubs and in pubs, by all classes. There is little doubt that they were also seriously and spiritedly discussed by the family at Griff, for Isaac Evans had "High Church" leanings, while Mary Ann held a completely opposite view at the time—at least in public. But to Maria Lewis, she wrote that she was

. . . unable to shape an opinion for the satisfaction of my mind . . . I do not mean that I have not preferences, but however incongruous a theory may be with my notions, I cannot find the comfortable repose that others appear to possess after having made their election of a class of sentiments.[10]

This admission is the first inkling of that doubt which would, within two years, scatter her own "comfortable repose" in religious conviction to the four winds.

Her study of ecclesiastical history was almost certainly an effort to clarify her own convictions so that she could defend them. There seemed to be no other way for her to ease her mind of this agitation. She had reached the point where she could no longer accept expression of her faith blindly; others had questioned it, and their point of view had been given credence by various individuals —her brother, for one—whose sincerity and integrity she did not question. Yet, she was skeptical of the answers these individuals provided:

> . . . their opinions are seconded by the extensive learning, the laborious zeal, and the deep devotion of those who propagate them, but a reference to facts will convince us that such generally has been the character of heretical teachers,[11]

she wrote to Maria Lewis in May 1839. Her researches brought her face to face with the newest scientific opinions and interpretations of the Bible; by September she was writing Miss Lewis that she was investigating works of geometry, chemistry, and geology, and also studying Latin, ". . . all arrested and petrified and smothered by the fact thickening succession of actual events, relative anxieties and household cares and vexations." [12] She was so preoccupied that the visit of Dowager Queen Adelaide —in whose escort her father participated from Griff to Coventry—received only barest mention. Her family must have felt considerable relief when, on her twentieth

birthday, Mary Ann bought a complete set of Wordsworth—for light reading!

By March of 1840 she had begun work on an elaborate
Chart of Ecclesiastical History, tracing the rise of
Christianity from the days of the Apostles to the Reformation. Mrs. Newdigate, she wrote Miss Lewis excitedly,[13] had given her personal blessing to the project
and had invited her to use the library at Arbury Hall;
Mary Ann hoped that the Chart eventually would be
published. But a brief, rather poignant allusion in a letter
to her beloved teacher, dated March 30th, indicates that
there had been a major distraction:

> . . . I trust in some degree, desire and prayer to be free
> from rebelling against Him whose I am by right, and
> whose I would be by adoption. I endeavoured to pray for
> the beloved object to whom I have alluded, (I must still
> for a little while say *beloved*) last night and felt sooth-
> ingly melted in thinking that if mine be really prayers my
> acquaintance with him has probably caused the first to be
> offered up especially in his behalf. But all this I ought not
> to have let slip from my pen.[14]

The "beloved object" has never been further identified, nor has it ever been known precisely why this, her
first romance, ended so sadly for her, or whether she
ended it herself. The young man may have been considered ineligible for more than one reason; Mary Ann
Evans was, after all, a young lady of considerable consequence in the community, and both her father and
her brother would have looked with disfavor on the
attentions of a suitor whom they considered, for financial
or other causes, unsuitable. However, the reason might
have been religion. Victorian girls took their religious
convictions very seriously and there was a similar situation in the life of Christina Rossetti who broke two en-

gagements because the men's religious beliefs did not agree with her own. It seems significant that, earlier in the same letter, Mary Ann mentioned Bulwer-Lytton's novel *Devereaux*, in which one of the characters was an atheist, and remarked that she had been "considerably shaken by the impression that religion was not necessary to moral excellence." [15] From her reference to hers being the first prayers "to be offered up especially in his behalf," it could be inferred that the "beloved object" was an unconvertible free-thinker; and however fascinating she might have found such an individual in a novel, she could not bring herself to consider him as a husband. At least, not in 1840. All this, however, is speculation. What is important is that, here again, is evidence that what Mary Ann Evans experienced, George Eliot remembered, and that this early romance undoubtedly had its share in the poignant delineation of Maggie Tulliver's hopeless love for Philip Wakem.

The ambitious *Chart of Ecclesiastical History* was soon abandoned, for another was published late in the summer of 1840, but Mary Ann's interest did not abate. She began an intensive study of German so that she could read the newest Biblical criticism written by German scholars immediately upon publication, instead of having to wait for it to be translated into English. Her flair for languages was amazing—she was already fluent in both French and Italian, and by October she was facilely translating a German poem. Eventually, she was to add Spanish, Greek, Latin, and Hebrew to the list, and she probably would have attempted Chinese had the opportunity to study that language presented itself. But perhaps she had a more cogent reason for her language studies than mere personal satisfaction. Again, change was to enter her life which might necessitate her earning her own livelihood. In May, she wrote to Maria Lewis, "I will only hint that there seems a probability of my becoming an unoccupied damsel, of my being severed from all the ties that have hitherto given my life a semblance of usefulness. . . ." [16]

Isaac was engaged to be married. The young lady was Miss Sarah Rawlings of Birmingham, who possessed a good income (Isaac would always be prudent!), and, as son and heir to his father's property, he would, of course, bring his wife to Griff, who would expect to take over Mary Ann's place as hostess and housekeeper. Robert Evans would, naturally, remain in his home in Victorian patriarchal fashion. But what about his unmarried daughter, who showed no signs of acquiring a suitable husband? Especially a daughter who for three years had held undisputed control over the household, and who, despite the difference in age between herself and her future sister-in-law, possessed a greater intellectual capability and social experience, and tremendous sensitivity as well? The idea of continuing to live at Griff under those circumstances must have been extremely unattractive to Mary Ann. She was resigned to spinsterhood, if need be, but not to becoming a nonentity. She thought briefly of going to stay with Chrissey at Meriden, for her sister had three children now, and, being none too strong, could use responsible help. At Meriden she could be useful; on the other hand, she hesitated to intrude upon "the serenity of that atmosphere." [17] Yet, much as she liked her brother's fiancée, she was honest enough to realize that she would in time bitterly resent having to defer constantly to her wishes. So her strenuous application to language study may have been more than a "beguilement" for her "capricious mind." [18] If worse came to worst, and the need arose, she could earn her living as a translator without losing her status as a lady, and thus be fairly independent.

At this point, however, Robert Evans himself took a hand in the proceedings. Just as, twenty-one years earlier, he had turned over Kirk Hallam to his eldest son, he now decided that Isaac was old enough to assume complete responsibility for Griff. His decision may have been motivated partly by a feeling that he did not want to see a daughter-in-law in his wife's place; also, he was sensible enough to realize that Mary Ann's presence there might be as difficult for his son's bride as it would be for herself. His love and protectiveness of his "little wench," though inarticulate, was very real. Besides, the days when he could actively supervise a large estate by himself were past. He was, however, still in great demand as a consultant, so he would lose nothing financially by retiring. By July, everything was settled to the satisfaction of all concerned. Mr. and Mrs. Isaac Evans would live by themselves at Griff, and he and Mary Ann would buy a house in Coventry.

House-hunting was the major concern that autumn, though Mary Ann, in between trips to Coventry, found time to read Tasso, Schiller, and Spenser's *Faerie Queene*, which delighted her. In October, she paid a visit to her future sister-in-law in Birmingham where she heard a performance of Handel's *Messiah*, which despite her deprecatory remarks in her letter to Miss Lewis, she obviously enjoyed in spite of herself. She had broken away from her rigid Evangelical convictions more than she herself realized, for she was also reading Thomas Carlyle's works with attention and interest—something that would have been impossible a few years earlier. It was as though the prospect of leaving Griff for a new home had led to a desire for new and different intellectual experience as well.

Maria Lewis came to spend the holidays at Griff, the last Christmas Mary Ann was to spend as a daughter in her former childhood home, and, as always, seems to have been able to put some of her former pupil's doubts at rest. Mary Ann's letters at the first of the year, despite references to headaches, were infinitely more cheerful than those preceding that visit. And her father had found a house—Bird Grove in Foleshill Road, Coventry. "I shall be incessantly hurried until and after our departure, but at present I have to be grateful for a smooth passage through contemplated difficulties," [19] she wrote Miss Lewis in February. To her Aunt and Uncle Evans she wrote, "I am thankful to say that my dear father looks forward to removal with great satisfaction, and this relieves me of my chief anxiety." [20]

On March 10, 1841, Mary Ann—accompanied by Isaac, who drove the gig—arrived at Bird Grove. A storm was brewing, but they managed to get the wagonload of furniture into the house before the first flash of lightning, and then Isaac left her alone, to face the formidable task of putting things in order. Her homesickness for Griff was acute; still, she was happy, because she was making a home for her father, and the one thing she wanted at this moment was to ensure his continued contentment and comfort. Besides, the break with her old home was not quite complete. Isaac would not be married until June, so there would still be a few weeks when she could ride over to Griff and walk under the tall elms. And people in Coventry were most friendly and welcoming; Mrs. Abijah Pears, her next-door neighbor and also a former student at the Misses Franklin's, had come to call almost immediately, with offers of help and good advice which Mary Ann accepted gratefully. And the Misses Franklin were still in charge of their school; they would be eager to see her again, so she need not feel quite a stranger. She would be able to continue her language lessons and to spend more time on her music, now that she did not have a dairy to supervise. Such may have been her thoughts while she cleaned and swept and dusted and polished to have all in readiness to welcome her father when he arrived on March 19th. But she did not know then that Coventry, and Mrs. Pears in particular, were to be instruments for setting her feet on a wholly unanticipated path toward a destiny she had not even glimpsed.

IV

In 1841, Coventry was a rapidly expanding town, already experiencing the new prosperity of the Industrial Revolution. It was also one of the most fascinating towns in England, famous for its medieval church spires, Elizabethan houses, and the story of Lady Godiva. From the second-floor windows of Bird Grove, Mary Ann could see a far panorama of the gently rolling Midlands; the immediate view at the front, however, was marred by the factories and the mean streets of the industrial district. The house itself was semidetached, which meant that their neighbors, Mrs. and Mrs. Abijah Pears, were literally next door—quite a change from the privacy of Griff. However, there was a garden, and while it did not give Mary Ann the opportunity for the long walks she had always enjoyed, an English spring was an English spring, even in Coventry. Her greatest joy was that her father had adapted to the change so easily. ". . . I can decidedly say that he was never before so happy as he apparently is at present," [1] she wrote to Martha Jackson in May. Her own health, too, was better than it had been for a very long time. And, though she missed Griff, she quickly discovered that life in town had its pleasures, too. Ladies came to call on Miss Evans and left their cards; she and her father were invited out to dinner. Social obligations, German and Italian lessons with Signor Brezzi, and visiting the poor, in addition to supervising the household, filled her days. Soon she was studying Greek and Latin with the Reverend Mr. Sheepshanks, the headmaster of Coventry Grammar School, and Mr. Simms, the organist of St. Michael's Church, came once a week to give her a piano lesson.

Her father also found himself busier and more interestingly occupied than ever before. Instead of merely acting as agent for properties, he was now constantly consulted by landowners throughout the county, who sent their carriages to take him to their estates, so that they might benefit from his expert opinion. He was frequently away during the week, which meant that Mary Ann spent a great deal of time alone. But she certainly had no time for loneliness. Apart from her lessons, she was still pursuing her theological reading; her latest enthusiasm was Isaac Taylor's *Physical Theory of Another Life*. Its central theme—that man's destiny in the after-world would be marked by a heightening and deepening of all his faculties, and that it therefore behooved him to attain the highest possible degree of wisdom and perception here and now—enthralled her. It suited exactly her own personal ideas, for there was no philosophical thought that did not interest her; and Taylor's conviction that there would be complete communion possible between minds, plus a limitless power of perceiving abstract truth and logic, held an enormous fascination. The marvelous possibility that some day complete knowledge could be hers filled her with excitement. That Taylor did not once mention specifically any Christian doctrine of immortality does not seem to have occurred to her. She did not realize that her religious ideas had been veering away from the rigid Evangelicalism espoused by Maria Lewis. Her study of church history had revealed the changes of teaching and emphasis in the Christian Church since the days of the Apostles; and when, in August, she read Charles Hennell's *An Inquiry into the Origins of Christianity,* which maintained that the Christian faith needed neither the supernatural nor the mystical to explain or support it, she was probably a little shocked, but in a sense her reading had prepared her for this point of view. Certainly, she was deeply stirred by it. In this way, the stage was set for a typically nineteenth-century religious crisis, but Mary Ann's would differ from those of Browning, or Tennyson, or Carlyle. Hers would result in a complete reversal of all her previous thought.

The instigator of this crisis was Mrs. Abijah Pears, her next-door neighbor. She was herself both Evangelical and Methodist, but her brother Charles Bray, a wealthy ribbon manufacturer who owned the beautiful Rosehill estate just outside Coventry, was a free-thinker. He was thirty years old, rather eccentric, and deeply interested in—among other esoterica—phrenology, a means of revealing character by a study of the conformation of the skull. At the moment, this so-called "science" was enjoying an enormous popular vogue, and Bray had the reputation in the community for being quite accurate in his character readings. He was also completely dedicated to all political and religious controversies. He wrote about both incessantly—indeed, where no controversy was to be found, he was not above starting one himself. (Many years later, he was to proudly proclaim himself as the prototype of Mr. Brooke in George Eliot's *Middlemarch*.) In 1836, he had married Caroline Hennell, and perhaps nothing indicates his personality more clearly than his taking Volney's *Ruins of Empire* on the wedding journey to read aloud to his bride. Mrs. Bray, sister of Charles Hennell, the author of *An Inquiry into the Origins of Christianity*, was a Unitarian; and, actually, her brother had written his book at her request. Though her own beliefs were hardly orthodox, she was nonetheless deeply distressed by her husband's free-thinking rationalism, upon which even the most cogent verbal arguments had had no effect whatsoever. To the group in residence at Rosehill must be added Sara Hennell, Mrs. Bray's elder sister, an extremely intelligent, widely read young woman, deeply religious according to her own Unitarian beliefs, who had written a number of philosophical treatises. A highly unorthodox household, it was nevertheless the center of intellectual life at Coventry. Carlyle, Emerson, and the Italian patriot Mazzini all visited there, and, no matter what the time of day or year, there was always stimulating discussion and argument, over which Charles Bray presided with vigorous enjoyment.

Mrs. Pears took Mary Ann to call at Rosehill in November of 1841. Her motive, ironically enough, was her brother's conversion to Christianity, which she thought young Miss Evans might accomplish. The Brays were not complete strangers to Mary Ann; Charles Bray had come to Griff several times to consult with her father, and she had met both him and his wife at the Pears's and at other social functions. But that November afternoon marked her first opportunity to become really acquainted with them. Mr. Bray greeted her jovially, immediately asking permission to do a phrenological reading of her head. Then he inquired as to whether she had read either his brother-in-law's book, or his own. Upon being told that she had read only Hennell's *An Inquiry,* he promptly loaned her a copy of his *A Philosophy of Necessity,* which fully elucidated his opinion of the law of consequences— a doctrine thoroughly familiar to his guest—and counseled "unembittered resignation to the inevitable." [2]

The effect of this visit on Mary Ann should not be underestimated. Quite literally fresh from the country, it was her first entree into so cosmopolitan a society, and the Brays' cordial reception delighted and flattered her. Even more important, for the first time in her life she found herself in her own intellectual milieu. In the presence of kindly people who not only understood what she was talking about, but also did not think it strange that she could understand and enjoy such subjects, her usual shyness and diffidence disappeared. She conversed animatedly and wittily. But the crucial discovery for her was that, although the Brays were at the opposite end of the pole from her, as far as religion was concerned, they were *good* people—indeed, far better mannered and more genuinely kind than many she knew who professed themselves Christians, whose laxness she had found shocking on more than one occasion.[3] The Brays were completely honest in their beliefs and lived by them conscientiously; but they were also quite willing to listen to another point of view, a quality in which she herself—up to that moment at least—had been conspicuously lacking. The Brays, for their part, were equally charmed with her. As Mr. Bray wrote later,

> I consider her the most delightful companion I have ever known; she knew everything! She had little self assertion; her aim was always to show her friends off to the best advantage—not herself . . . But there were two sides. Here was the temperament of genius which always has its sunny and shady side. She was frequently depressed—often very provoking, as much as she could be agreeable—and we had violent quarrels, but the next day, or whenever we met, they were quite forgotten, and no allusion was made to them.[4]

The meeting had come at a decisive moment in Mary Ann's life. Isaac had married Sarah Rawlings in June, and she had gone to Birmingham to be a bridesmaid. As when Chrissey was married, she was happy for her brother, but he was now completely removed from her immediate sphere. In August she had written to Maria Lewis,

> I have of late had a depression that has disordered the vision of my mind's eye, and made me *alive* to what is certainly a *fact*, though my imagination when I am in health is most adept at concealing it, that I am *alone* in the world . . . I mean that I have no one who enters into my sorrows or griefs, no one with whom I can pour out my soul. . . .[5]

The Brays supplied this lack completely and with astonishing speed. Even more surprising was the immediacy of her reaction to their religious ideas; she devoured Mr. Bray's *Philosophy of Necessity*, re-read the entire *Bible*, and gave Hennell's *An Inquiry* a second reading.

49

On November 13th, within days of her first visit to Rose-hill, she wrote to Miss Lewis,

> My whole soul has been engrossed in the most interesting of all inquiries for the last few days, and to what my thoughts may lead, I know not—possibly to one that will startle you; but my only desire is to know the truth, my only fear is to cling to error.[6]

She now began an intensive study of the new Biblical criticism. And the result *was* startling. A succinct entry in her father's Journal records it:

> January 2, 1842: Went to Trinity Church in the forenoon. Miss Lewis went with me. Mary Ann did not go.[7]

In the twentieth century, absence from Sunday Service is such a commonplace occurrence as to be unremarkable. But in 1842, to miss church for any reason other than real illness or grave cause was unthinkable in the class to which Mary Ann Evans belonged. And to decline to attend, and to give as the reason the unequivocal statement that she had lost her faith in church doctrine, which is precisely the reason she gave, was considered catastrophic. Robert Evans's first reaction was surprise, then bewilderment, then anger. Naturally, he blamed the Brays, and ordered his daughter to have nothing more to do with them. He found it difficult to believe that anyone, especially a young girl, could discard the convictions of a lifetime in eight short weeks, and his opinion was perfectly reasonable, considering the circumstances. He had not been aware that Mary Ann had been scrutinizing her beliefs for the past four years; he had paid little attention to the books she had been reading and did not realize that, in a sense, her introduction to Rosehill had merely hastened an inevitable conclusion. Also, there was a social factor to consider; to his mind, *nice* people definitely were not free-thinkers, and Mary Ann's insistent championing of her new friends, who evidently had turned her into a free-thinker, irritated him beyond expression. He had not altogether liked her strict Evangelicalism, but it was at least respectable, and he had felt that she was young enough to outgrow it in time. In any case, certainly *it* had not led a twenty-two-year-old girl to oppose her father, something quite incredible in that age of the paterfamilias par excellence.

Mary Ann, for her part, was anything but tactful or diplomatic about expressing her change of mind. She exulted in her sense of freedom from "the wretched giant's bed of dogma" [8] and embraced free-thinking as enthusiastically as she had once embraced Evangelicalism. ". . . I wish to be among the ranks of that glorious crusade that is seeking to set Truth's Holy Sepulchre free from a usurped domination. We shall then see her Resurrection," [9] she wrote grandiloquently to Mrs. Pears. (Her father had included their neighbors in his general anathema against the Brays, so she had resorted to letters.) She herself was not really clear about what she believed; she knew only that she no longer believed in "a fear of vengeance eternal, gratitude for predestined salvation, or a revelation of future glories as a reward." [10] Which just about covered the teaching of the catechism and the Thirty-Nine Articles besides! Still, she felt strongly that "the only heaven, here or hereafter, is to be found in conformity with the will of the Supreme, a continual aiming at the attainment of the perfect ideal. . . ." [11]

Her former fears about the state of her soul vanished when she reached the conclusion that established doctrines of damnation, salvation, and redemption were later interpretations and additions to the teachings of Jesus as set forth in the Gospels. She could say, now, "I am more and more impressed with the duty of *finding* happiness." [12] Her religion had brought her comfort, but little joy. In recent months, she had looked back longingly to the happy days of her childhood; now her new sense of release from "a narrow, self-delusive fanaticism which is only a way of escaping pain by starving into dullness all the highest powers of your nature," as George Eliot was to describe it in *The Mill on the Floss*,[13] revived some of the lightness of spirit she had so sadly missed.

Certainly, every effort was made to persuade her to forsake these new and dangerous ideas. Mrs. Sibree, wife of the Reverend John Sibree, minister of the Independent Chapel, had been one of the first ladies to call at Bird Grove, and had become very fond of Mary Ann. Deeply distressed, she asked a friend, the Reverend Francis Watts, who taught theology at Spring Hill College in Birmingham, to talk with the recalcitrant young woman. Mr. Watts was an excellent choice for the task; he had a remarkable knowledge of the new Biblical criticism and the latest theological positions, as well as being thoroughly grounded in the Christian faith, and he seemed to be just the sort of person who could deal with Mary Ann's doubts, for he had come through just the same kind of study as hers with his faith intact. He quickly learned, however, that—whatever her friends might think —Mary Ann's opinions were not the result of superficial reading or conversation. *"She* has gone into the question!" [14] he remarked, in amazement. Miss Rebecca Franklin sent a Baptist minister to Bird Grove; his comment was even more emphatic: "That young lady must have had the devil at her elbow to suggest her doubts, for there was not one book that I recommended to her in support of Christian evidences that she had not read." [15] Mary Ann continued adamant, despite "more than the usual amount of *cooled* glances, . . . so many hailstones that make me wrap more closely about me the mantle of determined purpose. . . ." [16] She would *not* go to church. Her father refused finally even to discuss the matter with her. She wrote him a letter, too, in which she claimed kinship with "some of the finest minds of Christendom in past ages," [17] in cherishing the teachings of Jesus, but finding "the system of doctrines built upon the facts of his life and drawn from Jewish notions to be most dishonorable to God and most pernicious in its influence on individual social happiness." [18]

Robert Evans was by now completely at sea over a situation which nothing in his near-seventy years had prepared him to meet. Angered by her continued stubbornness, he moved swiftly to break the impasse. He had, he said, bought Bird Grove to give his daughter a good home and a proper address, of which she was obviously unappreciative.[19] So, Bird Grove would be put on the market. He would live either with Chrissey and her husband at Meriden, or in a small cottage on the Aylesford estate at Packington. And Mary Ann might do as she pleased. He would wash his hands of her.

Mary Ann, confronted by an obduracy as great as her own, reacted first with tears and then with firm decision. She would go into lodgings at Leamington and support herself by teaching. But before she could begin to pack her book boxes, help came from a most unexpected source. Her brother Isaac, though he did not approve of her views, nevertheless recognized her integrity, and insisted that, before she made a final break, she was to come to Griff for a long visit. He then persuaded his father to delay selling the house until Michaelmastide; Robert Evans agreed with unexpected immediacy. Other friends came to Mary Ann's support; the redoubtable Miss Rebecca Franklin summoned the irate father to her parlor and minced no words in telling him how he would be censured for casting off his daughter.[20] People simply did not behave that way! Mary Ann's free-thinking views might be just another phase which eventually she would overcome; certainly, her conduct was otherwise above reproach, hardly justifying a parental "never darken my door again" ultimatum. Even Sarah, Isaac's wife, spoke to her father-in-law with complete candor, telling him that he could place no more effective barrier to Mary Ann's return to orthodox behavior than by "making [her] wordly interests dependent upon it."[21]

Mary Ann went to Griff at the end of March. Wisely, neither Isaac nor his wife apparently made any attempt to discuss religious matters with her. She was welcomed with open arms, and given the quiet and the solitude that she at that moment craved. She went for long walks and drew new strength from the familiar surroundings. She thought quietly and deeply. Her estrangement from her father genuinely grieved her, and she really did not want to make the separation permanent. A week after her arrival, she was writing to Mrs. Pears, "On a retrospect of this past month, I regret nothing so much as my own impetuosity of feeling and judging."[22] She was, after all, relatively young, and completely unworldly. And she was honest enough to recognize that, just as she now felt that her rigorous Evangelicalism had been wrong, ultimately she might want to modify her present, completely opposite views. She had reached these convictions by a process of logical reasoning, and had been very impatient of those who did not follow her logic; now she was beginning to feel that there might be a flaw in that logic, and to realize, quite suddenly, that there were, moreover, some areas of life and human relationships where reason

54

and logic do not always apply. Intellects could not always agree; abstract truths were frequent sources of division. But there were emotions, sympathies, what she later called "truth of feeling," [23] which could bridge wide gaps between the differing views and make possible a mutual acceptance without in the slightest infringing on an individual's personal convictions.

By the end of April, she was back at Bird Grove. She arrived in time to greet her Aunt and Uncle Evans who had come for a week's visit, but the situation was rather constrained. Samuel and Elizabeth Evans's strong Methodist views contrasted too sharply with her own, and she was doubtless relieved when they returned to Staffordshire, so that she could try to re-establish her old relationship with her father. To her great joy, this was not difficult, for Robert Evans was as eager for a reconciliation as she herself now was. There was no capitulation on either side, but "truth of feeling" and their real love for one another prevailed. Robert Evans agreed to let her hold whatever views about religion she wished—probably secure in the knowledge that she would never try to tell him about them—and her compromise was recorded in his diary on May 15th, 1842:

"Went to Trinity Church. Mary Ann went with me today." [24]

V

The crisis was past, though Mary Ann was to bear the mark of it as long as she lived. But she eagerly took up the threads of her life again. There were immediate family problems to claim her attention: Chrissey's husband, Dr. Edward Clarke, had had financial difficulties because of an illness that prevented his continuing his practice, and he had decided to move from Meriden to a smaller house at Barford, nearer Warwick. The entire Clarke family came to pay a farewell visit at Bird Grove in July, and, in that same month, Sara Hennell, Mrs. Bray's sister, arrived at Rosehill for an extended stay. Much to Mary Ann's joy, her father had lifted his interdict against the Brays, so she could with his knowledge and consent call upon Miss Hennell soon afterward. It was at this time that the two young women established the basis for a life-long friendship. Mr. Evans's personal feeling about the Brays was still ambivalent; he was not at all certain that they were the best examples for his daughter, nor that the works of Spinoza, which Mary Ann had begun to study intensively with Mrs. Bray, were the proper kind of read-ing for a "young female." But, at the same time, he real-ized that his daughter needed companionship, and the music and conversation at Rosehill meant so much to her that he did not have the heart to disapprove openly.

Isaac, however, was not at all backward about express-ing his opinion; he said unequivocally that his sister was ruining her chances of finding a husband. Her continued visits to a house where the owner could introduce only free-thinkers and radicals to her would make respectable, suitable young men wary, and the free-thinkers and the radicals would not be interested in courting her because she had resumed her church attendance.[1] He maintained vigorously that Mary Ann must have a husband—after all, she *was* twenty-three years old. He even suggested that his father leave Coventry altogether, thereby remov-ing Mary Ann completely from the pernicious influence of Rosehill. Robert Evans, however, refused. He did not want to pull up stakes again, now that the religious situa-tion had been resolved, and he finally told his son flatly that he had no objection to Mary Ann's activities. It is possible that his permission was motivated, at least in part, by a kind of subconscious realization that his daugh-ter, if she married at all, would have to marry a man on her own intellectual level, and such a man Isaac, for all his worthiness, would not be likely to know. "The little wench," he could easily see, would never be happy with a man like Isaac. Also, present events at Rosehill might turn Mary Ann's own thoughts toward matrimony more readily than any definite effort to place her "on parade."

Charles Hennell, Mrs. Bray's brother, had become engaged, and, in November of 1842, his fiancée, Elizabeth Brabant—nicknamed "Rufa" by Samuel Taylor Coleridge because of her beautiful reddish-blonde hair—came to visit her future in-laws. Mary Ann, by then considered one of the Bray family, was invited to all the engagement festivities, and she liked Rufa immediately. The daughter of Dr. Rufus Brabant, a physician of Devizes, a most remarkably learned old gentleman who had been at work for many years on a monumental work which, when completed, would—he said!—dispose of all the supernatural elements of Christianity, Rufa had served for several years as her father's secretary. She had also begun work on her own translation of Strauss's *Das Leben Jesu,* a rationalist biography of Jesus which had created a tremendous furor in Germany in 1840. She was precisely the kind of young woman Mary Ann would find congenial, and her liking evidently was reciprocated. When Rufa was married to Charles Hennell in November 1843, she invited Mary Ann to come up to London to be one of her bridesmaids.

Mary Ann was delighted at the prospect, not only of being in the wedding party, but also for the opportunity it would provide her for meeting Dr. Brabant. The elderly scholar was everything she had anticipated. His great learning fascinated her; he knew Strauss personally, and other contemporary philosophers whom she admired. She was perfectly contented just to be near him and listen to him talk. The only thing that kept her hero-worship from being embarrassing was the fact that it was so patently genuine. The great man was pleased by her obvious admiration, and he was also much impressed by the quality of her mind. After Rufa's wedding, he impulsively invited her to return to Devizes with him for an indefinite stay. He and his wife would be lonely without Rufa, he told her, and they would enjoy her company. It might be, too, that she could help with his work while his daughter was away.

Robert Evans's permission was asked, and he consented to a two-week visit. Mary Ann was in seventh heaven. The thought that she might actually be permitted to help this great man, as Rufa had done, made her ecstatic. She was welcomed with great kindness and courtesy by the doctor's blind wife, and with perhaps a bit more reserve by her sister, Sarah Hughes, who lived with them. Dr. Brabant told Mary Ann to consider the library her room; he nicknamed her "Deutera," "second daughter," promised that he would teach her more Greek, and said that she was to read to him daily in German. It is quite possible, considering her impulsiveness—though unprovable —that she really knelt at his feet, offering to devote her life to his service; such an action would have been quite in character. Her letters to Mrs. Bray reveal her excitement: "We walk and talk together, and I am never weary of his company. I have just written father to beg for a longer leave of absence. . . ." [2] To Sara Hennell she wrote, "I am in a little Heaven here, Dr. Brabant being its archangel." [3]

She did not, however, reckon with the possibility of female jealousy. Mrs. Brabant, though blind, was fully aware of her husband's interest in this young girl, and Sarah Hughes supplied with her eyesight what Mrs. Brabant would probably never have seen. She lost little time in telling her sister of these suspicions. Mrs. Brabant staged a disagreeable and angry scene and literally ordered Mary Ann out of the house at once, with the added thrust that if ever she set foot in their home again, she herself would leave it. This was hard enough, but, even harder, Dr. Brabant—far from taking any responsibility for the defense of Mary Ann or making any explanations to his wife—allowed her to believe that the entire situation had been Mary Ann's fault, and permitted Mary Ann to leave Devizes under a cloud, well before the original two-week visit had expired.

Mary Ann's humiliation was acute. In her idealism, she had considered Dr. Brabant as a superior being. Perhaps she had been a little indiscreet in her enthusiastic adoration, and the doctor may have behaved foolishly in his delighted acceptance of her attention, but only a most petty, almost poisoned mind could have attributed any conscious or unconscious desire to supplant Mrs. Brabant in any of her actions. She was genuinely shocked that such accusations could occur to friends whom she had considered on a higher plane. Even more, she was hurt to the quick by Dr. Brabant's easy acquiescence to Miss Hughes' suspicions. She had discovered her idol's clay feet under circumstances peculiarly painful, and this revelation she found it difficult to rise above. There is no doubt that the experience made a permanent scar, despite her later attempts to gloss it over: "If ever I offered incense to him, it was because there was no other deity at hand and because I wanted some deity *pour passer le temps*. I always . . . laughed at him in my sleeve," [4] she wrote to Sara Hennell in 1846, but this comment sounds suspiciously like *post hoc* wishful thinking. The truth of the matter would seem more likely to be found in her answer to a friend's question, many years later, when *Middlemarch* was making a sensation. Asked where on earth she had found the model for Mr. Casaubon, the elderly clergyman whom the heroine marries out of admiration for his seeming intellect, and in hope of helping him with his "great unfinished"—never to be finished—work, "with a humorous solemnity which was quite in earnest, she pointed to her own heart."[5] Again, what Mary Ann Evans experienced, George Eliot remembered later and used to create one of the most horrifying, sharply etched portraits of an academic fraud in all literature.

The episode at Devizes, however, did not in the slightest affect her friendship with the doctor's daughter. And when, in 1844, Rufa Brabant Hennell decided that she could not continue with her translation of Strauss's *Das Leben Jesu,* at her suggestion it was given to Mary Ann to complete. The Brabants were fortunate indeed in her willingness to accept such a commission. Translating the work would have been a formidable project for a most seasoned scholar to contemplate, for it was in thick volumes, written in the heavy, pedantic style so typical of nineteenth-century German scholars. Mary Ann had already read the work in the original, so she came to translation with some preparation; nevertheless, she quickly discovered that reading a text was one thing and translating it into good, idiomatic English quite another. She did like Strauss's approach; he did not deny Jesus of Nazareth historically, but insisted dogmatically that all those details of his life which could not be historically documented or scientifically proved (i.e., the miracles) must be regarded as "myth." Such statements as

The hero of a biography, according to modern conceptions, should be entirely and clearly human. A personage half human, half divine, may be a figure plausible enough

in poetry and fable, but is never in the present day chosen
as the subject of historical narrative.[6]

coincided precisely with Mary Ann's own present views.
She also liked Strauss's idea that Jesus was among those
who have shown "to mankind most purely and most
plainly what it ought to be." [7] In those respects, she was
pleased and excited at the prospect of presenting Strauss
to the English intellectuals.

She was, however, practical. The translation would
take considerable time—actually, it was to be her sole
occupation for two years. Such a book would not have the
popular appeal that would guarantee a large sale. Under
those circumstances, publishers generally preferred to issue the book "by subscription"; that is, interested individuals would contribute enough money to ensure that
printing and binding costs would be met. In March of
1844, Mary Ann wrote to Sara Hennell, "I shall be very
glad to learn from you the *particulars* as to the mode of
publication for Strauss—who are the parties that will find
the funds, and whether the manuscripts are to be put into
the hands of anyone when complete, or whether they are
to go directly from me to the publisher?" [8] Upon being
assured that funds had been promised and that John
Chapman was interested in publishing the work, she committed herself to the undertaking.[9] She even studied
Hebrew and Jewish history in order to acquire what she
considered the necessary background for her work. Her
father must have thrown up his hands in despair. Mary
Ann was becoming a "learned lady." Still, she could view
herself with a degree of humor; upon hearing from Mrs.
Bray that Strauss had been informed (probably by Rufa
Brabant Hennell) about her translation, she answered
wryly,

> I do not think it was kind to Strauss . . . to tell him
> that a *young lady* was translating his book. I am sure he
> must have some twinges of alarm to think he was depen-
> dent upon that most contemptible specimen of human be-
> ing for his English reputation.[10]

She did not, however, spend all of her time at her desk.
During July, the Brays took her with them on an excursion to the Cumberland Lakes, stopping at Manchester,
which she loathed: ". . . the streets and houses where
humans do actually live and breathe there are worse than
a book can tell," [11] and Liverpool, where she was entertained by Mr. and Mrs. James Martineau, brother and
sister-in-law of Harriet Martineau, the novelist. She had
just returned to Bird Grove when Mr. Bray arranged for
her to accompany him on a trip to London, to have James
Deville, the noted phrenologist, make a cast of her head.
Mary Ann's attitude toward phrenology seems to have
been one of tolerant amusement, though she was interested in it, as she was in everything else, and Mr. Bray's
comment, after Deville's phrenological reading, is certainly both significant and prophetic:

> She was of a most affectionate disposition, always requiring
> someone to lean upon, preferring what has hitherto been
> considered the stronger sex, to the other and more im-
> pressible. She was not fitted to stand alone.[12]

He could, of course, have reached the same conclusion
merely by his own observation of her. She was a rare
combination of almost masculine intellect and logic, and
sheer feminine dependency and intuition. Some of her
seemingly inexplicable actions can be explained psycho-
logically in the light of these paradoxical characteristics.

Back from London, she toiled at her translation all
through the autumn and winter. "I am thoroughly tired

of my own garb for Strauss's thoughts," she wrote Sara Hennell. "I am awfully afraid of my own translation, and I want you to come and comfort me." [13] By spring of 1845, she was even more disconsolate, for the promised subscription money was not forthcoming in the amounts anticipated.

> Glad am I that someone can enjoy Strauss! The million certainly will not, and I have ceased to sit down to him with any relish . . . I can possess my soul in patience about Mr. Parkes, though I should work much better if I had some proof sheets coming in to assure me that my soul-stupefying labor is not in vain.[14]

There was also a personal situation in her life at the moment that undoubtedly contributed to her general sense of restlessness and depression. She had met a young man, a picture restorer, whose identity remains unknown, whom her friend liked very much and to whom she had become strongly attracted. He definitely had been smitten with her, for he proposed immediately. Some biographers maintain that her father refused to sanction the match, and, almost certainly, Robert Evans would not have approved of a picture restorer—whose income would be both limited and fluctuating—as a son-in-law. But there seems, judging from the veiled references in the letters of Mrs. Bray and Mary Ann, to have been another reason—that Mary Ann herself, after a few weeks' acquaintance, decided that she did not love him enough, and that marriage to him would "involve too great a sacrifice of her mind and pursuits." [15] She evidently gave him his *congé* by letter, which he accepted gracefully enough; then she worried intensely over the possibility of having hurt his feelings with more brusqueness than she had intended. It wasn't that translating

Strauss meant more to her than marriage; she simply did not feel that happiness in marriage would be possible for either of them. Nevertheless, she regretted any lack of tact or consideration. "If circumstances could be repeated with the added conditions of my experiences, I should act very differently," she wrote soberly to Sara Hennell. "As it is I have of now dismissed it from my mind, and I only keep it recorded in my book of reference, article '*Precipitancy, ill effects of.*' " [16]

One day was memorable in the general gloom of Strauss, headaches, and pangs of conscience. In April, she was invited to a dinner in honor of Harriet Martineau at Bracebridge Hall, just outside Coventry, and found the celebrated novelist "one of those people whom one does not venerate less for having seen." [17] But, for the most part, the struggle with Strauss absorbed her completely. She had finished two volumes by the first of May, though she was not at all happy about the conclusion of Volume II. "They are not Strauss's best thoughts, nor are they put into his translator's best language, but I have not the courage to imitate Gibbon—put my work in the fire and begin again." [18] Volume III still faced her, and there would, of course, be the revisions. To add to all these difficulties, Chrissey's husband had finally gone into bankruptcy as a result of his illness; and their four children were sent to Mary Ann to look after during the household upheaval. The youngest, Clara Christiana Clark, was not yet a year old, and was a quite spoiled, demanding infant. "The young lady's smiles were abundant this morning, interspersed however with frowns which I am afraid she is taught to think as amusing as the smiles. To me, they are anything but interesting," [19] she wrote wearily to Sara Hennell. She had also undertaken to tutor Mary Sibree, the daughter of the woman who had tried to reconvert her to orthodoxy, in German and Italian. And still, "leathery brain must work at leathery Strauss," [20] she commented wryly, worrying about Strauss's Greek quotations—should they be translated into English or left in the original? By September, the proofs of Volume I were in her hands, but Volume II was scarcely begun.

The Brays became alarmed at her constant headaches and general exhaustion. They were planning a two-week tour of the Scottish highlands, and they begged her to join them. Sara Hennell came to Rosehill in October and added her own pleas to theirs. Mary Ann at first demurred; Chrissey's difficulties were far from settled, and she, too, was now at Bird Grove. Mr. Bray finally took matters into his own hands; he paid a call on Robert Evans and told him that Mary Ann must have a holiday, if she was not to become really ill. Reminded that Chrissey would be there to care for him and to manage the house, Mr. Evans quickly gave permission, and Mary Ann left for the Highlands on October 14th. The trip in every way was a thrilling experience for her, because she was seeing the native country of her idol, Sir Walter Scott. But when they reached Edinburgh, there was a letter waiting for her from Isaac, telling her that their father had fallen and broken his leg only a few hours after she had left Bird Grove. Mary Ann wanted to return at once, without even a glimpse of Abbotsford and Melrose Abbey, but the Brays dissuaded her, insisting that her strength was not equal to the journey unless one of them went with her. She did not want them to shorten their holiday on her account, so she continued with them. Much to her relief, when she reached home at the end of the month, she found that her father was recovering nicely, but her feelings of anxiety and guilt at not returning at once had been intense.

She had had a rest, however, and Strauss was taken up again with a right good will, until February 1846, when she admitted to being "Strauss sick." Translating his dissection of the Crucifixion made her physically ill, and only the small reproduction of Thorvaldson's statue of the Risen Christ, which she kept before her on her desk as she wrote, made it possible for her to continue her work.[21] Her father had not been well during the winter, and all the time she could spare from her desk had been spent in reading to him. The proofs of the first two volumes were a disappointment; they were full of maddening errors and the type used for the Greek quotations was so faint that it made her eyes ache. But she was cheered by the news that Charles Hennell had sent some of the proof sheets to Professor Strauss, and that the great philosopher had been so impressed with them that he had agreed to contribute a Latin preface to the finished work. He sent an appreciative letter to Mary Ann, as well, which delighted her, and mitigated to a considerable extent her anxiety and nervousness over the approaching publication date.

The Life of Jesus made its appearance on June 15, 1846, under the aegis of John Chapman, publisher, whose own interest in "radical causes" and books had established an immediate bond between himself and Mary Ann when they had met in London early that month. The book was published anonymously—it was not the kind that a lady would admit to having written—and was, for the most part, kindly reviewed. Mary Ann rejoiced: "All the world is bathed in glory and beauty for me now," [22] she wrote to Sara Hennell in October. Her success, as she had hoped, was bringing her new opportunities to use her pen. In December of 1846, she wrote the first in a series of little sketches for the Coventry

Herald, entitled "Poetry and Prose from the Notebook of an Eccentric," her first original work. There were six of these sketches, ironic commentaries on the social scene and its foibles, in the style of Addison and Steele's *Spectator Papers* but with a characteristic touch of her own humor and vivacity which anticipated the work of the future George Eliot. The most delightful is called "Hints on Snubbing," in which the "Eccentric" says,

> You can no more snub your betters than you can patronize them; on the contrary, toadyism towards superiors is the invariable attendant upon a large endowment of the snubbing faculty.[23]

She comments slyly on society's attitude toward writers: "All men of a thousand-a-year, who can afford to give champagne at their dinner parties, may feel authorized to snub any poorer genius of less magnitude than Dickens." [24] Newspaper editors may "choose for a victim any individual who presumes to avow an opinion in opposition to their own—and what is more, to act upon it." [25] "But," she cautions, "let everyone beware of snubbing on religious grounds in quarters where there is wealth, or fashion, or influence." [26] And finally, "As regards the snub domestic, gentlemen should by no means neglect one of the grand privileges of conjugal life, an unlimited power of snubbing their wives." [27] Not exactly Mrs. Poyser or Aunt Glegg, but the sketches do show a glimmering of the ironic wit which would ultimately delight her era.

Only one cloud dimmed her horizon at the beginning of the New Year (1847)—her father's illness. They had taken a holiday together at Dover during the summer, and she had noticed that his health was far more frail than she had realized. That autumn, a cholera epidemic had broken out in Coventry; Charles Bray had been desperately ill and Mary Ann had been exposed to the disease at Rosehill, but Robert Evans mercifully escaped. In April of 1847, he was well enough to allow her to pay a short visit to London, where she heard Bellini's *I Puritani*, and Mendelssohn's new oratorio, *Elijah*, with the composer himself conducting. She wrote about it enthusiastically to Mary Sibree, calling it a "glorious production" [28]—a far cry from the days when she had debated whether such music might be an occasion of sin. At the end of September, she took another short trip with her father, this time to the Isle of Wight, where, much to her joy, his strength and spirits seemed substantially to revive, and they returned to Bird Grove to pass a quiet, uneventful winter.

By April of 1848, however, Robert Evans was very ill. Repeated attacks of influenza had weakened his heart, and for days he lay almost in a coma, breathing heavily in hard, quick gasps. Then he would revive, and always call to his daughter to read aloud to him. He was pathetically dependent on her, though he refused to permit himself to admit it, and Mary Ann slept on a sofa in his bedroom, to be there at the instant that he needed her. She permitted no one to nurse him but herself. There seemed to be no hope for his recovery, then, quite unexpectedly, he rallied. At the end of May, he was able to go to St. Leonard's, near Hastings, where his doctors hoped he would be benefited by the sea air.

But he was much too ill—far more ill than anyone realized. In 1848 there were no X rays or cardiograms, no miracle drugs or oxygen tents. He had not been at St. Leonard's a week before the cough and shortness of breath returned, and he was actually worse than he had been at Coventry. There was nothing to do but to bring him home, which Mary Ann did, facing the cruel fact that he would never get well again. She made him as comfortable as possible, gave him the required medicines, read to him, played the piano for him, and did whatever gave him comfort or pleasure during that long, weary year, for Robert Evans was a strong man, even in weakness. She was terrified lest his mind crack under the strain—she could not have borne to see him live on mentally incapacitated.[29] She never left him; she refused to leave him, except once, when Ralph Waldo Emerson visited Rosehill and her longing to meet the celebrated American philosopher-poet overcame her scruples.[30]

To keep her mind occupied, she started another translation—this time of Spinoza's *Tractatus Theologico-Politicus*. Strangely enough, she seems to have been influenced by her father to undertake it; one day he had looked at her with penetrating lucidity and said, "I thought you were going on with the book." [31] He had heard her discussing the possibility of a Spinoza translation with Mrs. Bray before his illness, and his comment was his laconic way of giving his approval not only to it, but also the work she had already done. Mary Ann was moved to tears, and immediately returned to her desk during those hours when her father was asleep. But when he was awake, she was always beside him; ". . . my chair by my father's bedside is a very blessed seat to me," [32] she wrote to Mrs. Abijah Pears. And to Charles Bray, "Strange to say, I feel that these will ever be the happiest days of my life to me. The one deep strong love I have ever known has now its highest exercise and fullest reward— the worship of sorrow is *the* worship for mortals." [33]

Robert Evans died during the night on May 30, 1849. Mary Ann, exhausted by her ordeal, remained at his bedside, knowing now that she was indeed alone. Her cry, "What shall I be without my father?" [34] expresses poignantly her sense of bereavement and utter desolation.

She was no longer the "little wench." There was no one of her own blood to call her "my dear child." Isaac and Chrissey would certainly "do for her," but they had their own responsibilities on which she felt she should not intrude. Besides, there were practical matters to consider. Her father, like all Victorian fathers, had kept her in complete ignorance of all financial matters. She knew that she would inherit something, but would it be enough to make her independent? Could she remain at Bird Grove? Could she make her living, if she must, as a translator, or should she become a teacher? A maelstrom of thoughts battered at her benumbed mind. She was nearly thirty years old, unmarried and not likely to be married, a spinster in nineteenth-century England where women like herself were pitied and made objects of charity. She must, at that moment, have remembered Maria Lewis. Was that the only life possible for her now?

Fortunately, help came to her quickly. Her beloved friends, Mr. and Mrs. Bray, had been planning a tour of the Continent, and all arrangements were made for their leaving England that June. With their characteristic generosity, they insisted that Mary Ann come with them. She was really too numb to make any immediate decisions for herself, and legal matters would naturally be handled by Isaac, since he was the son of the family. A complete change of scene would give her an opportunity to put her situation into perspective and to consider alternatives quietly, without haste. Mary Ann was easily persuaded, for she thought she could not bear to be at Griff just now. So, on the 11th of June, five days after her father was buried in Chilvers Coton Churchyard, Mr. Bray, who had returned to Coventry for the funeral, took her to London to join his wife. On the following day, still dazed from shock and grief, she left London with the Brays for Paris.

VI

The Europe which greeted Mary Ann Evans that summer
was a continent still in a turmoil from the preceding
"Year of Revolution," 1848. From Paris to Rome, from
Spain to Poland, the fires kindled by successive uprisings
were still ablaze. Comparative peace reigned in France,
which had been first to depose her king, Louis Philippe,
and send him fleeing for his life across the Channel to
London. Louis Napoleon, nephew of Bonaparte, was now
President of the Republic; in a few years he would follow
his uncle's example and proclaim himself Emperor of

the French, but, in June 1849, his country was still luxu-
riating in unaccustomed democracy and political liberal-
ism. Not that the French armies were inactive—Garibaldi
was still fanning the flames of the Risorgimento, and
French troops were on the march to defend Rome and
the Papal States against him. Austrian forces were engaged in putting down revolts in Tuscany and Lombardy.
The people of Hungary had declared their independence
and had elected Kossuth as their head of state for a brief
time, until, with Russian assistance, Austria crushed that
flurry of democratic actions. With war actually in progress, or, in many cases, imminent, the world was not
precisely safe for travelers, so the Brays and Mary Ann
kept to well-patroled routes. From Paris they went by
rail and diligence to Lyons, then down the river Rhone
by steamer to Avignon. Nice and Genoa were fairly quiet,
and so was Milan, but, even so, they did not linger in
these cities very long. Turning north, they stopped at
Como, then went on into Switzerland—always a secure
haven—reaching Vevey at the end of July.

Had this journey occurred at any other time, doubtless
Mary Ann would have written numerous letters to her
family and friends, giving her opinions and observations
in great detail. Even during her father's illness she had
followed the Paris uprising of 1848 with interest, and her
heart and soul had been with the republican cause. "I
have little patience with people who can find time to pity
Louis Philippe and his moustachioed sons," [1] she remarked scornfully, shortly after that monarch's ignomin-
ious arrival in London. At that moment in her life, she
was profoundly anti-royalist: "Our little humbug of a
queen is more endurable than the rest of her race because
she calls forth a chivalrous feeling." [2] This remark is
startling, considering the conservatism of Mary Ann's

own family; however, it must be remembered that Victoria Regina was, in 1848, quite unpopular with her subjects, so perhaps Mary Ann was merely voicing current opinion. And the Brays, as "liberals," would have influenced her, doubtless, by their own great impatience with royalty. But Europe in June of 1849 inspired no comment on her part about any of the momentous events swirling around her. She was too emotionally exhausted to do more than to go amiably where the Brays led her; travel, the favorite nineteenth-century panacea for grief, did not help her at all. What she needed was a prolonged period of rest and quiet, away from familiar scenes that reminded her too vividly and constantly of her father, free from her brother's and sister's and in-laws' well-intentioned advice and endless questions and speculations about her future. She did not know herself what she wanted to do; indeed, she could not know. From a sheltered, protected life, she had been thrust into a world where she had to take all responsibility for herself. She did not know how to be independent. No doubt Charles Bray's remark, "She was not fitted to stand alone," haunted her, but, fit or not, she had that lesson to learn.

So she decided to stay in Switzerland. Geneva attracted her because of its beauty, and also because many artists and writers had found refuge there. The city boasted a university and a very intellectual society, which she might find congenial when she reached the point where she would feel able to be with people again. The Brays helped her to find a place to live; they settled upon the Pension La Vallière, a pleasant, exclusive family hotel in the suburb of Campagne Plongeon. Here they left her, promising to send her books and winter clothes to her as soon as they reached England. She refused to give any definite date for her own return. "I will never go near a friend again, until I can bring joy and peace in my heart. . . ." [3] She wrote to Sara Hennell, but, in the same letter, she begged her friend to write often. Despite her reluctance to be in England at that moment, she was nevertheless homesick, and she admitted it. She certainly did not intend to become a permanent exile, but she had no cognizance of her really great capacity for friendship.

The clientele of the Pension La Vallière was a very aristocratic one, and at first Mary Ann, diffident with strangers even in familiar surroundings, found herself the proverbial fish out of water. "The going down to tea bores me, and I shall get out of it as soon as I can. . . ." [4] She wrote the Brays two days after her arrival. "The Marquis and his friends play at whist—the old ladies sew, and Mde. Valliere [sic] says things so true that they are insufferable." [5] A week later, however, she had made friends with Madame la Marquise de St. Germaine, of whom she wrote, "the most charming person I ever saw with kindness enough to make the ultra-politeness of her manners quite genuine." [6] Though the Marquise was a devout Catholic, Mary Ann really enjoyed discussing religion with her. Young Baron de Herder, grandson of the philosopher Johann Gottfried von Herder, amused her by his heavy opposition to all gallantry; she was quite certain that he must be a Communist! [7] Her letters to the Brays during these weeks indicate that she was gradually regaining her interest in the world about her. On August 20th, she wrote anxiously that she hoped her black velvet dress and her fur muff and tippet had been packed in the box of winter clothes: "The people here dress and think more about dressing even than in England. You would not know me, if you saw me." [8] In the same letter, she confessed humorously that the Marquise had created a new hairdo for her:

75

She has abolished all my curls and made two things that stick out on each side of my head like those of the sphinx. All the world says I look infinitely better, so I comply, though to myself I seem uglier than ever—if possible.[9]

By August 28th, she was seriously considering the idea of spending the winter in Paris. The Marquise urged her, but she decided against it. She was already accustomed to Geneva, and besides, "people do not seem to think me quite old enough to ramble about at will . . . As long as people carry a Mademoiselle before their name, there is far less liberty for them on the continent than in England." [10]

Nevertheless, comfortable though she was at the Pension la Vallière, she felt that she would need to find a less expensive place to live. She wanted to be able to afford a small piano so that she could practice her music, and also to continue her language studies. It would definitely be more practical, as well, for her to be in the town of Geneva rather than in the outskirts, for snow-blocked roads were common in the winter, and the Pension la Vallière had been known to be isolated for weeks at a time. It was difficult to find a place congenial and respectable, as well as reasonable, for there seemed to be a huge influx of visitors that season, and accommodations even under normal circumstances were not more than adequate. It was not until October that she met Madame and Monsier D'Albert-Durade, whose pleasant home in the Rue des Chanoines offered a single apartment for one paying guest. They liked each other instantly, and Mary Ann, with a sigh of relief, moved in with baggage, boxes, books, and piano. She could not have been more fortunate in her choice; her winter at Geneva was to be one of the happiest periods of her entire life.

Alexandre Louis François D'Albert-Durade was a painter, one of the finest portrait artists in Geneva. He was a dwarf, only four feet in height, with a deformed spine, the result of a childhood accident; but he possessed an abundance of that quality which the French call *esprit*, and his genuine kindliness and eagerness for his friends to enjoy life as much as he did himself made his physical defect seem negligible. He loved music, and played the piano and sang well. He loved the theater, and frequently persuaded his guests to participate in play-readings as an evening's entertainment. The creative and intellectual society of Geneva found its way to the house in the Rue des Chanoines, and François D'Albert-Durade was at his best as host for supper parties and musicales, in which the "young English mademoiselle" automatically was included. With utmost tact, he and his wife made Mary Ann feel that she was not just a lodger, taken in to augment the family income, nor even a transient guest. She was a friend, who received from them the same kind of affectionate consideration that she had enjoyed at Rosehill. "M. and Mde. D'Albert introduce me to their friends as though they wished me to know them, as if they wished me to like their friends and their friends to like me," [11] she wrote delightedly to the Brays.

Nor was the situation even remotely similar to the unpleasant one which had upset her so terribly at Devizes. Madame D'Albert sensed immediately Mary Ann's need for wholehearted, loving acceptance, and proceeded to "mother" her. She insisted on her breakfasting in bed every morning, and scolded her if she caught her reading by the light of one candle. For Mary Ann was studying again—she was reading Voltaire and doing some mathematics every day "to prevent by brain from becoming soft." [12] She was also attending a course of lectures on

Experimental Physics, given by the noted Professor Auguste de La Rive, of the University faculty. Far from criticizing the "English mademoiselle" for constantly "having her nose in a book," Madame D'Albert promptly supplied her with a good lamp and five candlesticks, an unprecedented gesture for a thrifty Swiss housewife. She hung the walls of Mary Ann's room with pictures, one "the most beautiful group of flowers conceivable thrown on an open Bible" [13] which she herself had painted. She was lavish with affection. "She kisses me like a mother, and I am baby enough to find that a great addition to my happiness." [14] Moreover, there was conversation at the Rue des Chanoines to delight the most discriminating taste even when there were no visitors, and with the D'Albert-Durades Mary Ann enjoyed the same freedom that had meant so much to her at Rosehill. "I can say anything to M. and Mde. D'Albert. M. D'A. understands everything, and if Madame does not understand she *believes*—that is to say, she seems sure that I mean something edifying." [15] Small wonder that she loved Geneva. "Coventry is a fool to it," [16] she wrote the Brays.

The winter was severe; for two months Geneva was enveloped in heavy mist. By February, however, the weather had cleared sufficiently for her to see the Jura in all its glory, and soon she was taking some of the celebrated "walks" up the easier mountain slopes. Monsieur D'Albert had persuaded her to let him paint her portrait: "The idea of making a study of my visage is droll enough," [17] she commented. The portrait, which is now in the National Portrait Gallery in London, shows an intelligent-looking young woman, with light brown hair parted in the center, drawn smoothly across the top of her head and puffed out slightly at the sides—doubtless the Marquise de St. Germaine's idea of coiffure. The eyes are clear and honest, the lips curved in a slight smile. The nose is a little long—Mary Ann always despaired of her nose—but the general impression is one of charm, obviously arrived at without the use of cosmetics, combined with good breeding. She is wearing a dark dress—probably the famous black velvet—with a wasp waist, and the bodice is cut diagonally to reveal a beautiful lace guimpe with a round collar. Looking at this portrait, one can readily understand why Mary Ann Evans was considered an extremely elegant and beautiful young woman. It is not a face which might inspire love at first sight, but the qualities of sympathy, perception, and loveliness that her friends discovered in her are plainly revealed. Quite obviously, she had regained that serenity so characteristic of her, and the glint of humor in the eyes and smile indicates that her natural high spirits had been blessedly revived during those months at the Rue de Chanoines.

But the time had come when her obligations in England could wait no longer. She had also come to the realization that the small income her father had been able to leave her could not support her completely, even in Switzerland, unless she worked. There was no work of any kind she could do in Geneva; the city was full of translators whose reputations had been established over a period of years. In England, she did have some contacts with publishers, and, though her Strauss translation had been issued anonymously, her work was known to a few influential people like the Brays and Charles Hennell and John Chapman, who could be depended on for help. So, on March 18, 1850, she reluctantly left Geneva, accompanied by Monsieur D'Albert-Durade. He had intended to go with her only as far as Paris, but she seemed so completely helpless and lost—she had never in her life traveled alone—that he decided to escort her all the way to London. Here they parted, he to remain in London to look at the picture galleries, including Mr. Godfrey Windus's collection of Turner drawings which, in 1850, interested no one except Mr. Windus and John Ruskin. Mary Ann took the train to Coventry and went directly to Rosehill, where she rested for several days before starting on a round of family visits.

She found these visits very difficult. "My return to England is anything but joyous to me, for old associations are rather painful than otherwise to me," [18] she wrote to Martha Jackson from Griff in early April. Naturally, she missed her father terribly, especially at Griff, which, now completely in Isaac's hands, had taken on her brother's personality. He was not unwelcoming, and he was willing to do his brotherly duty by his unmarried sister; but he now had three children to consider as well as his wife, and he had no intention of permitting Mary Ann's ideas and ways to damage his ever-increasing reputation for substantiality in the community. Mary Ann quickly discovered that she was an interloper. "It was some envious demon that drove me across the Jura to see people who don't want me," [19] she wrote rather bitterly to Sara Hennell. No doubt if she had been willing to subside into the niche of a typical Victorian maiden lady, Isaac, albeit reluctantly, would have been amenable to her making her home at Griff. But Mary Ann Evans had tasted independence, and she realized that what would be a duty to Isaac would be to her a stifling existence. From Griff, she went to see Chrissey, where she wrote Mrs. Bray, "Dear Chrissey is much kinder than anyone else in the family and I am happiest with her . . . But I am delighted to feel that I am of no importance to any of them, and have no motive for living amongst them." [20]

She had always been so devoted to her family that it was both shock and grief to her to discover that they no longer wanted her, except on their terms. But this discovery also gave her the necessary impetus to put a half-devised plan into action.

John Chapman, who had published her translation of Strauss, was in the process of taking over the editorship of the *Westminster Review*. This quarterly magazine under John Stuart Mill had enjoyed a distinguished reputation as a political commentary, but it had lost some of its prestige under the present ownership. Chapman wanted to revive that prestige, and he also wanted to expand the magazine's format to include literary articles and reviews. Shortly after Mary Ann returned to Rosehill in June, he came up to see her. Then, in October, he came again, this time with Robert Mackay, a young theologian who would ultimately become a celebrated Plato scholar, who had just published his first book bearing the formidable title, *The Progress of Intellect as Exemplified in the Religious Development of the Greeks and Hebrews*. Chapman asked Mary Ann to write a review of this tome for the *Westminster Review,* so that he might judge her capabilities in that area and consider the idea of employing her on a regular basis.

A "review" in that era bore no resemblance to today's book review columns. The nineteenth-century reviewer was expected not only to discuss the book, but also to add such commentary and information from his own store of knowledge as might illuminate the subject further. Actually, a book review Victorian style was merely a "springboard" for the author's own essay on ideas that the book suggested to him. Some individuals even used the occasion for political partisanship; Lord Macaulay's review of Croker's edition of Boswell's *Life of Johnson* is a notorious example. Certainly no more difficult task could have been set Mary Ann than to review Robert Mackay's two-volume philosophical treatise.

But she was prepared for it. Mackay's thesis, the development of the idea of God, was a subject she had studied intensively and discussed frequently at Rosehill. She had probably read more widely and deeply in the general area of pre-Christian religious belief and practices than had most of her contemporaries; furthermore, she could write clearly and cogently on difficult subjects, as she had proved by her translation of Strauss's involved German into idiomatic English. She read Mackay's book and wrote the review within the month. In mid-November, Chapman summoned her to London for a conference; he paid for her article, promised its publication in the January issue of the magazine, and offered her a position on his editorial staff, starting in January 1851. Her living arrangements were easily settled: she would move into the Chapman house where several other staff members also had their lodgings. A "literary evening" which Chapman held in her honor was the crowning assurance of her acceptance in the world of London journalism. Tremendously excited by this almost miraculous change in her fortunes, Mary Ann returned to Rosehill to pack her trunk, then went to spend the Christmas holidays with Chrissey.

On January 8, 1851, she stood on the doorstep of Number 142 Strand. It was the year of the Great Exhibition, which was to show England's achievements in art and science to the world, and the city was already filled with anticipation over this great event. It was a most propitious time for anyone to be in London, especially someone like Mary Ann Evans who was, quite literally, beginning a new life with great expectations. At the moment, she probably thought only of the immediate possibilities—the *Westminster Review* and the concurrent opportunities her association with the magazine might offer. She could not have foreseen in the slightest that she had taken a momentous step on the road leading to her ultimate destiny.

VII

Early biographers of George Eliot were conspicuously silent concerning those first few months in 1851 when Mary Ann Evans took up residence at 142 Strand. Their motives were entirely praiseworthy; it was not customary in the nineteenth century to present any distinguished author, man or woman, in any but the most favorable light. Episodes which might be remotely discreditable were pointedly ignored. Christopher Wordsworth, nephew of the poet William Wordsworth and his first biographer, destroyed all letters and other documents testifying to his uncle's connection with Annette Vallon; and when James Anthony Froude published his biography of Thomas Carlyle in 1882, he was roundly castigated by the reviewers and by his friends for including so many details that were considered too intimate, too personal, to be made common knowledge. A number of "eminent Victorians" burned their private papers as a result of Froude's indiscretion, Robert Browning among them, and subsequent biographers bent over backward to avoid similar "scandalous revelations." In the twentieth century, of course, *post hoc* Freudian analysis is the fashion, and in their efforts to humanize their subjects many biographers have succeeded only in distorting the facts in the opposite direction. Nevertheless, it is necessary to reconstruct, as far as is possible at over a century's distance, the distressing events of January–March, 1851, because they shed considerable light on Mary Ann Evans's character and subsequent actions. Be it said at once that nothing in them redounds to her discredit. Her mistakes were the result of a naïvete that all her study had not eradicated, which expected that everything would operate according to the theories of life and living that she had absorbed in the protected security of Griff, Bird Grove, Rosehill, and even Geneva.

The situation at 142 Strand begins and ends with John Chapman—physician, author, and publisher—who combined a bibliophile's enthusiasm that in time was to make him one of England's leading bookmen, with a strongly sensual nature that made his private life, to say the least, colorful, even viewed by more liberal twentieth-century standards. A little younger than Mary Ann Evans, one of the handsomest men of his time—his nickname was "Byron," and he did his utmost to live up to it—he had studied medicine in Paris, and then at St. George's Hospital, London. Eventually, in 1857, he took his medical degree at St. Andrew's, Edinburgh. But books had always been his first love, and he was deeply interested in philosophy. In 1844, he wrote a book entitled *Human Nature,* which had a small *succès d'estime.* Shortly afterward, he bought the stock of a bookseller, moved his headquarters to 142 Strand, and, counting on the bookshop to provide him with a steady income, embarked on his own publishing career. By 1851, he had become editor and publisher of the *Westminster Review.* He knew the entire literary world of London: Froude, Dickens, Harriet Martineau, Herbert Spencer were his particular friends. In the great rambling house, the ground floor of which was taken up by the bookshop and editorial offices, while the family and assorted boarders had their rooms on the upper floor, John Chapman not so much lived as reigned.

His personal life can only be described as chaotic. He had married at a fairly early age, but his wife Susannah had never enjoyed robust health, and was at this time a whiny, unattractive woman who long since had lost all physical charm for him. She had never been the best of housekeepers, according to all reports, though this criticism should be tempered by the realization that housekeeping at 142 Strand would have given a most efficient woman pause. Susannah Chapman never knew whether ten or forty would sit down for dinner, and meals were served with a disregard for regular hours that kept the servants completely demoralized until they became accustomed to it. But the most astonishing problem of that household was the presence of Elizabeth Tilley, ostensibly the governess for the Chapman children but actually John Chapman's mistress. By 1851, he no longer felt the passion for her that had led him to bring her into his home (this he confided to his diary, a document unequaled for its frank assessment of its writer's comings and goings and personal emotional reactions) .[1] Nevertheless, she exerted an almost unholy influence over him, and above the ground floor her word was law.

It seems strange that Mary Ann Evans should willingly have gone there to live. Certainly, she was not unaware of the situation. It was common knowledge all over London; besides, Elizabeth Tilley had taken it upon herself to write a letter, or perhaps several, either to the Brays or to Mary Ann—the record is not clear on this point—in which she evidently did more than hint about her precise position in the household. Perhaps Mary Ann dismissed the matter as being no concern of hers. Her chief reason for going to London was the magazine, and her dealings with John Chapman were on a business, not personal, basis. She was "liberal" in her views, or thought she was, so apparently she was not shocked by this revelation of her employer's character, and, with the respect for personal privacy observed by her class, she doubtless felt that his domestic problems were his own affair. Also, it must be remembered that she needed the work. Like most naïve persons, Mary Ann was sure that she knew all there was to know about the "facts of life." To be a part of the *Westminster Review* seemed too fine an opportunity to reject simply because a governess had written a spiteful letter, which might not even be true.

It was all too true, as she quickly discovered. Elizabeth Tilley fumed with jealousy from the moment any newcomer of feminine gender set foot in the house, and so did Susannah Chapman. In such instances, the two women were always in agreement, joining forces against their "rival," and they proceeded to make Mary Ann Evans's life as miserable as possible, Elizabeth Tilley being the more successful in the joint effort. Mary Ann wanted a piano in her suite. Chapman went with her to help select it, and, when it arrived, spent the entire afternoon listening to her play Mozart. Susannah, the very next day, bought a very expensive piano for the family drawing room, and told her husband that, if he wanted to hear Miss Evans play, he could listen to her there. Chapman wanted to read German with Mary Ann to improve his command of the language; Elizabeth Tilley promptly decided that she needed German lessons, too. To keep the peace, Mary Ann played the drawing room piano and taught the governess to read German, but the undercurrent of jealousy and insinuation continued apace.

The situation did have its comic psychological overtones, which a W. S. Gilbert would have appreciated. A man beleaguered by petticoats is never a very heroic object; Chapman, faced by Susannah's sulks and Elizabeth's temper tantrums, tried every means at his command to placate them but invariably ended up in worse plight than when he began. He frequently fled to Mary Ann for sympathy which she, unwisely, always provided, and his gratitude that she neither pouted nor raged doubtless made him more emotional than he otherwise would have been. Mary Ann, whose own emotions were quickly stirred, apparently evidenced a sympathy for him which flattered and soothed his bruised ego, and, besides, he needed her for the *Westminster Review*. He had recognized at their first meeting that her first-class mind could be most useful in editing the magazine. He had already decided that she must write the Prospectus for the "new" magazine ("new," in the sense of his now being sole owner and publisher) and had put her to work writing a catalogue describing all the books he had published. She was a miracle at revising articles and reading proof. For her to leave for any reason whatever would be disastrous to the magazine.

Accordingly, he exerted himself to keep her from being lonely. Through one of his friends she received tickets for Michael Faraday's lectures at the Royal Society; he arranged for her to enroll in Francis Newman's (brother of John Henry Newman) course in geometry at the Ladies' College (now Bedford College) of the University of London. He took her to the theater—the Lyceum was directly across the street from 142 Strand—and to the opera; and she was always a guest at his Friday evening parties, where, in her familiar black velvet dress, she made quite a striking appearance. His efforts did not go at all unremarked by Susannah and Elizabeth. By the end of February, they had decided that he and Mary Ann "were completely in love with each" [2] and made their decision known.

Mary Ann now had to recognize that she was in a precarious position, far worse than the one at Devizes. At least, at that time, her father had been alive and served to protect her reputation; now she had only a most unsympathetic brother who would be quick to censure what he would consider the inevitable consequence of her going off to London on her own—though he had been glad to have her go. Even worse, her own honesty forced her to admit that she was far more attracted by John Chapman than she had realized. This attraction she might have managed to conceal, had not her loneliness and craving for affection made her respond to his overtures. Besides, the religious principles which earlier might have protected her she had forsaken. She was entirely vulnerable. Chapman used every means in his power to per-

suade her to continue to work with him; there is recorded
the veiled episode of his wife's bursting in on them, to
find Mary Ann in tears and Chapman holding her hand.
Another explosion followed, and, at this point, Mary
Ann knew that she could stay in London no longer.
Chapman escorted her to the train; later that day he
wrote in his remarkable diary,

> She pressed me for some intimation of the state of my feel-
> ings. I told her that I felt great affection for her, but that I
> loved E. and S. also, though each in a different way. At this
> avowal, she burst into tears.[3]

Right there in Paddington Station! It was an unwise
question, but the answer perhaps gave Mary Ann some
much needed insight into the character of a man like
Chapman. She had been humiliated at Devizes, but that
anyone could so deliberately inflict such hurt was still
inconceivable to her. And she was leaving London more
or less in disgrace, her proud banner of independence
dragging in the dust. Nor could she blame Chapman for
everything. With her clear-sighted honesty, she now saw
that she should not have given two jealous women the
opportunity to slander her, by permitting herself, since
he was so bound and guarded, even the slightest look or
gesture that could have been misconstrued.

She returned to Coventry, to the Brays, who took her
in without question. She had hardly been there two weeks
when, much to her surprise, Chapman wrote to her, asking her to continue with the catalogue of his publica-
tions. He also, for some unknown reason, enclosed a
packet of letters that his wife had written to him, filled
with slanderous insinuations about his relationship with
her. By this time, Mary Ann must have heartily wished
him, his wife, his mistress, and his catalogue in Jericho;
still, she had promised to undertake the task, and she

could not feel justified in breaking a promise. On April 4th, she wrote to him,

> . . . I consent to continue with the Catalogue, since I am ashamed of perpetual vacillations, on conditions that you state, or, rather, I should hope, re-state to Mrs. C. the fact that I am doing it not because I "like," but in compliance with your request. You are aware that I never had the slightest wish to undertake the thing on my own account. If I continue it, it will be with the utmost repugnance, and only on the understanding that I shall accept no remuneration.[4]

As has been said, Chapman needed her for the magazine, and her reprimand affected him not at all as long as she did the work. And she needed the income, but her pride was too great to permit her to accept it at his hand, though a few weeks later she did agree to accept £100 for making an abridgment of her translation of Strauss. At the end of April, she wrote what Chapman described as an "able and excellent"[5] letter to Susannah, evidently explaining her position unequivocally. The business relationship was resumed in a series of—according to Chapman—"cool" letters with no personal overtones, except one: she signed her letters to him "Marian Evans," while to others, for a time at least, she used "Mary Ann." It seems permissible to conclude from this that Chapman first called her "Marian," the name by which eventually she was generally known.

In May of 1851, their relationship had improved to the extent that Chapman came to visit her at Rosehill. He wanted to persuade Marian to return to London as assistant editor of the *Westminster Review*. On May 30th, they walked over to Kenilworth Castle together, and, for the first time, enjoyed the opportunity of uninterrupted conversation. But Chapman recorded later in his ubiquitous diary:

> I dwelt on the incomprehensible mystery and witchery of beauty. My words jarred upon her, and put an end to her enjoyment. Was it from a consciousness of her own lack of beauty? She wept bitterly.[6]

It is surprising, considering his ten-ton tact, that he did not ask her that question directly. Nevertheless, she was finally persuaded to return to 142 Strand. The prospect of an editorship was too alluring to refuse; besides, having had a taste of London life, she was eager for more. And she did not want to impose longer on the Brays. By September, she was once more at the Chapmans', hard at work on the first issue of the "new" magazine which had been announced for January 1852.

She had come to town at the beginning of one of the most brilliant "seasons" London had ever experienced. The Great Exhibition had opened in May, and the city was crowded with visitors from all over England, the Continent, and even America, come to view the wonders of English science and technology displayed at the Crystal Palace, which was the greatest wonder of all. The great glass and steel building, designed by Joseph Paxton, rose above the trees in Hyde Park, glittering in the sunlight by day, illuminated with gas torches by night. Of course Marian went to see it—surprisingly enough, in the company of Dr. Rufus Brabant, who had come to London for that specific purpose. She also went to the theater, to the opera, and to lectures, and was regularly in attendance at Chapman's Friday evenings. "I have got nothing done here, there are so many *distractions* . . ."[7] she wrote to the Brays on October 4th. A week later, she gaily reported having "made a conquest of a fat clergyman and a thin student," [8] though in a later letter, evidently in reply to an interested inquiry, she told Sara Hennell,

> The "thin student" is no such thing, but a beneficed clergyman, who admires Strauss, discusses the Immortality of the soul, and preaches "extrumpery" to his poor Dorset parishioners, who have seen nothing beyond their native hedgerows,[9]

thus effectively disposing of any romantic ideas in connection with that "conquest."

Rumors of romance were in the air in another quarter, however. Almost immediately after her return to London, she had renewed her acquaintance with Herbert Spencer, sub-editor of the *Economist,* the offices of which were across the street from the Chapman establishment. He was one of the Friday evening regulars, and his intellect and liberal views attracted Marian's interest. He, too, seemed quite taken with her, and was her frequent escort to plays and operas. Sometimes they were accompanied by Spencer's friend, George Henry Lewes, whom Marian described quite casually to the Brays in October of 1851 as "a sort of miniature Mirabeau in appearance." [10] She was not overly impressed with Lewes at that moment, but Spencer's name recurs so constantly in her correspondence that it is easy to see why many of her friends assumed that they were engaged. Spencer, however, did not propose. "Physical beauty is a *sine qua non* with me; as was once unhappily proved where the intellectual traits and emotional traits were of the highest," [11] and it has been suggested that the lady might have been Marian Evans.

Whatever Spencer's attitude may have been, it does not seem to have disturbed Marian overmuch. She was immersed in work that demanded every ounce of strength and energy she possessed. As Chapman's assistant, she had to read hundreds of articles submitted for publication and work with the more temperamental authors. She had what might be called a ringside seat for the Martineau battle—the war of words waged by Harriet, the novelist, and her brother James, the theologian. Both were stubborn and opinionated individuals, who, over the years, had come to dislike each other cordially. Both were frequent contributors to the *Westminster Review*, and each was quick to take umbrage at any editorial advantage shown the other. Then, in order to judge the book reviews commissioned for publication, Marian had to read the books; her desk was piled high with weighty volumes of history and philosophy, side by side with the latest "silly novel" of some anonymous lady novelist. The *Westminster Review* took all knowledge for its province; Marian had to proofread articles on the Irish Question, the Mormons, "The Atomic Theory Before Christ and Science," strikes, prison reform, female education, and "The History of the Beard." Her own intellectual curiosity and thoroughness were such that it may be assumed that she tried to become as knowledgeable as possible in all these areas herself. In addition, she was a frequent contributor to the Belles Lettres section of the magazine. It is no wonder that her letters occasionally mention headaches and eyestrain.

Because she lived in Chapman's house, she was involved in his business affairs apart from the *Westminster Review*. Chapman had long been at war with the Booksellers' Association over their price-fixing policies, especially on books sold abroad. He felt that the price of a book was the publisher's prerogative, and he had gradually gathered considerable support, not only from his fellow publishers but also from authors who had long resented the current practice of the booksellers of pricing their books as low as possible to ensure quick sales. On the evening of May 4, 1852, there was an historic meeting at 142 Strand. Charles Dickens presided; Wilkie Collins, Tom Taylor (the editor of *Punch*), P. M. Roget (of Roget's *Thesaurus*), Herbert Spencer, George Henry Lewes, Robert Bell (editor of Bell's *English Poets*), and George Cruikshank the illustrator were among those present. There was also political support; a number of M.P.'s sent messages, among them William Gladstone. The meeting was a tremendous success; Chapman's speech, which Marian helped him to compose, was wildly applauded, and at midnight she saluted him with a rousing version of "See the Conquering Hero Comes" on the piano.[12] A week later, Gladstone carried the fight to the floor of the House of Commons. His motion failed, but his speech attracted considerable attention, so it is possible to say that Marian Evans had a small part—if indirect —in his eventual rise to the position of Prime Minister.

Her letter to the Brays telling of this exciting meeting contained one rather ominous note: "So now I hope poor Mr. Chap. will have a little time to attend to his business which is needing him awfully—in fact, his private affairs are wearing a melancholy aspect." [13] An understatement, certainly, for, despite the success of the *Westminster Review,* there never seemed to be enough ready money on hand to publish it, and Chapman had gotten into the habit of borrowing from his book publishing budget to meet the needs of the magazine. This robbing Peter to pay Paul could not continue indefinitely, and, while Chapman managed to stave off disaster for a time, he was finally forced to admit insolvency. Meanwhile, books were announced for publication and had to be delayed because the money allocated to them had been used for the *Westminster Review*. Marian fumed at this practice, especially when she herself became a victim of it. In 1853, Chapman asked her to translate Ludwig Feuerbach's *Das Wesen des Christentums* (*The Essence of Christianity*). She had agreed to undertake it, and the book was advertised, but publication had to be delayed. "I don't think you are sufficiently alive to the ignominy of advertising things . . . which never appear," [14] she wrote to Chapman sharply in December. And she told him unequivocally that she had rather he published the work and not pay her, than pay her a translator's fee and not publish.

Family difficulties grieved and perplexed her, as well. Chrissey's husband, Edward Clarke, had died just before Christmas of 1852, and Marian spent the early months of 1853 trying to help her sister decide what was the best thing to do. There were six children to care for. Isaac had given them a house to live in, but he was not known to be generous, and Marian debated going there to live with them. But she decided against it: "To live in that hideous neighborhood amongst ignorant bigots is impossible to me," [15] she wrote Mrs. Bray. She had seen Isaac briefly at Chrissey's, and he had flown into a rage when he discovered that she had arranged to return to London, to her job, without consulting him. He told her never to "apply to him for anything whatever—which, seeing I have never done so, was almost as superfluous as if I had said I would never receive a kindness from him." [16] Yet, she dared not bring Chrissey and the children to London, as long as her own financial state was so precarious. She suggested that they all go to Australia, where one of Edward Clarke's former patients had offered to sponsor the eldest boy,[17] and even offered to go with them and see them settled, but Chrissey would not hear of leaving England. Her own quarrel with Isaac, Chrissey's difficulties, and the endless problems of the *Westminster Review* made Marian desperately ill—headaches, an incurable cough, and rheumatism constantly plagued her. She tried to carry on with her usual schedule, but under a terrible emotional strain that occasionally broke through her deceptively serene exterior. Noah Porter, later President of Yale University, who was for a brief time a guest at 142 Strand in 1853, recalled seeing her once ". . . give way to a mood of abstraction during which the tears streamed down her strong yet gentle face." [18]

Still, in the eyes of the many people she knew, she was in an enviable position. She was an unmarried woman who had succeeded in supporting herself, often aiding a sister who was greatly dependent on her. She was greatly admired and respected by a wide circle of friends and acquaintances, and, despite her many personal difficulties and her general exasperation with the *Westminster Review*, she was certainly enjoying London. The reason is not hard to find. "Mr. Lewes especially is kind and attentive," she wrote to Mrs. Bray, "and has quite won my regard after having a good deal of my vituperation. Like a few other people in the world, he is much better than he seems—a man of heart and conscience wearing a mask of flippancy." [19] The "miniature Mirabeau" had come frequently to 142 Strand since their first meeting in October 1851, at first in the company of his friend Herbert Spencer, then more and more by himself. By spring of 1853, he had become her closest friend in London; by autumn of that year, he would have become the focus of her entire life.

VIII

The relationship between Marian Evans and George Henry Lewes is rightly considered to be the single most important influence of her life. Had she never met him, there would have been no George Eliot. She was an established writer in 1853, of course, but, without the inspiration and the encouragement that Lewes constantly provided, it is doubtful that she would ever have attempted fiction, or persevered in it after the first attempt. If, as some critics have maintained, her novels were written as a kind of reparation and expiation for having de-fied the moral standards of Victorian England, it has also been said that, in a sense, the final outcome justified her decision. Her decision was one which did shock and outrage society, and deeply grieved her few devoted friends, who, remembering her love and friendship of long standing, nevertheless continued to stand by her. Yet, viewed in context of her character and actions up to the moment of their meeting, her consent was inevitable; and it is a tribute to her essential integrity, and to Lewes's devotion, that, as the years passed, society in general—even royalty —came to accept their situation as unique, certainly, but not scandalous. That she endured considerable pain and anguish of spirit is true; the numerous women in her novels who suffer remorse over moral transgressions are obviously drawn from her own emotional reactions. Maggie Tulliver, Hetty Sorrel, Mrs. Transome, Gwendolyn Harleth—all testify to the author's firm belief in the disastrous wages of sin, and her intense preoccupation with morality had a deeply personal basis.

To make matters worse—in public estimation, at least —the George Henry Lewes of 1853 seemed the person least likely to attract a striking young woman of thirty-four, already on her way to becoming a celebrity. Born in 1817, he was the son of an actor, John Lee Lewes, known as "Dandy Lewes." John Lee was evidently not much of an actor, though he was for a brief period the manager of the Theatre Royal in Liverpool. He had literary pretensions of a sort—he published two volumes of run-of-mill poems before his death in 1823 or 1824. His widow remarried in 1825, but not much is known about her second husband except that he was a retired sea captain named John Willim. George Henry was the last of three children; both his elder brothers had died young, and his own childhood had been anything but secure. For reasons unascertainable, he was shuttled about from school to school; for a brief period in 1827 he was sent to a school in Brittany, and he also studied at a school at St. Helier on the island of Jersey. Though he was only ten years old at that time, he was apparently very precocious. In Brittany, he acquired his great love of French language and literature (he was eventually to become almost bilingual). He especially loved French drama, an interest doubtless inherited from his actor-father and stimulated by secret Sunday night excursions to the theater at Nantes. About 1830, he returned to England, and was enrolled at Dr. Burney's school in Greenwich.[1] He left there in 1833, and this was his last connection with any kind of formal education.

But his restless intellect would not permit him to be satisfied with the meager amount of knowledge he possessed. Adrift at sixteen, he went up to London, where he worked as a notary's clerk, then in a merchant's counting house, and finally decided to study medicine. In the 1830's there were no medical schools; incipient doctors learned their profession by "walking the wards" and attending such lectures as busy, overworked staff members had time to give them. Student life was rugged, and only the hardiest survived. But there was time for amusement, too—Lewes went regularly to a pub in Red Lion Square, where a congenial group met for the serious discussion of philosophy, science, literature, and politics. Here, one of the group, a Jewish watchmaker named Cohn, introduced him to the works of Spinoza. Perhaps Lewes fell upon Spinoza with such enthusiasm ". . . partly because he was an outcast, for as I was then suffering the social persecution which embitters all departure from accepted creeds, I had a rebellious sympathy for all outcasts." [2] He had long since parted from any orthodox religious beliefs, and his scientific bent made him impatient with the unprovable. Yet, Spinoza's mysticism appealed to his imagination and intellect. Whatever the reason, he literally devoured the works of the German philosopher, and he began to study German. He also attended the theater constantly—Macready was having a brilliant season at the Drury Lane—and he tried his hand at writing tragedies. It was at this time that he met Leigh Hunt, the poet and critic, who encouraged him in his literary aspirations, and William Bell Scott, later to be associated with Rossetti and the Pre-Raphaelite Brotherhood.

He continued his medical studies in a desultory fashion until about 1837. The theoretic aspects of biology and anatomy continued to interest him greatly, but he was never possessed of sufficient scientific detachment to endure the sight of pain and suffering, so he finally decided that he had no vocation as a physician. His studies in Spinoza had led to his reading other philosophers; and, in 1838, having realized that Germany was the country where the most important philosophical inquiries were being conducted, he impulsively decided to go abroad. It was a rash decision for a penniless youth of twenty-one, and must have struck most observers as the height of irresponsibility. At his age, other young men were already properly settled. He seems to have supported himself in Berlin by giving English lessons, meanwhile perfecting his own command of the German language and reading widely in contemporary German philosophy as well as the latest commentaries on Plato and Aristotle. Certainly he attended the theater—his language study could justify that extravagance—where he saw the works of Schiller and Goethe in performance. Doubtless it was at this time that he learned to know and love Goethe's works, a knowledge and a love that were to find fruition in his biography of that poet, playwright, and philosopher, which was not only remarkable in its day but also is still considered an excellent and important source of information.

In 1841, he returned to England, still adrift, not knowing precisely what he wanted to do. He tried his hand at being an actor, but physically he was not up to the requirements of the huge stages and auditoriums of that period, to say nothing of the rehearsing required to keep perhaps three plays going at once. He was not very tall, his head seemed too big for his slight frame, and his voice was weak. Among his own circle of friends—mostly actors and journalists—he was notable for his ugliness, but also for his wit, and especially for his exuberant enthusiasm which was quickly aroused but seldom sustained. He acquired a reputation for eccentricity; he affected French dress and manners, and seems to have been willing to do almost anything to call attention to himself—a characteristic attributed to him long after he had outgrown it. "If Lewes were to appear riding on the back of a white elephant down Picadilly, I should not be surprised," [3] was Thackeray's assessment of him at this period.

Then, with the same impetuosity that characterized everything else he did, he fell in love. The lady was Agnes Jervis, daughter of Swynfen Jervis, M.P. for Bridgeport. She was only nineteen and exquisitely beautiful; Lewes must have exerted all his charm to win her, for she had many admirers in her circle, a higher stratum of society than Lewes's own, and perhaps this was part of her charm for the impecunious young man who was now trying to be a journalist. Certainly he adored her and considered her quite faultless. He was not aware, on that February day of 1841, when he married her at St. Margaret's, Westminster, that Agnes's beauty concealed a fickle disposition and a great susceptibility to flattery. In fact, he seems to have been proud of her attraction for other men; and, in the early years of their marriage, he was too occupied in trying to provide for her and their four sons, who were born in quick succession, to be overly observant.

Had he been more so, it is doubtful that he would ever have been persuaded to let Agnes set foot in the Phalanstery. This was an establishment in Queen's Road, Bayswater, which Thornton Hunt, son of Leigh Hunt, had inaugurated early in 1842. Thornton Hunt had been considerably intrigued by the works of Pierre Fourier, a French socialist philosopher, whose theories had greatly influenced the leaders of the French Revolution. The Phalanstery was an attempt to duplicate the independent familial community that Fourier advocated; in this huge rambling house, Thornton Hunt and his family, his sister Jacinta and her husband John Glidden, another sister, Anastasia, and her husband and children, and two younger, unmarried sisters made their home. They were an interesting family, and George Henry Lewes often enjoyed spending an evening with them, because he could always be assured of stimulating conversation, music, and the amateur theatricals he enjoyed. Conventional Londoners looked on the Phalanstery rather askance, for Thornton Hunt's appreciation of the ladies was quite notorious, and not all the females who visited there, sometimes for weeks on end, came under the heading of family friends. But Lewes had no qualms about bringing Agnes with him, especially since she so obviously enjoyed the change from their own drab lodgings. Nor does Thornton Hunt, the head of the household, seem to have paid her any special attention at first. Perhaps Lewes thought that proper formality would prevail because Agnes *was* his wife and Hunt was his best friend, for there were certain rules that friends, even the most unconventional, observed.

Of one fault Lewes could not be accused: lack of industry. Unlike Marian Evans, he had no influential literary friends in 1841 who might have given him an easier entrée to publishers, nor did he have the prestige of a University degree. Neither were his in-laws disposed to be helpful beyond an occasional new dress for Agnes or toys for the children. A married man in 1841 was expected to assume full support of his wife and family. Lewes had only his knowledge of Continental literature and philosophy, a command of two foreign languages—French and German (he had begun to study Spanish as well) —a deep interest in science and in the theater, and a flair for putting words on paper. He also possessed an instinctive critical perception and intuition, and a delightful wit. So began his days and months at his desk, toiling over articles on French drama, the decline of good acting in the English theater, German philosophy, French metaphysics, Historical Science, and German poetry. These he sent out to the magazines, and received the beginning author's usual flood of rejection slips. But, finally, the *Westminster Review* took some of them; so did the *Edinburgh Review*. An article on Goethe, published in the *British and Foreign Review* in 1843, brought his work to the attention of John Stuart Mill, who wrote him a commendatory letter, which led to a warm friendship. Through Mill, Lewes became interested in the works of Auguste Comte, the French philosopher, whose *Cours de Philosophie Positive,* with its thesis that no system of thought was valid unless it was based on scientifically proved fact, further provable by its intrinsic usefulness to humanity, had given rise to a new philosophy called Positivism. Lewes embraced Positivism with a convert's zeal, and praised Comte highly in two articles for the *British and Foreign Review*. His efforts to present Positivism to the British public won for him a few words of praise from its originator; in a letter to John Stuart Mill, Comte spoke of Lewes as a "loyal and interesting youth." [4]

By 1844, after three years of unremitting labor, Lewes was beginning to be known as an authority on philosophy. Charles Knight, a London publisher, was at that time issuing a series of inexpensive books, "Knight's Weekly Volume Series," which sold for a shilling a copy; and he commissioned Lewes to write a history of philosophy for him. *The Biographical History of Philosophy* was published in four parts, in 1845 and 1846. Much to Lewes's amazement, it was an immediate success. Students at Cambridge adopted it as their personal textbook, for he had refused to write it in the ponderous manner affected by most authorities. Instead, he approached the subject in context of the lives of great philosophers, rather than attempting to describe systems of thought in isolation from the minds that had conceived them. It was a daring, welcome idea, and the popularity of the book can be gauged by the fact that four new editions—each one revised by the author—were published during his lifetime.

In the flush of this success, Lewes decided to abandon philosophy and try fiction. Two novels, *Ranthorpe*, published in 1847, and *Rose, Blanche, and Violet,* 1848, quickly sent him back to writing articles. Both books were little more than pot-boilers, based more or less on his own experience, with impecunious would-be poet-heroes, and fair, though equally impecunious, damsels, who fluttered and fainted in the approved nineteenth-century circulating library manner. The reviewers treated both books with deserved severity, though Charlotte

Brontë and Edgar Allan Poe had some kind words for *Ranthorpe* because of the picture it gives of London literary and theatrical life, as lived by those struggling to gain a foothold in it. But Lewes had no gift for fiction. His characterization showed none of that flair for mimicry which enlivened evenings at the Phalanstery, and his conversational brilliance turned to heavy sententiousness on the printed page.

So, when he was offered a lecture engagement in Manchester, in February 1849, he accepted it with alacrity. For several weeks he lectured on philosophy every evening to this provincial audience, except for March 10th, when he appeared at the Theatre Royal in the role of Shylock. He had never given up the idea of becoming an actor; a few roles in the plays put on by Charles Dickens' amateur theatrical company had only whetted his appetite. When opportunity for a professional appearance came his way, he snatched at it, but, unfortunately, he was no more successful in Manchester than he had been in London. The critics panned his Shylock roundly, saying that his performance lacked "force"—a polite way of saying that he might just as well not have been on the stage.

He did not intend, however, to forsake the theater. On April 14th, the *Manchester Guardian* announced the opening of a new play, *The Noble Heart*. The author and leading actor was George Henry Lewes. The play—a high-powered melodrama set in sixteenth-century Spain —has a plot equaled only by the opera *La Gioconda* for complexity. A Spanish nobleman, Don Gomez de la Vega, in love with a girl of humble origin, persuades her to marry him, even though she is in love with a soldier away at the wars, in order to save her father from financial ruin. On the wedding day, the soldier appears, and Don

Gomez discovers that he is his own son. He is furious, but finally is persuaded to let the young couple marry, while he retires to the desert to become a hermit. The highly bombastic role of Don Gomez de la Vega was not improved by Lewes's delivery, but the play did have a limited success. In February of 1850, it was given a London production—prudently, the manager of the Olympic did not permit Lewes to appear in it—and it played nine nights to enthusiastic audiences, despite the conspicuous lack of enthusiasm on the part of the critics.

Lewes, however, had other irons in the fire by this time that were absorbing his full attention. For several years, he had discussed with Thornton Hunt the possibility of launching a weekly newspaper, and the time at last seemed right for such a venture. They had canvassed their own circle of friends and acquaintances in London for support, and Lewes, in both Manchester and Edinburgh (where he had played Shylock again in November 1849), had obtained the interest and promises of guarantees from many influential people. All involved in the project were liberal, free-thinking individuals, quick to see the need of a publication that would ask questions about political, civic, educational, and economic matters, and provide a forum for discussion and exchange of ideas as well. Literature would not be neglected—it could not possibly be, with Lewes as one of the editors—and literary criticism, it was promised, would be impartial and unbiased, without the political overtones that led Conservative magazines to praise Conservative writers, and Radical magazines to do the same, without regard as to whether the book, the poem, or the play in question deserved that praise.

The *Leader* made its first appearance in April of 1850 and quickly attracted some of the foremost intellectuals of the time as contributors. Herbert Spencer, James Anthony Froude, and Charles Kingsley—all were published in its columns. It was read by all classes, from the halls of Parliament to the "reading rooms" established for working men in Liverpool and Glasgow. No subject was barred from its pages: Free Trade, copyright law, taxation, educational reform, mesmerism and spirit rapping (then enjoying a great vogue in London), philosophy, science—week after week, the *Leader* attacked, reproved, approved, rebutted, and served as a kind of journalistic gadfly. Letters especially came under Lewes's scrutiny: "How few men of letters *think* at all," [5] he wrote caustically in one review. Silly novels by silly lady novelists were his special target: "Judging from *Lady Selina Clifford,* we venture on some such verdict. Lady Dormer has nothing to say—and says it." [6] Thackeray he admired greatly; he also approved of Charlotte Brontë, and he called *Moby Dick* "a strange, weird book, full of poetry and interest." [7] He encouraged George Meredith by a kindly review of his first volume of poems, but said that Matthew Arnold's *Empedocles on Etna* was "altogether a mistake," [8] a view with which Arnold concurred, and he removed *Empedocles* from subsequent editions of his poems.

But some of Lewes's most interesting and really delightful writing was done under the pseudonym of "Vivian," in a weekly column where he could exhibit his wit and comic flair with a lighter touch than he customarily employed in the articles signed "G.H.L." Very quickly, "Vivian" acquired a personality of his own—a charming young man-about-town, constantly involved in tangled romances (carefully detailed in the column) , and a perpetual theater-goer. In fact, "Vivian" became the *Leader's* drama critic, and, under his mask, Lewes fired darts at playwrights, actors, managers, and audiences that would never have hit their mark had they been submitted to an orthodox review. For instance, the following remark from his review of *Angelo:*

> It is very probable that a woman having stabbed herself would make grimaces similar to those that distort Mrs. Sterling's countenance, but it was impossible for me to behold them with any other feeling than that of seeing a woman before me suffering from colic.[9]

Perhaps the most unusual and amusing chore that "Vivian" undertook was to review the plays of "Slingsby Lawrence," who was also George Henry Lewes! Lewes was still determined to succeed in the theater, and he had found a mine of material in French comedies which he translated and adapted for the Vestris company at the Lyceum Theatre. The best of these, *A Game of Speculation,* was translated, rehearsed, and produced on twenty-four hours' notice. Naturally, "Vivian" attended all the opening nights of his "lucky, but overestimated friend Slingsby Lawrence," but his frank impartiality in judging the plays had "made for a coolness between us," so he begged his readers not to expect any opinion in the column. Whereupon, he quoted the favorable reviews from the *Times* or the *Morning Post,* again commenting on the luck of his "intimate enemy." Playgoers who attended the opening of a Slingsby Lawrence play invariably turned to "Vivian" first when the next issue of the *Leader* arrived. And those same playgoers were certainly intrigued, if not scandalized, at the sight of the author in a front-row stall, frequently accompanied by the assistant editor of the *Westminster Review,* Miss Marian Evans.

For, of course, everyone knew that George Henry

Lewes was a married man. What everyone did not know was that, by 1851, his marriage existed only in name. Intimate friends had shared his grief when his youngest son, St. Vincent, had died of whooping cough in March of 1850, and had been anxious with him over the possible effect of this tragedy on Agnes, who was expecting another baby. The infant arrived safely in April 1850, two weeks after the *Leader* had made its first appearance. Within a very few days, Lewes discovered that the child's father was his best friend, Thornton Hunt.

The effect upon him was catastrophic. Naturally, he could tell no one. Faced with the visible consequences of his own "liberal" views, and doubtless feeling greatly responsible for them because he had continued his friendship with Hunt after his marriage—despite his friend's known reputation—he felt that he could do nothing else but forgive his wife, and he registered the child's birth under the name of Edmund Alfred Lewes. For a time, the reconciliation seemed permanent; then, in October 1851, Agnes bore Hunt a daughter, Rose Agnes. From that moment, Lewes ceased to regard her as his wife. But because he had once forgiven her and had attempted a reconciliation, he had under the law condoned her offense, and, therefore, a divorce was impossible, even if he had possessed the financial resources to get an Act of Parliament passed in his favor (the only means of divorce at that time). Nor was there any possibility for even an attempted reconciliation, for Agnes Lewes was determined to remain with Thornton Hunt, despite the fact that Hunt also was married and showed not the slightest inclination to divorce his wife. In fact, Mrs. Hunt had borne her husband a son within a few weeks after the birth of Rose Agnes. Agnes Lewes, bemused and fascinated, remained Hunt's mistress for five years and had two other children by him—both registered under the name of Lewes, as were Rose Agnes and Edmund Alfred —before their connection was broken. She was to outlive her husband and all her children, supported by Lewes as long as he lived, and afterward by Marian until her death, when Lewes's daughter-in-law and grandchildren cared for her, no doubt wondering how this fretful woman, eighty years old, could possibly have been the center of a scandal half-a-century before.

Scandal it certainly was. For a man to leave his wife was a most serious breach of morality, and, had Agnes given the slightest indication that she wanted her husband to remain, he probably would have done so. But, in the face of Agnes's adamant refusal, Lewes went into lodgings by himself during the winter of 1851, later describing those months as "a very dreary, *wasted* period of my life. I had given up all ambition whatever, lived from hand to mouth, and thought the evil of each day sufficient." [10] The shock of his wife's infidelity deeply affected him; never too strong physically, he began to suffer from excruciating headaches. And he still had to work with Thornton Hunt every day on the *Leader*. He still had to support himself and Agnes and the five children, though Hunt had been persuaded that he must, in decency, contribute to the support of his own son and daughter. The *Leader* had to be published, deadlines had to be met, articles had to be written and edited, "Vivian" must continue on his airy way without respite. The few friends who knew the truth of the situation rallied to his support, but Lewes refused to divulge many details even to them, for the sake of his own children. He preferred them to think that their father was responsible for the breach, rather than lose respect for their mother. But the very fact that those friends, like Herbert Spencer and John

Chapman, were known liberals, only made the entire affair seem that much more deplorable. "That blackguard, Lewes" found more than one door shut in his face, as he accepted the brunt of condemnation.

It was at this time that he first met Marian Evans. Her description of him as a "miniature Mirabeau" implies that she was not especially attracted to him. But she quickly discovered in him an intellect that matched and complemented her own, and her sympathies, always quickly aroused, soon made her one of his staunchest partisans and defenders. Just when and how he told her the complete story of his unhappy marriage is not known. It is generally supposed that he poured out his heart to her on a winter afternoon when he and Spencer had come to call on her; Spencer had to leave early for another appointment and Lewes remained behind. His name occurs frequently in Marian's letters during 1853, but no personal details are mentioned—a rather surprising omission, considering her usual openness about all her concerns to friends like the Brays and Sara Hennell. Then, on October 17th, she moved from 142 Strand to lodgings at 21 Cambridge Street, Hyde Park Square. It is almost certain that Lewes was a major factor in her decision to find a place to live where she would not be under such constant—if friendly—observation. In November, she told John Chapman that she wanted to give up her editorship; he persuaded her to continue until April, and she also agreed to finish the translation of Feuerbach. It was generally known that she had been helping Lewes considerably with his editorial work for the *Leader;* in April 1854, when he collapsed from nervous exhaustion, she wrote his literary reviews for him while he went to Hampshire for a rest cure. ". . . I really hope this total cessation from work in obedience to a peremptory order will end in making him better than he has been for the past year," [11] she wrote Mrs. Bray on April 18th. In May, evidently in reply to a question about her plans, she wrote Charles Bray, ". . . I might want to go to the Continent or twenty other things." [12] Clearly she was drawing near to a momentous decision.

It is impossible, at over a century's distance, even to hazard a guess at her thoughts during those weeks, except to say that she was well aware of what the world's immediate judgment was. She had intruded herself upon Lewes; she was the "other woman" who had callously and deliberately destroyed a marriage. For, even though some of the truth had been circulated about Agnes Lewes and Thornton Hunt, custom and current standards of morality demanded that, no matter how much a marriage resembled "unholy deadlock," it *must* be preserved. There had been criticism enough when Lewes had left his wife, but it would be infinitesimal compared with the storm that would break were he and Marian to decide to publicly live their lives together. Ironically, there would have been less condemnation if—as some people erroneously supposed—she had been his mistress. But such an idea would have been entirely repugnant to Marian Evans. Their relationship could not be sullied by slyness and intrigue. If they were to live together, it must be openly, in the eyes of the entire world.

She doubtless considered gravely the effect such an action would have on those who admired and respected her; what sort of example it would be to those who looked to her as the upholder of honor and integrity that she had always prided herself as being—attributes very, very important to the world at large in 1854. She had made a niche for herself in a most difficult profession. Would she be able to continue writing and have her work published, as she *must* do?—for Lewes would have to devote most of his income to Agnes and the children. Editors were sensitive to reader opinion, and might not risk publishing anything by a woman whose actions were considered justly censurable. And what of Lewes's position? That he had become quite as respected a writer as herself would be quickly forgotten. He would, indeed, be "that blackguard" who had deserted wife and children for a more inviting, more exciting companionship.

Against all these obstacles, however, she must weigh other, equally important factors: that they were deeply in love with each other; that their temperaments were completely compatible; that Lewes was the only man who had reached both her heart and her mind so completely. She was thirty-five years old. She had been lonely in the past—she knew much about loneliness. Without Lewes, that loneliness would be unbearable. If she had never met him, she might have continued as she had begun; having met him, and having known the happiness and the comfort he had brought to her, she could not endure the thought of going on alone.

Lewes returned from Hampshire in June, in time for the production of Slingsby Lawrence's new play, *Sunshine Through the Clouds.* Marian went with him, and wrote Mrs. Bray that it "makes one cry rather too much for pleasure." [13] One wonders just how much of her weeping was called forth by the play, and how much by her own emotion. She had worked hard in Lewes's absence; her translation of Feuerbach was ready for publication in July, and she was released from any professional obligation to remain in England. She had resigned her editorship, but Chapman, in whom she finally confided, had assured her that he would print and pay for any articles that she cared to write.

South Farm, Arbury, Warwickshire, where George Eliot was born, November 22, 1819. Print from Olcott's *George Eliot.*

South Farm, Arbury, Warwickshire, some years later when changes had been made to the house.

Chilver's Coton Church, where George Eliot was christened. It was also the model for the "Shepperton Church" in *Scenes from Clerical Life*.

Robert Evans, George Eliot's father. From Olcott's *George Eliot*.

George Eliot about the time she was beginning her literary career.

An early sketch of George Eliot done by her friend Mrs. Bray. Once in the possession of Warwick H. Draper.

George Eliot from an original pencil sketch done about 1847. The outline was traced round a shadow thrown by a cast and filled in by her friend, Sara Hennell.

Quietly, soberly, she and Lewes made their plans. They would go to Germany, because Lewes was working on his biography of Goethe, now, and he needed the resources of Weimar. Every contingency was considered, and, so far as possible, settled. Provision must be made for Lewes's three sons; it was decided that they would remain with their mother until school age, and that he would be fully responsible for them financially. They would not be told about the situation until they were older. Lewes would visit them frequently, but alone. For the time being, Marian would not enter that part of his life, but to that part she did enter she would bring and use all the best of her beliefs and the training of her early youth. One poignant fact had to be accepted. There could be no children. Marian Evans and George Henry Lewes knew that they themselves must be strong enough to accept the consequences of their decision, but they could not foist those consequences upon the innocent.

On the 19th of July, 1854, Marian wrote to the Brays and Sara Hennell:

Dear Friends—all three
I have only time to say goodbye and God bless you. Poste Restante, Weimar for the next six weeks, and afterwards, Berlin.

Ever your loving and grateful,
Marian [14]

On the following day, she and Lewes left England.

IX

About ½ past ten, Liszt called, and after chatting pleasantly for some time, invited us to go and breakfast at his house, the Altenburg.[1]

Marian Evans and George Henry Lewes arrived at Weimar between three and four o'clock in the morning on August 2nd, after a tedious ten-hour train journey from Frankfurt. They had come to Germany via Antwerp and Brussels, and stopped first at Cologne, where Dr. Brabant, also vacationing on the Continent, had met them. Through his good offices, Marian attained her lifelong ambition of meeting Strauss—a meeting, however, that proved to be better in anticipation than actuality. "Strauss looks so strange and cast down, and my deficient German prevented us from learning more of each other than our exterior which in the case of both would have been better left to the imagination," [2] she wrote humorously to Charles Bray. At Cologne they had taken the Rhine steamer to Mainz, where they found little to hold their attention, and they left almost immediately for Frankfurt, which had a greater attraction because Goethe had once lived there. But they were both impatient to reach Weimar, where Goethe's memory had been so lovingly enshrined. Lewes was eager to get to work on his biography, and Marian, now that the first excitement of her "elopement" had passed, felt a corresponding need to be at her desk. Not that she regretted her decision in the slightest. "I am happier every day . . . Affection, respect, and intellectual sympathy deepen," she wrote to Mr. Bray on August 30th.[3]

Weimar, at first glance, was disappointing.

A walk in the morning in search of lodgings confirmed the impression that Weimar was more like a market town than the precinct of a court . . . One's first feeling was—how could Goethe live here in this dull, lifeless village? [4]

But once they had settled at 62–a Kaufgrasse, and could devote more time to leisurely sight-seeing, they discovered the magnificent Belvedere chaussée—the two-mile avenue lined with chestnut trees leading to the summer palace; they visited the imposing Schloss with its beautiful park, and discovered the endless "walks" through forest and field.

To anyone who loves Nature in her gentle aspects, who delights in chequered shade on a summer morning and in a walk on a corn-clad up-land at sunset, within sight of a little town nestled among the trees below, I say—come to Weimar! [5]

Marian rhapsodized. More important, of course, were the omnipresent memories of Goethe, Schiller, Wieland, and Herder—and, "Above all, Liszt is here!" [6] The great composer-pianist far exceeded vacationing royalty as an attraction; he lived in royal splendor in a magnificent house presented to him by the Grand Duke, invitations to which were coveted, for he wanted only interesting people about him. The fact that "Herr and Frau Lewes" were included at breakfasts at the Altenburg, at which the maestro or one of his artist pupils always provided a piano recital, while titled personages clamored at the gates, is indicative both of Liszt's perspicacity and the Leweses' genuineness. Naturally, Marian went into ecstasies over Liszt's performances: "For the first time in my life I beheld real inspiration—for the first time I heard the tone of the piano." [7] And the fact that Liszt accepted both Marian and Lewes so wholeheartedly guaranteed them social acceptance everywhere in Weimar. Some might cavil that Liszt's cordiality to them was due to his own rather equivocal situation—the presence at the Altenburg of Princess Wittgenstein, who was attempting to obtain an annulment of her marriage at Rome in order to marry the composer, did not go unnoted. But, in general, an admiring public countered such criticism with the opinion that, after all, Franz Liszt was Franz Liszt. One should, of course, frequent the Altenburg himself, but if he could not, the next best thing was to be on friendly terms with those who did.

So the Leweses were invited to the home of Gustave Schöll, the director of the Free Art Institute, where artists and scholars, visiting or resident, regularly congregated;

and the Marquis de Ferrière le Vayer, the French ambassador, whom Marian described as "intensely French," [8]
regaled them at his receptions with hilarious anecdotes
about his experiences as First Secretary of the Embassy
at Peking. In September, when the theaters opened, they
attended a performance of Verdi's *Ernani,* which Liszt
conducted, and they also heard three of Richard Wagner's
operas. Wagner's work was the subject of much controversy in musical circles—indeed, it had been due entirely
to Liszt's patronage and assistance that any of his operas
had been performed at all. The Leweses did not enjoy
Lohengrin: "G. however, had not the patience to sit out
more than two acts of 'Lohengrin'; and indeed, I, too,
was weary." [9] *Der Fliegende Holländer,* however, Marian
found delightful, and she would have enjoyed hearing
Tannhäuser again. And she appreciated Wagner all the
more after a performance of Weber's *Der Freischütz,*
which seemed stagy and artificial by comparison. But she
did not become a Wagner worshiper:

> If it were admissable for a person entirely without techni-
> cal qualifications for judgment to give an opinion on
> Wagner as a musician, I should say that his musical in-
> spiration is not sufficiently predominant over his thinking
> and poetical power, for him to have the highest creative
> genius in music. [10]

Wagner's ideas concerning opera she admired, but, for
her taste, too frequently his ideas were overpowered by
the musical expression, making the listener concentrate
on the opera's meaning, rather than experiencing it
emotionally.

> . . . the composer who is pre-eminently a musical genius,
> on the slightest hint of a passion or an action, will have
> all other modes of conception merged in the creation of

music, which is for him the supreme language, the highest order of representation.[11]

she wrote in an article for *Fraser's Magazine*, a statement penetrating and interesting not only because it indicates her perception and understanding of a field apart from literature, but also because it reflects her belief in "truth of feeling" as a criterion, not only in human relationships, but also in art. Twenty-three years later, she met Wagner in London at a dinner party, and listened to him read his libretto of *Parsifal;* she and Lewes were also invited to the final rehearsal of the London performance of *Tristan und Isolde.* There is no indication that her first reaction to his music underwent any change, but the very fact that she still, in 1877, was interested in a composer considered so avant-garde and controversial is indicative of the breadth and scope of her mind, as well as the fact that her partisanship of "rebels," as long as they remained true to their gifts and had some genuine contribution to make to the world, had not in the least abated.

Marian had great need of the warmth with which she was received at Weimar, for, as might be expected, her open departure from England with Lewes had raised a storm of condemnation. As she had feared, innuendo at the least and open accusation at worst named her the cause of Lewes's separation from his wife, and letters from London indicated that rumors were painting the entire situation in the blackest colors, making it far, far worse for her than it really was. She had expected this, but she had not taken into consideration how much the mud-slinging, particularly that which was picked up at random, cruelly, to make the slingers feel virtuous in their own sight, would hurt; nor could she accept quite as meekly as she had believed possible the fact that her reputation was being demolished. Fortunately, Lewes was a man capable of decisive action. He wrote at once to his closest friends, Thomas Carlyle and his physician Arthur Helps, with complete candor, explaining that the reason —aside from their great love for one another—for his and Marian's decision was Agnes's preference to live with Thornton Hunt and her refusal to remain as his wife and the mother of his children. Unequivocally and indignantly he exonerated Marian from any and all blame. Carlyle replied at once with "a letter of noble sympathy," [12] and both he and Arthur Helps undertook to counteract the scandal in every way they could. Marian, heartened by Lewes's devotion and the promised help of his friends, wrote to Charles Bray:

> It is possible that you have already heard a report prevalent in London that Mr. Lewes has "run away" from his wife and family. I wish you to be in possession of the facts which will enable you to contradict this report when it reaches you. Since we left England, he has been in constant correspondence with his wife; she has had all the money due to him in London; and his children are his principal thought and anxiety. . . . I have seen all the correspondence between them, and it has assured me that his conduct as a husband has not only been irreproachable, but generous and self-sacrificing far beyond any standard fixed by the world. . . . I have been long enough with Mr. Lewes to judge of his character on adequate grounds, and there is therefore no absurdity in offering my opinion as evidence that he is worthy of high respect.[13]

As for the rumors about "her part in Lewes's separation," she added, ". . . the only influence I should ever dream of exerting over him as to his conduct towards his wife and children is that of stimulating his conscientious care for them, if it needed any stimulus." [14] Her chief concern was that Mrs. Bray and Sara Hennell should also know the truth, whatever their reaction might be:

> I am quite prepared to accept the consequences of a step which I have deliberately taken, and to accept them without irritation or bitterness. The most painful consequence, I know, will be loss of friends.[15]

The strain which her relationship with Lewes placed on this special friendship was great. Charles Bray responded promptly and affectionately, but his wife and sister-in-law were both dismayed and deeply grieved. Sara Hennell sent a letter filled with reproaches for the "serenity" with which Marian had given them up,[16] to which Marian replied in hot denial: "My love for you rests on a past that no future can reverse, and offensive as the words seem to have been to you, I must repeat that I can feel no bitterness towards you, however you may act towards me." [17] Sara was mollified, though she still felt a certain constraint: "Your letter to Charles today seems to show you very happy now—but I have a strange sort of feeling that I am writing to someone in a book and not to the Marian that we have known and loved for so many years." [18] Gradually, however, their correspondence was resumed on its old footing. Mrs. Bray did not write until months later, and her letter, evidently rebuking Marian for her disregard of the marriage bond, forced Marian to an even more frank and definite defense:

> Assuredly, if there be any one subject on which I feel no levity it is that of marriage and the relation of the sexes—if there is any one action or relation of my life which is and always has been profoundly serious, it is my relation to Mr. Lewes. . . . Light and easily broken ties are what I neither desire theoretically, nor could live for practically.[19]

And then she added bitterly, "Women who are satisfied with such ties do *not* act as I have done—they obtain what they desire and are still invited to dinner." [20]

She had reason to know the truth of this last assertion, for, by the time she wrote this letter, she and Lewes had returned to England. After the freer atmosphere of Weimar and Berlin (where they had stayed from November until March 1855), she knew by direct experience how very rigorous Victorian respectability could be. Between March and October, they changed their address five times. Nothing in Marian's letters indicates that they were ever specifically asked to move, but the implication of so many changes is inescapable, especially in the light of her letter to Bessie Rayner Parkes:

> Your address to me as *Miss Evans* was unfortunate as I am not known under that name here. We find it indispensable to our comfort that I should bear Mr. Lewes's name while we occupy lodgings, and we are now with so excellent a woman that any cause of removal would be a misfortune. If you have the occasion to write to me again, please bear this in mind.[21]

Within the year, her letters carried the signature "Marian E. Lewes." As far as she was concerned, George Henry Lewes was her husband—she spoke of him in that manner—and their relationship was as sacred and binding as any legal marriage could be. Their devotion to each other was visible for all to see; and, while it took time, gradually their close friends came to accept the situation as the only possible solution for two individuals who deeply and honorably loved each other, to whom the law gave no better recourse. A major factor in this acceptance was the reaction of Lewes's sons, when they finally learned about Marian. They adored her, and called her "Mother" without hesitation. She gave them all the attention that she would have lavished on children of her own; and that the three boys really needed her care and concern—having received little enough from their own mother—was, in itself, sufficient justification for agreeing that the decision had been wise.

Estrangements, brief or lengthy, from friends were difficult, but the worst consequence Marian was required to bear was, of course, her family's shocked outrage. She did not write to Isaac and Chrissey until May 1857, nearly three years after she had consented to live with Lewes as his wife; and her letters were couched in the most discreet terms, saying only that she had been married, that she had known her husband for some time previous to the event, and that she hoped for their good wishes for her happiness. In return, she received a letter from Isaac's solicitor, demanding full particulars. She had to tell the truth, which she did, frankly and honestly. Isaac was appalled. He immediately broke all ties with her, and also forbade Chrissey to answer her sister's letter. His reaction has often been severely criticized, but it must be seen within the social framework of the times. Isaac Evans was a pillar of Victorian respectability, whose sister had brought disgrace on the family. In 1857, there was only one course for such a pillar to take, and that was to cut off the offender from the family circle without mercy. Had Lewes seduced and abandoned her, the affair might have been managed more easily; Isaac could have prosecuted the man at law, or shot him, and received Marian as a repentant prodigal. But Marian had—incredible as it seemed to him—committed herself to this situation of her own free will and choice. Isaac's views, naturally, were dictated by his background, upbringing, and inborn rigidity. He had objected to Marian's going to London in the first place; he had, according to his lights, stood back of her during the regrettable episodes of Dr. Brabant and John Chapman, but this—this was too much! He would not—he *could* not accept it, nor could any other man in his circumstances. He was not to break his silence for twenty-three years.

The breach with her beloved brother was the greatest sorrow that Marian ever had to endure. Fortunately, her love for Lewes, and his for her, was sufficient to overcome, in large measure, a consequence as inevitable as her own decision had been. And, by the time she wrote to Isaac in 1857, she had found another source of comfort and strength. She had discovered that she could write fiction. She had published her first story.

Almost from the beginning of their relationship, Lewes had urged her to try her hand at fiction. While they were at Weimar and Berlin, he had been most insistent; but they needed money, especially for his family, and articles for the *Westminster Review* offered a more certain source of income than stories which might not be published. Also, she was at that time more interested in Lewes's finishing his biography of Goethe than in any work of her own. She continued to write for both the *Westminster Review* and the *Leader,* during the summer of 1855, in lodgings at Park Shot, Richmond, where they both had to work in the same room and the scratching of another pen had nearly sent her out of her mind. When *The Life of Goethe* finally appeared in October, she had been caught up in the book's immediate success, too delighted with Lewes's accomplishment to work on any new kind of writing for herself.

Then, in May 1856, Lewes embarked on another project—a book on marine biology. Marian went with him to Ilfracombe on the Bristol Channel; their luggage included a huge hamper filled with tall glass jars, intended to serve as a seaside vivarium. "There can hardlier be an uglier town—an uglier cluster of human nests lying in the midst of beautiful hills," [22] she wrote in her Journal, but the walks were pleasant and the specimens of marine life plentiful. Days were spent searching for zoophytes, molluscs, annelids, and sea anemones; Marian waded into shallow coves with her skirts pinned above her knees and her sleeves rolled up to her elbows. "You would laugh to see our room decked with yellow pie dishes, a *foot pan,* glass jars, and phials," she wrote to Charles Bray, "and still more to see the eager interest with which we rush to our 'preserves' in the morning to see if there has been any mortality among them in the night." [23] The trip was providing benefits other than research; Lewes's health was becoming more robust in the bracing Devonshire air, and the singing in his ears which had endured for so long had disappeared.

On June 26th, they crossed the Bristol Channel by packet steamer to Swansea, where they took the train around the coast to Tenby. Here they continued to collect marine specimens, and Lewes began work on his series of articles entitled "Seaside Studies," which *Blackwood's Magazine* had promised to publish. Marian had finished an article on Victor Hugo's latest volume of poems, *Les Contemplations,* and dispatched it to the *Westminster Review,* so for the moment her pen was not scratching in counterpoint to her husband's. It was at this moment that Lewes urged her to sit down and write a story. In fact, he ordered her to begin at once! He reminded her that she had written a fragmentary chapter of a novel and had read it aloud to him in Berlin. He had been struck by its remarkable evocation of a Staffordshire village, with its farmhouses and fields, and of the people who lived there. He told her that he *had* a few doubts about her ability to write dialogue, and of her "dramatic power"; [24] still, she had written brilliantly *about* novels and certainly knew as much as anyone in England about what a novel should be, if not more.

Marian, quite understandably, had her own doubts as to her ability. Criticism and fiction are two entirely different things, requiring almost completely opposite qualities of consideration, application, and concentration. She was concerned also lest her ear for dialogue, which was so carefully attuned to catch the slightest falsity in the work of other writers, might not serve her when she tried to write it herself. Also, though she could detect faulty plot construction instantly, she was not certain that she could construct a plot, much less a faultless one. She was already planning an article for the *Westminster Review* on "Silly Novels by Lady Novelists"; there were many of these in circulation already, and she had no wish to add to their number. She did not want to contribute to the general impression that "to write *at all* is a proof of superiority in a woman." [25]

Apart and aside from her own self-doubtings, there was the undeniable fact that the novelists whom she respected were giants. Dickens, Thackeray, Charlotte Brontë, Elizabeth Gaskell—even Miss Martineau—anything she might write in fiction which would be above the "silly novel" category (and it would have to be, if she wrote at all) would be compared with works like *David Copperfield, Vanity Fair, Villette,* and *Mary Barton*. The competition would be tremendous. And what could she write about? Her life, so far as she could see, had not provided the kind of raw material that kept the public on tenterhooks for the next installment, as Dickens managed to do; nor had she experienced the Manchester mill strikes that had provided the background for Elizabeth Gaskell's *Mary Barton;* nor had she any of the Brontë mystical and passionate emotion. Drama, pathos—these were what Victorian readers demanded from their novels, plus a moral. Marian felt that she was well equipped to provide the third, but the first two gave her pause.

Nevertheless, Lewes insisted that she make the attempt. "You have wit, description, and philosophy," he would say. "These go a long way towards the production of a novel." [26] He told her that if, in his opinion, the story was good enough, he would submit it to *Blackwood's Magazine,* but it was more likely that she would have to "lay it aside and try again." [27] Marian began to listen to him seriously, and to consider just what she might do. According to her own account, the title of her first story, "The Sad Fortunes of the Reverend Amos Barton," flashed into her mind as she lay in bed one morning, half asleep. She told Lewes, who promptly replied, "Oh, what a capital title!" The impression given is that the story was written to fit the title, but it is more likely that, in casting about for material, she recalled the Reverend John Gwyther, of Chilvers Coton, whose young wife had died in heartbreaking circumstances. Emma Gwyther had been a close friend of Marian's mother, who had done what she could in the way of food and freely bestowed advice to help the impoverished clergyman and his large family. It is possible, though not provable, that the recent success of Anthony Trollope's *The Warden,* published in 1855, had played its part in recalling those distressing days to Marian's memory; she had been a young girl of seventeen at the time of Mrs. Gwyther's death, and had heard her mother's pungent remarks about a clergyman's salary being too small to permit his wife to have any servants or even sufficient food and clothing. Even though

Mr. Gwyther's Evangelical tendencies had annoyed his parishioners, decency was decency, in Mrs. Evans's opinion, and Marian herself had experienced that unpopularity that Evangelicals endured from the more orthodox.

So, when she returned to Park Shot in September, she set to work. Once inspiration came, the fire was quickly kindled. Other recollections returned to her, and she told Lewes that she felt her first work should not be a three-volume novel, but a series of short novellas about various clergymen she had known or heard of, the entire series to be called *Scenes from Clerical Life*. Lewes liked the idea, but prudently told her to finish "Amos Barton" first and see how it went. A week later, she read aloud the opening section. One doubt was immediately erased from her husband's mind—definitely she could do dialogue! The acid test, however, would be Milly Barton's death. Could she handle pathos?

> One night G. went to town on purpose to leave me a quiet evening for writing it. I wrote the chapter from the news brought by the shepherd to Mrs. Hackit to the moment when Amos is dragged from the bedside, and I read it to G. when he came home. We both cried over it, and then he came up to me and kissed me, saying, "I think your pathos is better than your fun." [28]

On November 6, 1856, George Henry Lewes wrote to John Blackwood, the editor of *Blackwood's Magazine*, in Edinburgh:

> May I trouble you with an ms of "Sketches of Clerical Life" which was submitted to me by a friend who desired my good offices with you? It goes by this post.[29]

Six days later the reply came—the one for which every author prays: "My dear sir—I am happy to say I think that your friend's reminiscences of Clerical Life will do." [30]

Part I of "The Sad Fortunes of the Reverend Amos Barton" appeared in *Blackwood's Magazine* on January 1, 1857. It was published anonymously, and it was a sensational success. Completely unknown and unheralded, Marian Evans Lewes—later George Eliot—was hailed as one of the finest novelists yet to appear in that generation of giants. At the age of thirty-eight, she had found her vocation—the work for which her entire life had been the preparation.

X

It is difficult for a twentieth-century reader to understand the enthusiastic reception of "The Sad Fortunes of Amos Barton." Most critics now dismiss it along with "Mr. Gilfil's Love Story" and "Janet's Repentance" (the other stories in *Scenes from Clerical Life*) as mere spadework, interesting only as the tentative first attempt of a new, uncertain author, which gives little promise of her future greatness. Certainly the bare outline of "Amos Barton" reveals that it was little better, if no worse, than the dozens of other stories published in the magazines of that period, quickly read and as quickly forgotten. Amos

Barton is the curate of Shepperton, struggling to support a wife and six children on eighty pounds a year. He is a conscientious, dedicated man, completely undynamic, and possessed of a sincerity in his religious views that leads him always to say the wrong things to the right people. As a result, his parishioners are impatient with him, and, with few exceptions, do little to make his life or theirs any easier or happier.

Then, a certain Countess Czerlaski, a worldly and apparently wealthy woman, who has recently come to Shepperton to live with Mr. Bridmain, her half-brother, interests herself in the Bartons; but her interest does more harm than good. Tongues wag over Amos's association with her, though he remains blind to the gossip. Suddenly, the Countess discovers that Mr. Bridmain is going to marry below his station; in a fit of petulance, she flounces out of the house and moves bag and baggage into the vicarage. Here she proceeds to keep everything in a turmoil by her whims and demands. Through all of this, Milly Barton, Amos's wife, steadfastly refuses to believe the ugly rumors circulating about her husband; and, though she is expecting her seventh child, she waits on the Countess hand and foot. Eventually, the Countess, who is good-hearted if heedless, realizes the situation and leaves. Shortly afterward, Milly dies in childbirth. The townspeople, now touched by the curate's grief and ashamed of their scandal-mongering, try to make up for their past unpleasantness, but it is too late. Just as his parishioners have come to value him, Amos Barton must leave Shepperton, because the vicar has decided that he wishes to spend his declining years there. Amos accepts a curacy in a northern manufacturing town, and returns to Shepperton only once more, in his hold age, to visit Milly's grave.

There is nothing in the plot of this story calculated to excite an audience nurtured on television and Cinerama, nor did it, in all probability, attract the "backstairs readers" of its own day who doted on sensational melodrama and the "penny dreadfuls." It is a simple story about very ordinary people—and therein lies its success. Marian Evans, in writing it, was evoking from her memories people she had known in a place she had loved. For Shepperton was Chilvers Coton, and the church, minutely described in the opening chapter, was the one where she had been baptized and which she had attended as a child. Already it had changed, but Marian re-created it as it had been:

> No benches in those days; but huge roomy pews round which the devout churchgoers sat during "lessons" trying to look anywhere else than into each others' eyes. . . . And the singing was no mechanical affair of official routine; it had a drama. . . . The innovation of hymn-books was as yet undreamed of; even the New Version was regarded with a sort of melancholy tolerance, as part of a time when prices had dwindled and a cotton gown was no longer stout enough to last a lifetime.

Nostalgia, combined with sly irony, is here, indicative of the future capability of George Eliot.

And the people were real, including the Countess, though whether her actions were or were not precisely as the story depicts them, it is impossible to say.[1] That Amos Barton was a most extraordinary hero, Marian was well aware: he was extremely commonplace, very run-of-the-mill, almost unnoticeable.

> Yet these commonplace people—many of them—bear a conscience and have a sublime prompting to do the painful right; they have their unspoken sorrows and their

sacred joys; their hearts have perhaps gone out towards
their first-born, and they have mourned over the irreclaim-
able dead. Nay, is there not a pathos in their very insignifi-
cance—in our comparison of their dim and narrow existence with the glorious possibilities of that human nature
which they share?

This statement, contained in this early work, is the statement of George Eliot the novelist's creed.

In other words, the world of George Eliot is not the
fashionable society depicted so brilliantly by Benjamin
Disraeli, nor the underworld of London so powerfully
delineated by Charles Dickens. It is not Trollope's Bar-
chester, or Hardy's Wessex, nor is it the turbulent, dark
Yorkshire moorland of Charlotte and Emily Brontë. It is
not her own creation, except as the novelist always trans-
forms reality into art. With the single exception of
Romola, George Eliot's world is the England she knew,
lived in, and loved, and even *Romola,* for all its medieval
Florentine setting, is really more English in spirit than
Italian. People she knew, events she had heard of or
witnessed—these comprise the source from which her inspiration flowed.

And they were recognized as such. Those who lived in
Warwickshire, who knew the actual events and people,
immediately realized that "Amos Barton" and the other
Scenes from Clerical Life must have been written by
someone who was familiar with the locale and its people.
Long before Marian had to reveal that she was George
Eliot, the Brays had suspected it. Her brother knew at
once who had written "Amos Barton," though he stubbornly maintained his silence.[2] As for other readers, they
recognized the truth and the sincerity of the story; the
reality of the characters struck them as remarkable. They
sympathized with Milly Barton, were infuriated with the

selfish Countess, and, like John Blackwood, wanted to kick Amos.[3] But Amos's blundering obtuseness struck them as *right;* his behavior was precisely what might be expected from such a man, and his suffering, due to his lack of shrewdness and self-interest, finally evoked sympathy rather than ridicule.

There was humor, too. In the opening scene at Cross Farm, Mrs. Patten, the elderly lady "who had got rich by the negative process of spending nothing," who is entertaining guests at tea with her views about the minister, is an ancestress of the redoubtable Aunt Glegg in *The Mill on the Floss.* "When Mr. Barton comes to see me, he talks of nothing but my sins and my need for mercy," she complains.

> "Now, Mr. Hackit, I've never been a sinner. From the fust beginning, when I went into service, I al'lys did my duty by my employers. I was as good a wife as any in the county —never aggravated my husband. The cheese factor used to say my cheese was al'lys to be depended on. I've known women as their cheese swelled a shame to be seen, when their husbands had counted on the cheese–money to make up their rent; and yet they'd three gowns to my one. If I'm not to be saved, I know a many as are in a bad way."

Homely, commonplace—familiar. The words are set down in the dialect that Marian had heard in her own home as a child. Miss Maria Lewis had managed to erase the Warwickshire from her speech, but not from her ear. Then, there is Mrs. Hackit—kindly, sharp-tongued, eminently sensible—the kind of woman Marian's mother had been:

> . . . Mrs. Hackit regulated her costume by the calendar, and brought out her furs on the first of November, whatever might be the temperature. She was not a woman weakly to

accommodate herself to shilly-shally procedures. If the season didn't know what to do, Mrs. Hackit did.

Mrs. Hackit is loud in denunciation of Amos because of his seeming dalliance with the Countess; she even gives him a "piece of her mind." But when Milly is dying, she goes at once to the vicarage, saying to her husband as she hurries out the door, "If I don't come back tonight, I shall send back the pony-chaise, and you'll know I'm wanted there." She is the sort of woman that everyone, even in these days of bureaucratic charity, can recognize —first to be sharp in criticism of what she considers wrong, but first to go where she can not only offer help, but also give it.

Of course, readers of 1857 were deeply moved by Milly's death. It was an age that did not shrink from pathos and tragedy. Women frequently died in childbirth, so Marian Evans was definitely writing "realistically" here. But, compared with others of its kind, this death scene is not harrowing, nor is it sensationalized. It is beautifully done, with great restraint. An even more poignant moment, however, is the brief sequence where Amos visits his wife's grave for the last time before leaving Shepperton:

He stood for a few minutes, reading over and over again the words on the tombstone, as if to assure himself that all the happy and unhappy past was a reality. For love is frightened at the intervals of insensibility and callousness that encroach by little and little on the dominion of grief, and it makes efforts to recall the keenness of the first anguish.

Gradually as his eyes dwelt on the words, "Amelia, the beloved wife," the waves of feeling swelled within his soul. . . .

"Milly, Milly, dost thou hear me? I didn't love thee

enough—I wasn't tender enough to thee—but I think of it all now."

Amos's words are old-fashioned to modern ears, especially spoken in the words of that earlier day, but his grief is genuine and the scene rings true. And, since writers draw upon their own emotional experiences and their recollection of them, it seems reasonable to suppose that, in this moment, Marian was subconsciously recalling her own experience with grief. Victorians were far more willing to express their emotions than is generally realized; they were willing to have their hearts touched; they were willing to weep. "The Sad Fortunes of Amos Barton" fulfilled these requirements perfectly for the readers of *Blackwood's Magazine* in January of 1857.

No sooner had Marian received her copy of the magazine, and rejoiced with Lewes that the editor had put her story on the first page, than she wrote to John Blackwood, "I hope to send you a second story by the beginning of February." [4] Already she was at work on "Mr. Gilfil's Love Story," and she dispatched the first part to Edinburgh on February 11th, signed with the name "George Eliot"—"George" from her husband's name, and "Eliot" because it had such "a fine rolling sound." [5] For "Mr. Gilfil's Love Story" she turned in memory to Arbury Hall, and the stories she had heard, especially from the housekeeper, about Sir Roger Newdigate, fifth baronet, who had lived there in the late eighteenth century, and had rebuilt the simple Elizabethan manor into the enormous Gothic hall which had so fascinated her as a child. There had been a young girl then, too, named Sally Shilton, a collier's daughter, whose beautiful singing voice had attracted the notice of Lady Newdigate. Lady Newdigate brought Sally to Arbury Hall and educated her; later, the girl had married the Reverend Bernard Ebdell, vicar of Chilvers Coton. As she had done in "Amos Barton," Marian lovingly, almost sensuously, re-created Chilvers Coton—again called Shepperton—and Arbury Hall metamorphosed into Cheverel Manor:

> . . . the castellated house of grey-tinted stone, with flickering sunbeams sending dashes of golden light across the many shaped panes in the mullioned windows, and a great beech leaning athwart one of the flanking towers, and breaking, with its dark flattened boughs, the too formal symmetry of the front; the broad gravel walk winding on the right, by a row of tall pines, alongside the pool—on the left branching out among the swelling grassy mounds, surmounted by clumps of trees, where the red trunk of the Scotch fir glows in the descending sunlight against the bright green of limes and acacias; the great pool, where a pair of swans are swimming lazily with one leg tucked under a wing, and where the open water lilies lie calmly accepting the kisses of the fluttering light-sparkles; the lawn with its smooth emerald greenness, sloping down to the rougher and browner herbage of the park, from which it is invisibly fenced by a little stream that winds away from the pool and disappears under a wooden bridge in a distant pleasure ground. . . .

England could boast no more stately "stately home" than this!

But any resemblance to the actual events that transpired in 1788 end with the description of the surroundings. Instead of telling what had actually happened, Marian tried her hand at constructing a fictional plot. The young girl, Sally Shilton, becomes Caterina Sarti, an Italian orphan whom Lady Cheverel discovers when she is visiting in Milan. Caterina grows up at Cheverel

Manor and is beautifully educated, especially in music, for she has an exquisite voice. The young curate, Mr. Gilfil, is desperately in love with her, but she is in love with Captain Wybrow, Lord Cheverel's nephew and intended heir. She believes that Wybrow is serious in his attentions to her, but he is, in reality, only amusing himself. When she discovers that he is engaged to marry another, she becomes frantically jealous; and finally, in a moment of near-madness, picks up a dagger and goes to meet him in the rookery, intending to kill him. To her horror, when she arrives, she finds him lying on the ground, dead of a heart attack. Unable to believe that she has not killed him, she runs away from Cheverel Manor. Mr. Gilfil finds her and manages to convince her that, no matter what she had thought of doing, she could not possibly have killed Wybrow—that she is not a murderess. He eventually persuades her to marry him, but she dies within a year after the wedding, leaving him to live out his life alone at Shepperton, where her room in the vicarage is kept as a locked shrine, sacred to her memory.

This short résumé does not seem adequate grounds for Lewes's enthusiasm in his letter to John Blackwood which accompanied the first part of the manuscript: "By post you will receive an installment of Eliot's new story which I think even better than the first part of 'Amos Barton' . . . You would never believe the work I have to make him credit his own genius." [6] "Mr. Gilfil's Love Story" is not as good as "Amos Barton"; the attempt to re-create an earlier century is not so successful because the author is not at ease in the surroundings she chose. She knew and had experienced Shepperton; she had only seen and heard of Arbury Hall and its people. The plot worried John Blackwood—he felt, for instance, that

Caterina's behavior toward Wybrow was a little too "openly devoted," [7] and he was very much concerned about the heroine's actually taking up the dagger. He feared that readers would lose sympathy for her. But Marian refused to alter a syllable. "My artistic bent is directed not at all to the presentation of eminently irreproachable characters, but of mixed human beings in such a way as to call forth tolerant judgment, pity, and sympathy. And I cannot stir a step from what I *feel* to be *true* in character." [8] Nevertheless, despite her reliance on "truth of feeling," the story does not quite "come off." Caterina's jealousy has an unfortunately melodramatic ring, and Wybrow's death—though adequately prepared for by carefully spaced references to his weak heart—seems almost too convenient. And his attitude of patronizing carelessness toward Caterina makes her fixed affection for him seem unbelievable and inconsistent. Still, as Marian wrote to her editor, "inconsistencies and weaknesses are not untrue." [9]

The story does hold a certain interest, however, because the relationship between Caterina and Wybrow definitely foreshadows the similar relationship between Hetty and Arthur Donithorne in *Adam Bede,* and Mr. Gilfil's pursuit of Caterina might also be considered a kind of preparation for Adam's search for Hetty. The characters are drawn with a sure hand—for instance, the description of Captain Wybrow (who is a preliminary sketch for Henleigh Grandcourt in *Daniel Deronda*):

> The face, however—it is difficult to say why—was not pleasing. Nothing could be more delicate than the blond complexion—its bloom set off by powdered hair—than the veined overhanging eyelids which gave an indolent expression to the hazel eyes; nothing more finely cut than the transparent nostril and the short upper lip. . . . Impos-

sible to say that this face was not eminently handsome; yet, for the majority of both men and women, it was destitute of charm.

After this passage, Caterina's infatuation seems all the more incredible, but that an impressionable young girl should fall violently in love with an unworthy man is certainly not lacking in truth. Nor is the following vignette, depicting Caterina's jealousy as she watches Captain Wybrow with his fiancée:

> . . . her eyes *would* steal to the opposite side of the fire-place, where Captain Wybrow had seated himself close to Miss Assher, and was leaning with his arm over the back of a chair in a most lover-like position. Caterina began to feel a choking sensation. She could see almost without looking that he was taking up her arm to examine her bracelet; their heads were bending close together, her curls touching his hand—now he was putting his lips to her hand. Caterina felt her cheeks burn—she could sit no longer. She got up, pretending to be gliding about in search of something, and at length slipped out of the room.

The reality of Caterina's emotion can still be, to use the contemporary phrase, "identified with." It is one of the commonplaces of certain human response.

While "Mr. Gilfil's Love Story" has no Mrs. Hackit or Mrs. Patten among its characters, there are still touches of humor supplied by the servants at Cheverel Manor and by Mr. Gilfil's feminine parishioners. We meet the latter in the Prologue, where they are attending the rector's funeral and are discussing the impropriety of certain newcomers who do not appear in black bombazine on such occasions and for weeks thereafter. They evidently regard it as a matter of class, or well-bred piety.

> "Some folks can't a-bear to put off their colours," [Mrs. Higgins] remarked, "but that was never the way i' *my*

family. Why, Mrs. Parrot, from the time I was married until Mr. Higgins died, nine years ago come Candlemas, I *niver* was out o' black two years together."

"Ah," said Mrs. Parrot, who was conscious of inferiority in this respect, "there isn't many families as have had so many deaths as yours, Mrs. Higgins."

Mrs. Higgins, who was an elderly widow, "well left," reflected with complacency that Mrs. Parrot's observation was no more than just, and that Mrs. Jennings very likely belonged to a family which had no funerals to speak of.

In mid-March, assured by Blackwood that "Gilfil will be even more generally popular than Amos," [10] Marian and Lewes set off for the Scilly Isles and another marine biology expedition. Lewes had the idea that "it would be supremely delightful to be at the Scilly Isles for the spring equinox," [11] but bad weather delayed them at Penzance for a week. The sun shone on the morning of the 26th when they finally boarded the packet *Ariadne,* but a storm blew up midway across the Channel, and they were both desperately seasick. However, upon reaching St. Mary's, they found comfortable lodgings—though the servant girl, upon "nearer acquaintance had great resources of stupidity in her." [12] Marian was soon enjoying her first sight of the granite coast and the unusual colorings of the rocks, but she had "many a wet and dirty walk," [13] for the weather was terrible. In the evenings, she and Lewes read aloud to each other from Elizabeth Barrett Browning's *Aurora Leigh* and Mrs. Gaskell's new biography of Charlotte Brontë. During the day, while Lewes fished for marine specimens, Marian finished "Mr. Gilfil's Love Story" and blocked out the third story of *Scenes from Clerical Life,* "Janet's Repentance."

On May 18th, having exhausted all the resources of marine life that St. Mary's afforded, the Leweses packed their portmanteaux, bottles, jars, books, and Marian's manuscripts, and set out for Jersey. Their rather circuitous route gives an interesting insight into nineteenth-century travel conditions, and also what was required for anyone wishing to do scientific research. They had to return to Penzance by packet-boat, then go to Falmouth by omnibus, next by steamer to Plymouth (in a thick fog, during which they were nearly ran aground), and finally by another steamer to St. Helier—five days for a journey that can now be accomplished by helicopter in under an hour. "Such hedgerows in this island! Such orchards, white against the green slopes, and shady walks by the woodside," [14] Marian rhapsodized to Sara Hennell. She and Lewes settled down at Gorey, a fishing village about five miles from St. Helier, close enough to enjoy the local society, composed mostly of retired military personnel, but sufficiently remote to afford them needed privacy and quiet for their work. It was at Gorey that Marian finally nerved herself to the task of writing her brother about Lewes.

It is dangerous, particularly at a century's distance, even knowing as much as possible about the personality and the background of an individual, to surmise what was in an author's mind at the moment of setting words on paper. However, this much is documented: Marian was working on "Janet's Repentance" at the time that she wrote to Isaac. The cruelty shown by Dempster to his wife in that story has often been considered a little too excessive to be real; Blackwood himself urged Marian to "soften" it a little. Dempster is, as he said, "rather too barefaced a brute." [15] Marian, however, replied that "everything is softened from fact, so far as art is permitted to soften and yet to remain essentially true." [16] Knowing how intensely personal and subjective a writer she was, it does not seem too incredible to suppose that some of the "fact" might have reflected her own feeling about Isaac's treatment of herself.

Like the other stories in *Scenes from Clerical Life,* "Janet's Repentance" is drawn from the author's memory. When she was at school in Nuneaton, she had heard the gossip about John Buchanan, a prominent lawyer of the town, who drank to excess and treated his wife Nancy so brutally that eventually she too took to drink. The Buchanans were the originals of Robert and Janet Dempster. The third leading character, Mr. Tryan, the minister who is libeled and persecuted because of his strongly Evangelical views, was drawn from the Reverend John Edmund Jones, who had gone through a similar experience at Nuneaton, and died of consumption at the age of thirty-four. So closely did the story follow the actual events of Jones's life that, when Parts I and II were published, his brother remonstrated with Blackwood, saying that he was "utterly at a loss to conceive who should have written the statements or revived what should have been buried in oblivion." [17] Marian answered his letter, via Blackwood, insisting that *her* Mr. Tryan was an "ideal character," adding rather impishly, "If Mr. Jones's deceased brother was like Mr. Tryan, so much the better. . . ." [18]

One can understand readily why Blackwood demurred at the general tone of "Janet's Repentance." It is the somber story of Janet Dempster, an essentially good and gentle woman, who is driven to degradation by her husband, who wants only to maintain his position of influence in Milby, and fears anyone who offers the slightest competition. His fears, not his religious convictions, are at the root of his persecution of Mr. Tryan, in which his wife at first willingly assists. Then, when a public demonstration threatens Mr. Tryan's life, and Janet is most completely in the grip of the brandy bottle, the two meet, quite by chance. Janet is struck by the minister's obvious sincerity and his genuine spirituality. On a winter night, when her husband, in a drunken rage, puts her out of the house dressed only in her nightgown, and she must suffer the humiliation of asking a neighbor to give her clothes and shelter, she sends for Mr. Tryan. Through his friendship, she is able to break her addiction, and through her own tremendous sense of remorse because of her weakness, she eventually becomes an even finer person than she might otherwise ever have been. When her husband is thrown from his carriage, which he has insisted on driving alone despite his intoxicated condition, she returns to him, to nurse him through an appalling attack of delirium tremens—most graphically and realistically described. (Marian may have had her husband's assistance in writing this episode.) When he dies of a massive cerebral hemorrhage, he has one final moment of lucidity, and, though he cannot speak, Janet *feels* that he, too, has been redeemed from his own degradation. She asks, "Robert, do you know me?"

> He kept his eyes fixed upon her, and there was a faintly perceptible motion of the lips, as if he wanted to speak.
> But the moment of speech was forever gone—the moment for asking pardon of her, if he wanted to ask it. Could he read the full forgiveness that was written in her eyes?

Robert Dempster dies before the question is answered, but, to George Eliot, the fact of Janet's willing forgiveness is more important than her husband's acknowledgment of it. Her devotion to him in his illness, and her really heroic struggle and triumph in overcoming her own besetting temptation, are witnessed by the townspeople of Milby, who credit the change in her to Mr. Tryan. Overnight, their attitude toward him is sharply reversed, and, when he dies, he is genuinely and sincerely mourned.

Perhaps one reason why "Janet's Repentance" was not so well liked as either "Amos Barton" or "Mr. Gilfil's Love Story" is that it was a little too close to reality for comfort. Marian, in answering Blackwood's anxiety, told him that

> . . . the real town was more vicious than my Milby; the real Dempster was far more disgusting; the real Janet alas! had a far sadder end than mine . . . There is nothing to do with the story as I see it, but either to let Dempster and Janet and the rest be as I *see* them, or renounce it as too painful.[19]

Life in English provincial towns in the 1830's, the period of the story, *was* often bleak and dreary, especially for women like Janet Dempster, with some schooling but little opportunity to discover or use any other talents they might possess. They could look forward only to marriage, or possibly to becoming a governess; like Janet, frequently they married unwisely. Once married, society demanded that they remain married, no matter how their husbands treated them. Court records of the period are filled with complaints against drunken wife-beaters, but, after all, there was a law on the statute books permitting a husband to beat his wife, provided that the stick was no larger than the circumference of his little finger. No measure was given to limit his brutality. So, while Milby superficially sympathized with Janet Dempster, it was a man's world, and a double standard in conduct was winked at. The persecution of Mr. Tryan by Dempster and his cronies also had its roots in fact; readers of "Janet's Repentance" would have recognized its counter-

A page of the original manuscript of *Adam Bede,* not actual size.

The best known likeness of George Eliot. From an etching by Rajon, after the portrait by Sir Frederick Burton. Circa 1864.

George Henry Lewes in 1840. From a pencil drawing by Anne Gliddon.

John Blackwood, George Eliot's publisher, who did so much to further her career.

George Henry Lewes, the man with whom George Eliot lived as husband and wife and who was her common law husband.

part by hearsay, if not actual witness. Evangelical clergy in the Church of England sometimes endured much at the hands of congregations, as did the "ritualist" clergy during the high tide of the Oxford Movement. That particular aspect of the story, perhaps, has as much relevance for the twentieth century as the nineteenth.

But the first readers of "Janet's Repentance" found its reality, unrelieved by the kind of humor Dickens could provide in a similar situation, almost too overpowering, and the story can justifiably be criticized on the same grounds today. True, there are some glints of George Eliot's humor, especially in her description of Mr. Tryan's petticoat brigade: Miss Pratt, who wrote a verse in his honor beginning "Forward, young wrestler, for the truth!" and Mrs. Linnet, who wore her spectacles "chiefly for the purpose of seeing what others were doing," and, when reading the biography of a missionary, "turned to the end to see what disease he had died of." But the author's personal involvement with the religious struggles of her characters is too evident, and the general tone of the story is gloomy, even for the nineteenth century.

However, John Blackwood eventually came round to Marian's point of view, and, by the time the last installment arrived, he was quite enthusiastic about "Janet's Repentance," though "Amos Barton" was still his favorite. He was eager to continue the series, but Marian declined. "I have a subject in mind which will not come under the limitations of the title 'Clerical Life,' and I am inclined to take a larger canvas for it and write a novel," [20] she wrote to him on September 5th, shortly after her return to Richmond from Jersey. Accordingly, it was decided to drop the series entirely and publish the three stories in book form early the following year. "I rejoice to think that you are going to devote your powers to a Tale on a great scale," Blackwood encouraged. "With a larger canvas, your exquisite sketches of character will all come into full life and take their legitimate share in the story." [21] On October 17th, Marian replied:

> My new story haunts me a good deal, and I shall set about it without delay. It will be a country story—full of the breath of cows and the scent of hay. But I shall not ask you to look at it till I have written a volume or more, and then you will be able to judge whether you prefer printing it in the Magazine or publishing it as a separate novel when it is completed.[22]

There is no evidence to support any conjectures as to the way Marian's—now George Eliot's—mind ran during those crucial weeks. However, it is obvious from the differences in the three stories in *Scenes from Clerical Life* that in them she had deliberately tried three quite different approaches to fiction. In "Amos Barton," she had written somewhat in the style of Elizabeth Gaskell's *Cranford,* which she had read and enjoyed—a simple story of country life, with little plot, dependent chiefly on characterization for its interest. In "Mr. Gilfil's Love Story," she had used Thackeray's historical approach, retreating to his favorite eighteenth-century setting, and had attempted to write about county aristocracy. And in "Janet's Repentance," she had used the more melodramatic style favored by Charles Dickens. Of the three, "Amos Barton" had been the most successful, even with her editor. Character drawing, then, was her particular forte, combined with an ability to re-create a world she really knew. A full-scale novel would give her the opportunity to develop both these more fully; she would have the needed time to explore motivations, and show —rather than merely tell—the consequences of her characters' actions. Also, one fault in her last two stories was that she had let them be printed before they were completely written. Hence her comment to Blackwood that she would not let him see any of the new work until at least the first volume was done. Charles Dickens was famous for writing and publishing his novels in installments, but she could not work that way—at least, not yet. She had to consider a novel as a complete entity, to revise and re-write as the book took shape, without subjecting the earlier chapters too quickly to the finality of print.

Almost certainly, she discussed the entire project with Lewes. She had already told him what would eventually become the novel's climax, when she was working on "Amos Barton," thinking that she might use it for the *Clerical Life* series, and he had agreed that it would make a good story. That he gave her every encouragement now cannot be doubted. And she herself was ready. She had served her apprenticeship; she knew the kind of book she wanted to write. On October 22, 1857, she wrote in her Journal, "Began my new novel, 'Adam Bede.' " [23]

XI

Of all the novels written by George Eliot, none has been more universally acclaimed than *Adam Bede*. Many readers have a special affection for *The Mill on the Floss,* and critics—especially since the eminent F. R. Leavis named it a novel "in the great tradition"—have tended to consider *Middlemarch* her masterpiece. But readers and critics alike have agreed on the quality of *Adam Bede*. George Eliot in her other works frequently equaled it, but, in a sense, never really surpassed it. In her own time it was hailed as a fresh, new approach to fiction; the passing of a century has made its novelty familiar, but has not dimmed its excellence. The author herself recognized its uniqueness when she wrote in her Journal shortly after publication, "Shall I ever write another book as true as 'Adam Bede'?" [1]

The germ of the novel was an anecdote which Marian's aunt, Mrs. Samuel Evans, had told her during a visit to Griff in 1839. Mrs. Evans was a devout Methodist, and, in the early days when women were permitted to do so, had preached to congregations in the open air, in fields or town squares—wherever people would gather to listen. In one of these towns, a young girl waited in prison, condemned to be hanged for the crime of child murder. She had stubbornly refused to confess her guilt —had, indeed, refused even to admit that she had borne an illegitimate child—but the evidence against her was so overwhelming that her conviction was a foregone conclusion. Mrs. Evans, hearing of the girl's obduracy, had gained admittance to the prison, and, after a night of prayer and exhortation, had brought her to confess and repent. The next morning she had accompanied her to the scaffold and had remained at her side until the end.

The story had impressed Marian deeply as a young girl; she had, as has been noted, considered using it as one of the *Scenes from Clerical Life*. But as she considered it further, it quickly outgrew the limitations of a single story. Episodes from her father's early life recurred to her, and the character of the honest young carpenter, Adam Bede, soon evolved as the hero. The girl was already there in embryo; the seducer was probably the next character to come to mind. When she started to write, the Adam Bede–Hetty Sorrel–Arthur Donithorne triangle was firmly established, so the novel began as an exploration of the causes and motives leading to Hetty's crime, which would be the climax. To Lewes must be given the credit of Dinah Morris's becoming a leading character. Marian introduced her in the third chapter, and when she read it aloud to her husband, he, quickly and perceptively realizing that much of the book's interest would center in the lovely, dedicated Methodist preacher, suggested that she be developed more fully. Marian immediately concurred and wrote the rest of *Adam Bede* with this idea in mind.[2] Lewes was quite correct. Most readers remember Dinah as the most vivid character in the novel; next to Maggie Tulliver she is the favorite of all George Eliot's heroines.

The story of *Adam Bede* is, perhaps, too well known to need more than brief summary. Its intrinsic melodrama has been noted, as has its similarity in plot to many other nineteenth-century novels. Adam Bede, the honest young workingman, is in love with Hetty Sorrel, a "farmer's lass," who, in turn, is deeply in love with Arthur Donithorne, the young squire. Adam catches his rival kissing Hetty in the wood; outraged, he quarrels with Arthur—who also happens to be his employer—and demands that he either marry Hetty honorably or tell her in no uncertain terms that he has never had such an intention. Arthur chooses the latter course, and leaves town to join his regiment. Heartbroken, Hetty accepts Adam's proposal of marriage, then discovers that she is going to have a baby. In desperation, she goes to Windsor, where Arthur's regiment has been stationed, only to discover that it has been sent to Ireland. Unwilling to return to her family, she wanders from town to town, finding shelter where she can, until the baby is born. Meanwhile, Adam has been searching frantically for her; finally, he and her family receive word that she is in prison, charged with murdering her child. There is a trial, and she is sentenced to death. During all this time, she has kept obdurate silence; it is not until her Methodist cousin, Dinah Morris, manages to come to her prison cell that she is persuaded to confess and seek forgiveness. Dinah goes to the scaffold with her on the following morning, where, at the last moment, Arthur appears with a reprieve commuting the death sentence to transportation for life. Eventually Adam, recovering from his grief, realizes that little Hetty would never have been the wife for him even if she had not transgressed, and that it is Dinah Morris whom he truly loves. At the end of the novel, he and Dinah are married.

The important thing about *Adam Bede*, however, is not the plot itself, but rather the way in which it seems to evolve so naturally and inevitably from the characters and their surroundings. The heavy author's hand, so evident in novels by Ainsworth and Bulwer-Lytton (and even, occasionally, in Dickens) is wholly absent here. George Eliot throughout consciously observed a psychological truth expressed by one of her characters, Mr. Irvine, the rector of Hayslope Church, in conversation with Arthur Donithorne:

> "A man can never do anything at variance with his own nature. He carries within him the germ of his most exceptional action; and if we wise people make fools of ourselves on any particular occasion, we must endure the legitimate conclusion that we carry a few grains of folly to our ounce of wisdom."

It is from these "germs of most exceptional actions" that the conflict in *Adam Bede* is derived. Adam, for example, is good, patient, an excellent son, an honest workman. His outburst of cold anger against Arthur, which culminates in the all-but-fatal blow, and his corroding hatred engulf him when he learns what has happened to

Hetty, the girl he loves and hopes to marry. Both are foreshadowed by his "flush of anger" when he discovers that his father has gone on a drinking spree, leaving work promised for the next day not even begun. His own dedication to his work has a grimness about it; there is little time in his life for joy. He is a strong man, a pillar of rectitude, and his inner struggle when he weighs his high moral standards against his instinctive desire to be near Hetty during her trial is wholly convincing. He has been hurt beyond endurance by two people whom he trusted implicitly, and he goes to see Hetty at the last only at the gentle insistence of Dinah Morris. His confrontation with her just before the gallows cart arrives is poignantly drawn.

> It seemed to Adam as if his brain would burst with the anguish of meeting Hetty's eyes in the first moments; but the sound of her voice uttering these penitent words touched a chord which had been less strained; there was a sense of relief from what was becoming unbearable, and the rare tears came—they had never come before, since he had hung on Seth's neck in the beginning of his sorrow.

Then there is Adam's final meeting with Arthur Donithorne, when he learns that the young squire has determined to leave Hayslope, so that his presence may not be a constant reminder and hurt to Hetty's family. Adam has managed to forgive Hetty, but he still hates Arthur. "A man should make sacrifices to keep clear of doing wrong; sacrifices won't undo it when it's done," he says coldly. But when Arthur cries in anguish, "Perhaps you've never done anything to repent of in your life, Adam; if you had, you would be more generous," Adam is finally brought to admit that he, too, has suffered regret and remorse for wrong-doing of his own:

"It's true what you say, sir: I'm hard—it's in my nature.
I was too hard with my father for doing wrong . . . I've
known what it is in my life to repent and feel it's too late.
I felt I'd been too harsh to my father when he was gone
from me—I feel it now, when I think of it. I've no right
to be hard towards them as have done wrong and repent."

These words come hard to a hard man, but though he is
still aware that ". . . deeds carry their terrible consequences . . . consequences that are hardly ever confined
to ourselves," his heart has been touched by compassion.
He is able to forgive Arthur, too, and his sorrow, though
deep, is bearable now that hatred is gone.

Like Adam, Arthur Donithorne grows in stature
through adversity. He is not the typical villain-seducer;
he is completely unlike the callow Captain Wybrow.
Handsome, charming, generous, likeable—he has every
potentiality for good. His flaw is that he cannot bear to
be uncomfortable. He is attracted to Hetty because she
is so pretty; she possesses "a spring tide beauty; it was the
beauty of young frisking things, round limbed, gambol-
ling, circumventing you by a false air of innocence."
When he meets her—almost by accident—in the wood,
he teases her about her current suitor, Craig the gar-
dener, and is astonished to see that what he intended as
a pleasantry brings tears to her eyes. A pretty girl in
tears makes him uncomfortable, so he kisses her, to make
himself feel better. He is quite unprepared for Hetty's
whole-hearted acceptance of his embrace, and he realizes
at once that she is taking the situation more seriously
than he intended. Yet, he cannot bear to have her think
that he would be guilty of trifling with her, and, actually,
he is more smitten than he wants to admit. His struggle
to resolve the dilemma between what he knows he ought
not do, and what he finds very pleasurable, is genuine;

he drifts along the line of least resistance, trying to convince himself that Hetty must know that he cannot possibly marry her, even while he realizes that he has given her every reason to expect that he will. His reaction when Mr. Poyser, Hetty's uncle, proposes the toast to him on behalf of the manor tenants at his coming-of-age fête is most skillfully handled:

> Arthur felt a twinge of conscience during Mr. Poyser's speech, but it was too feeble to nullify the pleasure he felt in being praised. Did he not deserve what was being said of him on the whole? If there was something in his conduct that Poyser wouldn't have liked if he had known it, why, no man's conduct will bear too close an inspection; and Poyser was not likely to know it; and, after all, what had he done? Gone a little too far, perhaps, in flirtation, but another man in his place would have acted much worse; and no harm could come—no harm *should* come, for the next time he was alone with Hetty, he would explain to her that she must not think seriously of him or what had passed. It was necessary to Arthur, you perceive, to be satisfied with himself: uncomfortable thoughts must be got rid of by good intentions for the future.

It is Adam's rage that wakens him out of his rationalizing, to what he "must shrink from believing in—the irrevocableness of his own wrong-doing." Still, he cannot bring himself to believe that there will be any worse consequences for Hetty than grief at his breaking-off with her: "He resolutely turned his eyes from any bad consequence that was not demonstrably inevitable." It is not until he learns that Hetty is on trial for murdering their child that the appalling consequences of his own vanity and weakness are fully revealed to him, but if one feels contempt for him, one also feels pity for his desperate efforts to make what amends he can. He saves

Hetty's life, but the broken, ill, middle-aged man of the final chapter—such a tragic contrast to the gay young squire at his coming of age—is proof of George Eliot's conviction that "Consequences are unpitying," and that "inward suffering . . . is the worst form of Nemesis."

Hetty Sorrel also carries within her the seeds of her own special Nemesis. The phrase "false air of innocence" is the clue to her character. She is a "distracting, kitten-like maiden" when Arthur Donithorne sees her in the dairy making butter.

> And they are the prettiest attitudes and movements into which a pretty girl is thrown when making butter—tossing movements that give a charming curve to the arm, and a sideward inclination of the round white neck; little pattings and rolling movements with the palm of the hand, and finishings that cannot at all be effected without a great play of pouting mouth and the dark eyes.

But the reader remembers the "false air of innocence," and recognizes that her coquettish gestures in butter-making are, at least to a degree, calculated. Hetty is quite used to the thought that people enjoy looking at her, and she is perfectly aware of Arthur's manifest interest. She is equally cognizant of Adam's devotion to her: "She liked to feel that this strong, skilful, keen-eyed man was in her power, and would have been indignant if he had shown the least sign of slipping from under the yoke of her coquettish tyranny. . . ." But her dreams and fantasies will not allow her to accept the realities of her world; she is almost pathetic in her willingness to meet Arthur secretly in the wood, to accept the trinkets he gives her which she cannot wear openly, finally to give herself to him completely in her self-delusion that he will marry her and bring her into his world. Her stunned dismay when she receives Arthur's farewell letter evokes great sympathy, for, despite her superficiality and vanity, she is lovable as a foolish willful child is lovable:

> Slowly Hetty read the letter; and when she looked up from it, there was a reflection of a blanched form in the old dim glass—a white marble face with rounded childish forms, but with something more than a child's pain in it. Hetty did not see the face—she saw nothing—she only felt that she was cold and sick and trembling. . . .
>
> The shattering of all her little dream-world, the crushing blow on her new-born passion, afflicted her pleasure craving nature with an overpowering pain that annihilated all impulse to resistance and suspended her anger. She sat sobbing until the candle went out, and then, wearied, aching, stupefied with crying, threw herself on the bed without undressing and went to sleep.

And she does possess a sense of honor. When she discovers that she is to bear Arthur's child, she knows that she must not deceitfully marry Adam. Tragically, she does not want to marry Arthur, either. She sets out on her lonely, dreadful journey to Windsor because it is the only thing she can think of to do, and she sells the jewelry her lover has given her for food and lodging. Hetty is not intrinsically wicked. It is made quite clear that her crime is not premeditated; she kills her baby in a moment of utter desperation which would lead a twentieth-century jury to acquit her on the grounds of temporary insanity. Her confession to Dinah is harrowing in its broken directness.

> "I did do it, Dinah . . . I buried it in the wood . . . the little baby . . . and it cried . . . I heard it cry . . . ever such a way off . . . all night . . . and I went back because it cried . . . I didn't kill it—I didn't kill it myself.

I put it down there and covered it up, and when I came back it was gone. . . ."

And then comes the pitiful plea, "Dinah, do you think God will take away the crying and the place in the wood, now I've told everything?" At this moment, even the most cynical reader must share Adam's feeling that Hetty *cannot* be punished to the full extent of the law, and almost joins in the shout from the crowd gathered at the scaffold, when Arthur rides in at full gallop, waving her reprieve.

Adam, Arthur, Hetty—all three are believable human beings, possessed of virtues that are overwhelmed by their respective frailties. But, in a sense, Dinah Morris is George Eliot's greatest achievement in characterization in this novel, because she is wholly—and convincingly—good. The novelist usually finds evil more easy to depict than goodness; it is difficult, especially in this particular era, to make goodness interesting. But George Eliot succeeds triumphantly with Dinah; the quiet, serene young woman in her sober Methodist garb dominates every scene in which she appears, because she possesses such genuine humility and compassion. She is strong without being hard; and, especially in the final chapters, where she unexpectedly weeps—much to her family's amazement—because Adam cannot realize that he loves her, she is entirely feminine. And when at last Adam does propose, and she decides that she can marry and still serve God as her conscience dictates, her acceptance is precisely what one would expect of her:

> "My soul is so knit to yours that it is a divided life that I live without you. And at this moment, now you are with me, and I feel that our hearts are filled with the same love, I have a fulness of strength to bear and do our heavenly Father's Will that I had lost before."

Sentimental? Some have deemed it so, but the words come naturally to Dinah Morris as the author created her. It must be remembered, too, that she was created for a reading public that expected and wanted their heroines to be good, and for a time when—judging from letters and diaries—engaged couples were not embarrassed at the idea of including God in their love.

But there is even more to *Adam Bede* than a tightly woven plot and superbly drawn leading characters. There is the Warwickshire landscape, faithfully and beautifully delineated, and the effect of life in both hall and cottage, done in the manner of the Dutch painters whom the author so admired. Mrs. Poyser's dairy is doubtless a memory picture of the dairy at Arbury Farm, just as Mrs. Poyser herself is a fictional replica of Christiana Pearson Evans. Her salty comments on life and love are as down-to-earth as the farm she lives on:

> "I allays said I'd never marry a man as had got no brains; for where's the use of a woman having brains of her own if she's tackled to a geck as everybody's a-laughing at? She might as well dress herself fine to sit back'ards on a donkey."

The scene in which she speaks her mind to old Squire Donithorne is a comic gem, as is the moment at the harvest supper when she obliquely remarks on Adam's diffidence in "speaking for" Dinah:

> ". . . men are mostly slow, their thoughts overrun 'em, and they can only catch 'em by the tail. I can count a stocking top while a man's getting his tongue ready."

And Dinah receives the benefit of her notice, too. "However, I'm not denying women are foolish. God Almighty made 'em to match men." But Mrs. Poyser is not the only memorable figure in George Eliot's rustic chorus. There is Lisbeth Bede, Adam's mother, lugubrious and caustic by turns; Farmer Poyser, who knows his own worth and is not above telling it; and Bartle Massey the schoolmaster (a faithful portrait, even to the name, of the man who had taught Robert Evans), who struggles to teach grown men to read, write, and cipher in the evenings after their work is done, who dislikes women on principle, and willingly expresses his views on the subject. Background characters they may be, but they provide the context for the main action of *Adam Bede,* and make that action seem more believable a part of universal human experience.

The book was written with comparative speed—it took Marian a little over a year to get it down on paper. There were interruptions; her time during the autumn of 1857 was divided between the new novel and correcting proofs for *Scenes from Clerical Life* which *Blackwood's Magazine* published in book form on January 5, 1858, to an almost universal chorus of praise. Marian had the excitement of receiving letters from Jane Welsh Carlyle and Charles Dickens, sent to "George Eliot" in care of the publishers, for she was still determined to conceal her identity. Jane Carlyle, known for her sharp tongue and incisive wit, almost rhapsodized, calling *Scenes from Clerical Life*

> . . . a *human* book—written out of the heart of a live man, full of tenderness and pathos without a scrap of sentimentality, of sense without dogmatism, of earnestness without twaddle—a book that makes one *feel friends,* at once and for always, with the man or woman who wrote it.[3]

She admitted a deep curiosity about the author's identity. Charles Dickens hit nearer home; he loved the book, and said,

. . . I should have been strongly disposed, if I had been left to my own devices, to address the said writer as a woman. I have observed what seem to me to be such womanly touches, in those moving fictions, that the assurance on the title page is insufficient to satisfy me even now. If they originated with no woman, I believe that no man before had the art of making himself, mentally, so like a woman since the world began.[4]

Sales, nonetheless, were slow, which discouraged Marian greatly. Lewes kept her at her desk, however, and when John Blackwood came to call on them in February, thirteen chapters of *Adam Bede* were ready for his perusal.

It was on this occasion that Marian revealed her identity as George Eliot. Blackwood came in the afternoon, and chatted amiably with the Leweses about *Scenes from Clerical Life*. Finally, he asked Lewes the direct question, "Well, am I to see George Eliot this time?" Marian quietly left the room and her husband followed her. A moment later she returned, and publisher met author for the first time. Blackwood, indeed, had suspected that Mrs. Lewes was George Eliot, but he promised that her secret would be implicitly kept. Five days later, he returned for a second visit, and Marian gave him what she had finished of *Adam Bede*. It is easy to imagine her trepidation at this moment, and her sense of relief and infinite gratitude when, after reading the first page, the taciturn Scot looked up and said, smiling, "This will do." [5] He read the rest on the train back to Edinburgh, and wrote at once on arrival there, asking when more of the book would be ready.

On April 7, 1858, the Leweses left England to spend the summer in Germany. Living was cheaper there, and Lewes wanted to pursue some scientific inquiries for a new book on human physiology. They stopped at Nu-

remberg en route, which Marian described as "one pro-
tracted *oh!*" [6] and reached Munich on April 12th, where
they found lodgings. Her description of them is as de-
lightfully minute as the one of Mrs. Poyser's dairy:

> . . . Two time pieces under glass shades, several crucifixes
> also under glass shades, several bouquets of artificial flow-
> ers under glass shades, a *Schranke* with glass doors crammed
> full of the most brittle and tiny articles to be found in
> German shops, selected apparently for their brittle-minute-
> ness, and seventeen bad pictures.[7]

While her husband made contact with various professors
at the University, Marian worked on *Adam Bede*. One
aspect of the novel perturbed her as the weeks went on;
Lewes had been saying that Adam was too passive a character, and should be "brought into more direct collision
with Arthur." [8] Inspiration finally came; the scene in the
wood flashed into her mind, and "the fight came to me as
a *necessity* one night at the Munich Opera when I was
listening to *William Tell*." [9] By the time they left Munich in July, she had reached the dance scene at the
coming-of-age festival.

The Leweses traveled through the Tyrol, stopping at
Salzburg, down the Danube to Vienna, then to Prague,
through Saxon Switzerland to Dresden. Here, despite a
violent attack of intestinal flu, Marian worked steadily
and uninterruptedly, "with great enjoyment." [10] On
September 2nd, they returned to England; six days later,
Volume II was on its way to Edinburgh. The final volume evidently "wrote itself," for it was in John Blackwood's hands by the end of November. Even before he
had seen the final chapters, he offered a handsome contract and decided to delay publication until after Christmas so that there would be no competition whatever for

this novel from any others issued especially for the holiday season trade.

Adam Bede was published on February 1, 1859. The reviewers were wildly enthusiatic, starting with the usually reticent London *Times:* "There can be no mistake about *Adam Bede*. It is a first rate novel, and its author takes rank at once among the masters of the art." [11] No further proof of its popularity is needed than the fact that it was in its sixth edition by August. Nineteeth-century book editions were not large by contemporary standards—between two and three thousand copies was the general run—but, even at a most conservative estimate, twelve thousand copies in six months could be called a success. The book was read and quoted by the Prince Consort; it was even quoted by Charles Buxton on the floor of the House of Commons.[12] Letters came in from Dickens, Mrs. Carlyle, James Anthony Froude; Charles Reade proclaimed it "the finest thing since Shakespeare." [13] Even Queen Victoria, who generally preferred "dear Mr. Dickens," owned that she had enjoyed "Mr. Eliot's country novel." It is amusing to read letters from Marian's friends, the Brays and Sara Hennell, asking her if she had yet read *Adam Bede*. When the book was read aloud to an old, half-blind farmer in Staffordshire who had known Robert Evans, he sat up far into the night, listening, exclaiming every now and then, "That's Robert! That's Robert to the life!" [14] And Isaac Evans, who read the book at Griff, told his intimate friends that no one but his sister could possibly have written it.[15]

What was Marian's reaction to all this furor? Deep gratitude.

I sing my "Magnificat" in a quiet way, and have a great deal of deep, silent joy, but few authors, I suppose, who have had a real success, have known less of the flush and sensations of triumph that are talked of as the accompaniments of success.[16]

Visible "sensations of triumph" might have betrayed the secret of her identity, and, besides, they were out of character for the professional writer she had become. Also, she was already at work on her next book. In December of 1858, she had written John Blackwood that "I have not yet made up my mind what my new story is to be, but I must not lie fallow any longer when the new year is come."[17] Obviously, some ideas were simmering in her mind. Her Journal entry for January 12, 1859, reads, "We went into town today and looked in the 'Annual Register' for cases of *inundation*."[18]

The story of Maggie Tulliver had begun.

XII

The Mill on the Floss, however, was not begun with the immediacy and the ease that characterized the beginning of *Adam Bede.* In the first place, having grown weary of lodgings, the Leweses had decided to buy a home, so house-hunting was the first order of the day. It was not until mid-February that they were finally settled at Holly Lodge in Wandsworth, a suburb of London on the Thames. The house, which Marian described as "a tall cake, with a low garnish of holly and laurel," [1] was comfortable, but large, and she experienced all the usual problems and frustrations of the housewife, particularly in the matter of good household help, which was almost impossible to obtain.

> Is there Balm in Gilead? In other words, is there a servant in your neighbourhood who would like a place near London? A servant of high character and with the general knowledge of the "general servant?" [2]

she wrote with wry humor to Mrs. Bray. To make up for this, however, they had very pleasant neighbors in Wandsworth; Dr. and Mrs. Richard Congreave lived near by, and they too were greatly interested in Auguste Comte and Positivism. Lewes found them especially congenial, and Mrs. Congreave quickly became one of Marian's most devoted friends.

In the midst of all the upheaval of moving, a letter came from Chrissey. Marian's joy at this breaking of a two-year silence was immediately submerged by grief, for her sister was slowly dying of tuberculosis.

> My object in writing you is to tell you how very sorry I have been that I ceased to write, and neglected one who, under all circumstances, was kind to me and mine. *Pray believe* me, when I say it will be the greatest comfort I can receive to know that you are *well* and *happy*. Will you write once more? [3]

Chrissey had begged. Naturally, Marian wrote at once: as she said in a letter to Sara Hennell, "The past is abolished from my mind. I only want her to feel that I love and care for her." [4] She longed to go to Meriden at once, but circumstances prevented the two sisters from meeting again before Chrissey's death on March 15th. Marian was deeply saddened, but comforted and grateful in the thought that there had been a reconciliation between them. The emotional strain was too great, however, to permit her to work at her novel, which she realized would require "time and labour," [5] and, above all, peace and serenity of mind.

She did have a story, however, written "one morning at Richmond, as a resource when my head was too stupid for more important work," [6] which she took out, polished off, and sent to Edinburgh at the end of April. She described it as a "slight story of an outré kind," [7] and, indeed, had it not been signed *George Eliot,* it would be difficult to assign it to her. It is a peculiar tale, reminiscent of Poe and Hawthorne, and especially of Wilkie Collins, about a man who possesses the gift of second sight and a unique ability to read the thoughts of others. He leads a strange, dual existence—one in the actual world and the other in the inner world of subconscious reality. Though he knows, through his mysterious gift, that the girl who enthralls him is shallow, vain, and eager only for the position he can give her, he nonetheless marries her and lives miserably ever after. There is a maid in the house who hates her mistress, but, strangely enough, Latimer's powers do not permit him to read her thoughts. It is only after her death, when the doctor, who is interested in such scientific experiments, revives her by means of a blood transfusion, that the secret is revealed: the maid had seen her mistress hide the poison with which she intended to murder her husband. The story breaks off abruptly, for Latimer, who has foretold to the instant the time of his death, has written this account as a kind of last confession. Blackwood did not altogether like "The Lifted Veil," though he owned it was well written, and he did not publish it in the magazine until July. ". . . I think you must have been worrying and disturbing yourself about something when you wrote it," [8] he said kindly, which, of course, was true.

Chrissey's death had deeply affected Marian, and, in addition, there was the constant, nagging exasperation of Joseph Liggins.

The "Liggins controversy," which only the firmness and the common sense of both Marian and John Blackwood kept from becoming a major scandal, arose from the great speculation over the identity of George Eliot. Some people had already shrewdly guessed that the author was a woman—Dickens and Jane Welsh Carlyle among them—but their interest was kindly, not prying, as was that of Elizabeth Gaskell, who wrote to Marian under the pseudonym, ". . . I have had the greatest compliment paid me I ever had in my life. I have been suspected of having written 'Adam Bede.' " [9] Bulwer-Lytton, too, was certain of George Eliot's feminine identity, but he was congratulatory and restrained in his curiosity. John Chapman had actually asked Lewes in so many words whether or not Marian *had* written a novel; Lewes emphatically denied his right to inquire.[10] Barbara Smith Bodichon, a friend from *Westminster Review* days, who had since married and gone to live in Algiers, had guessed immediately that Marian was the author on the basis of a few extracts printed in reviews of *Adam Bede*. ". . . I *know* that it is you," she wrote exultantly to Marian in April; "that YOU, *that you* whom they spit at should do it!" [11] Madame Bodichon's comment pinpoints the reason why both Marian and her husband wanted the incognito to be preserved for as long as possible. True, the fact that a woman had written *Adam Bede* might have hindered the book's success; despite the acknowledged excellence of both Charlotte Brontë and Elizabeth Gaskell, women were still considered in the guise of W. S. Gilbert's "that singular anomaly, the lady novelist." [12] As Lewes had written John Blackwood, "When

Jane Eyre was known to be a woman's book, the tone noticeably changed." [13]

But the main factor was, quite obviously, the equivocal situation in which Marian had placed herself. Not that she regretted her decision: "He is the prime blessing that has made all the rest possible to me—giving me a response to everything I have written, a response that I could confide in as proof that I had not mistaken my work." [14] But, at the same time, she recognized that, to solid Victorian respectability, she was "that dreadful woman," responsible for destroying a marriage and now living in flagrant violation of all morality. No book signed by her own name could hope for a fair hearing. And since, in the leisurely nineteenth century, it sometimes took almost a year for all the major quarterlies and monthlies to publish reviews, the longer George Eliot remained a mystery, the better the chances of *Adam Bede.* Once the book had been praised in print, and once continued good sales were assured, no awkward revelations could harm it. But, judging from Babara Bodichon's letter to Marian, the Lewes ménage was still the object of censure, so secrecy seemed imperative.

However, shortly after *Scenes from Clerical Life* was published in book form, a certain Joseph Liggins, who had lived in Warwickshire during the 1820's, was suggested as the author by none other than the Reverend John Gwyther, the original Amos Barton. Naturally, he had noted the first-hand knowledge of the people and the events depicted in the stories, and he remembered Liggins during his curacy at Chilvers Coton as having literary aspirations. Very quickly, a group of dissenting ministers tracked Liggins down, and Liggins, who seems to have been something of a ne'er-do-well, saw an opportunity to make a name for himself that ability and circumstances hitherto had denied him. He freely claimed the authorship not only of *Scenes from Clerical Life*, but of *Adam Bede* as well, embroidering his claim to the latter by the assertion that he had given the manuscript to John Blackwood some ten or twelve years before, and that Blackwood had kept it all this time before publishing it, denying him any compensation whatever.[15] A very audacious statement, but of the type that can be made to sound plausible by a suave and clever liar. Marian, when asked by Warwickshire friends, said that she did remember Liggins "as a vision of my childhood—a tall, black-coated, genteel young clergyman-in-embryo." [16] She refused to take the matter seriously, however, thinking that time would put an end to such patently ridiculous and untruthful allegations.

Then, a letter appeared in the London *Times* on April 13th from a Reverend H. Anders, saying unequivocally that Liggins and George Eliot were one and the same. Some reply was necessary, since the affair had been made public, so Lewes wrote a letter in Marian's name, signing it "George Eliot," emphatically denying Liggins's claim to authorship. But the stream of letters, both to the *Times* and to John Blackwood, insisting that Liggins *was* the author, did not diminish. By the end of April, a group of "interested friends" had organized a committee to raise a fund for his support.

"The myth about Liggins is getting serious, and must be put a stop to," Marian wrote firmly to Blackwood on April 20th. "We are not bound to allow sums of money to be raised (or perhaps a place given) on a false supposition of this kind." [17] Meanwhile, the *Leader* had published an entire column about "George Eliot's" letter to the *Times*—an almost unprecedented action in the history of journalism—insisting that authors had no right to anonymity, and demanding that "George Eliot" reveal himself. The *Critic* carried a similar statement. Blackwood, in reply to Marian's request that he take some action, wrote to her, "The articles were contemptible, and any notice of such things would only glorify the creatures who had written them." [18] He advised silence and restraint, cautioning that if the incognito could be preserved until after the new book—which Marian was trying to write—was published, they would have ridden out all possible storms and be on firmer ground.[19] Marian in reply suggested humorously that Liggins be requested to write a chapter of a novel: ". . . that chapter may possibly do what my denial has failed to do." [20] This letter amused Blackwood so much that he forwarded it to the *Times* for publication on June 6th, 1869.

The rumors, however, gained momentum; the committee to assist Liggins openly solicited subscriptions to the fund. John Blackwood himself wrote a stern letter of protest to the *Times,* but, far from quieting the storm, it only fanned the flames. The Reverend Mr. Quirk, curate of Attleborough near Nuneaton, wrote to the editor, demanding to see a sample of George Eliot's handwriting. When this was supplied, he was forced to admit that it in no way resembled Liggins's, but he still most obnoxiously continued to maintain that Liggins was the author. "I am fond of Liggins, compared with Quirk," [21] said Marian, even though the Reverend Mr. Quirk had been a friend of her sister Chrissey's.[22] And Lewes remarked succinctly, "[Liggins] is a cunning imposter and has credulous fools to deal with." [23]

Matters came to a head in June, and Marian decided

that the secret must be revealed, at least to those close friends who could always be counted on to stand by her—the Brays and Sara Hennell. After a performance of *The Messiah* at the Crystal Palace, she and Lewes dined with them. "I told them that I was the author of *Adam Bede* and *Clerical Scenes,* and they seemed overwhelmed with surprise." [24] As she had hoped, once they recovered from their amazement, their sympathy, understanding, and respect were immediate. Then Marian wrote a very strong letter to the *Times,* calling Liggins an imposter and a swindler.[25] The *Times* editor, J. T. Delane, sent a proof copy to John Blackwood, who immediately wrote to Marian, advising her to reconsider: "The letter is an excellent one, but by the public, who does not know all the aggravations in the case, would be looked upon as being too strong coming from *you* and might divert sympathy to Liggins." [26] Marian, on second thought, agreed. And she also decided that the secret of her authorship need not be kept from the public any longer. As Lewes said, quite practically, *Adam Bede* was a resounding success, and "they can't now unsay their admiration." [27]

Once Marian's identity as George Eliot was made general knowledge, there were, of course, other storms to be weathered. The *Athenaeum* attacked her savagely,[28] saying that the entire Liggins controversy had been a publicity stunt, calculated to help the sale of *Adam Bede.* The facts, however, were so manifestly opposite that their attack missed its mark completely. The chorus of praise for George Eliot drowned out all detractors; Liggins quickly faded into the background, though Mr. Quirk did not capitulate until September. It had been a nerve-wracking experience, but Marian emerged the stronger for it, and she was doubtless relieved—she, who hated subterfuges of any kind—that the need for concealment was over. Peace and quiet were once again hers, and she could at last work at her usual sustained pace.

> Resumed my new novel, of which I am going to re-write the first two chapters. I shall call it provisionally "The Tullivers," for the sake of a title *quelconque,* or perhaps "St. Ogg's on the Floss." [29]

It is always interesting to speculate why any author chooses to write a particular book, and *The Mill on the Floss,* following so closely upon *Adam Bede,* provides ample ground for such speculation. Marian Evans herself never told why, in so many words, but it seems reasonable to surmise that *Adam Bede,* with its reminiscences of her father's life, had also made her recall her own girlhood. In January, she had gone to the National Register to look up cases of inundation; her known admiration of Dickens's novels, and her specific mention of *David Copperfield* in several letters, indicate that the storm in which Steerforth meets his death might have influenced her mind in that direction. Also, in 1845, she had briefly visited Gainsborough-on-Trent, where the spring tide develops a bore with a wave front up to four feet high. It is said that she stood in a corner of the garden of Morton Hall, watching the river in fascination, listening to the boatmen cry, "Ware Aegir!" [30] Interestingly enough, Sara Hennell wrote to her mother in September of the following year (1846) that "Miss Evans looks very brilliant just now—we fancy she must be writing her novel." [31] There is no direct evidence to support any surmise that the visit to Gainsborough had suggested a locale, if not a plot, but the very specific reference to inundations in 1859, for which that area was famous, almost irresistibly suggests some deep impression which had lain dormant for nearly fifteen years.

Chrissey's death must have revived memories which she drew upon when she began to create the character of Lucy Dean. But an even more subtle influence was perhaps at work—an innate need to somehow justify herself and her own choice of action. Not that her heroine would risk the indignity of being ostracized to live with a married man—Victorian reticence would forbid such a blatant admission. But she could show how a child could become the kind of young woman who still lived by the finest dictates of her own conscience and integrity, even though it might involve going against the customary moral outlook of society.

And so Maggie Tulliver was born. She is George Eliot's most endearing heroine, for she is the novelist herself—as a passionate, generous, impulsive child; as a confused adolescent faced with her first tragedy; as a young girl radiantly in love for the first time; and as a truly noble woman who refuses to compound one wrong by a second, or to succumb to what "society" would dictate as the right course for her to follow. *The Mill on the Floss* is Maggie's book; we see the world of St. Ogg's through her eyes. George Eliot knew well what life on the land was like—Dorlcote Mill is not too far removed from Arbury Farm—and she had also experienced the life of a small provincial town during her days at Coventry. She was equally at home in the Tulliver parlor and the Dean drawing room, and she saw both with a compassionate yet penetrating insight which stripped the surface civility and complacency to bare both the hypocrisy and the gallantry beneath.

The story of *The Mill on the Floss* is also unique, for it lacks the "sensational novel" quality that characterized *Adam Bede*. Here, it is the clash of personalities and the probing of human motives that absorb the reader's attention. We understand Maggie's bewilderment at being the "outsider" among the Dodson clan—for it is the Dodsons, her mother's family, whose standards dominate her world. She is a brunette, not a flaxen-haired beauty like her cousin Lucy, whose curls are never rumpled and whose dress is never soiled—except for that moment when Maggie, in a fit of jealousy, pushes her into the brook. Maggie is emotional and impetuous, and shows no sign in the early chapters of the great beauty she will become. Her reaction to correction is either tears or a burst of rage; she runs away and tries to join the gypsies—just as Mary Ann Evans did—because her adored brother has treated her so harshly. When her father is made bankrupt through an unfortunate lawsuit, and the mill is taken from him to pay his debts, Maggie draws comfort from a volume of St. Thomas a Kempis and determines to renounce every thought of earthly ease with all the passionate determination that has characterized her entire life. Then she has a brief interlude of happiness; she falls in love with Philip Wakem, the crippled son of the lawyer who has ruined her father. (Monsieur D'Albert-Durade probably supplied some of Philip's characteristics.) Because of her brother Tom's hatred of all the Wakems, Maggie meets Philip secretly; when Tom, thanks to the observant and reportorial eyes of the town, learns of it, he forces her to choose between Philip and himself.

Maggie, from a sense of duty and old affection, chooses her brother. But the scene is set for tragedy. Philip's warning, "You will be thrown into the world some day, and then every rational satisfaction of your nature that you deny now, will assault you like a savage appetite," is fulfilled in the cruelest possible way. Maggie's cousin Lucy, whom she dearly loves and who loves her, invites her to pay a long visit; and, in the Dean household, the finest in St. Ogg's, Maggie finds herself in a milieu for which her own experiences have illy fitted her. Naturally, she meets Stephen Guest, Lucy's fiancé, who is violently attracted to her. To her horror, she finds herself equally attracted to him. She struggles with her feelings, emotion vying with her sense of loyalty to Lucy, and to Philip Wakem whom she has promised to marry if marriage should ever become possible for them. Then, one day, Stephen takes her rowing on the river. They are unexpectedly alone, for neither Philip nor Lucy can accompany them. The tide carries them far past the proper landing point, and they are unable to return to St. Ogg's.

At this point, Maggie's emotional turmoil reaches its climax. Convention decrees that a girl in such a situation must marry the man who has compromised her, and Stephen is eager to marry her. Marriage, even under such circumstances, would resolve everything respectably.

> If Miss Tulliver, after a few months of well chosen travel, had returned as Mrs. Stephen Guest—with a post marital *trousseau,* and all the advantages possessed even by the most unwelcome wife of an only son, public opinion, which at St. Ogg's, as elsewhere, always knew what to think, would have judged in strict consistency with those results . . . What a wonderful marriage for a girl like Miss Tulliver—quite romantic!

In this ironic comment we hear the echo of Marian Evans's own bitter words, "Women who are satisfied with such ties do *not* act as I have done—they obtain what they desire, and are still invited out to dinner." For Maggie refuses to marry Stephen, despite his protestations. "I have never said, 'They shall suffer, that I may have joy,' " she tells him, thinking of Lucy and Philip.

> "Oh, I can't do it," she said, in a voice almost of agony— "Stephen, don't ask me—don't urge me. I can't argue any

longer—I don't know what is wise; but my heart will not let me do it. I see—I feel their trouble now: it is as if it were branded on my mind. *I* have suffered, and had no one to pity me; and now I have made others suffer. It would never leave me; it would embitter your love to me . . . It is not the force that ought to rule us—this that we feel for each other; it would rend me away from all that my past life has made dear and holy to me. I can't set out on a fresh life and forget that: I must go back to it, and cling to it, else I shall feel as if there were nothing firm beneath my feet."

So she returns to St. Ogg's, ". . . without a *trousseau*, without a husband—in that degraded and outcast condition to which error is well known to lead; and the world's wife, with that fine instinct which is given her for the preservation of society," rejects her entirely. Her brother will not allow her to enter the house:

". . . I will sanction no such character as yours: the world shall know that I feel the difference between right and wrong. If you are in want, I will provide for you—let my mother know. But you shall not come under my roof. It is enough that I have to bear the thought of your disgrace: the sight of you is hateful to me."

She takes refuge with Bob Jakin, the "bird frightener" turned packman, and his wife, while the town does its worst. Even the minister, Dr. Kenn, can do nothing to change the collective mind of the ladies of St. Ogg's; and, when added rumors begin to fly about his own association with her, he is forced to advise her to go away. Stephen Guest writes a letter to his sisters, completely exonerating her; they believe him, but they equally believe that Maggie hopes to marry him, and that her renunciation was momentary, born of fear, not conviction. Only Lucy, who has been very ill as a result of her fiancé's conduct, manages to elude her family and friends—who are determined that she shall not see her cousin—and comes to Maggie with words of understanding and reconciliation: "—you have had more to bear than I have—and you gave him up when . . . you did what it must have been very hard to do."

"Lucy," said Maggie, with another great effort, "I pray to God continually that I may never be a cause of sorrow to you any more."

She pressed the little hand that she held between hers, and looked up into a face that was bent over hers. Lucy never forgot that look.

"Maggie," she said in a low voice that had the solemnity of confession in it, "you are better than I am. I can't . . ."

She broke off there and said no more. But they clasped each other again in a last embrace.

From this moment, events move swiftly. The river, under pelting rains, rises and overflows its banks; Maggie's first thought is for her mother and brother, perhaps marooned at Dorlcote Mill. After getting Bob Jakin and his wife and baby to safety, she takes a boat and starts rowing up-river. She reaches the Mill, to find that her mother, fortunately, is away, and Tom is there alone. Under the imminence of impending tragedy, Tom breaks the wall he has built within himself, and, for the last time, calls her by his old pet name for her, "Magsie." They do not survive the flood, but brother and sister are reconciled.

It is customary for critics to maintain that, while the first two volumes of *The Mill on the Floss* are among the finest that George Eliot ever wrote, the final volume, beginning with Maggie's appearance at the Deans' in St. Ogg's, is too foreshortened and contrived. The author recognized this deficiency herself; as she wrote to Monsieur D'Albert-Durade when they were discussing his translating the novel into French,

> My love of the childhood scenes made me linger over them; so that I could not develop as fully as I wished the concluding "Book" in which the tragedy occurs, and which I had looked forward to with much attention and premeditation from the beginning.[32]

The flood *does* come rather unexpectedly and suddenly; though floods are mentioned, as is the Round Pool—"that wonderful pool which the floods made a long time ago" —where Mrs. Tulliver tells Maggie that she'll "tumble in and be drowned some day." But so much happens between these foreshadowings and the final catastrophe that they are almost forgotten. Still, the flood does make for an effective and affecting means of bringing Tom and Maggie together once more, which was the author's intention. Perhaps she wondered, as she wept over her sheets of foolscap,[33] whether it would take a similar tragedy to reconcile herself and Isaac.

According to many critics, however, the major flaw of the novel is the character of Stephen Guest. Again, his entrance is prepared for—the author periodically mentions him before he appears, and we know that he is young, handsome, and very rich. Admittedly, he is not so fully developed as the other characters, but, if it comes to that, neither is Philip Wakem. Both men are designed as foils for Maggie, and it is simply because Philip is seen earlier in the story, as a schoolboy, that we think we know him better. What we do see of Stephen is certainly sufficient for the demands of the novel, and the scene in which this vain, rather spoiled young man is confronted with the fact that, for once in his life, he cannot have something that he thinks he wants—Maggie

—is superbly done. And no author ever depicted better the sudden rise of physical attraction between a young man and a young woman.

In the first moment they were both too much agitated to speak; for Stephen had learned from the servant that the others were gone out. Maggie had started up and sat down again, with her heart beating violently; and Stephen, throwing down his cap and gloves, came and sat beside her in silence. She thought Philip would be coming soon; and with great effort—for she trembled visibly—she rose to go to a distant chair.

"He is not coming," said Stephen in a low tone. "I am going in the boat."

"Oh, we can't go," said Maggie, sinking into her chair again. "Lucy did not expect—she would be hurt. Why is not Philip coming?"

"He is not well; he asked me to come instead."

"Lucy is gone to Lindum," said Maggie, taking off her bonnet, with hurried, trembling fingers. "We must not go."

"Very well," said Stephen, dreamily, looking at her, as he rested his arm on the back of his chair. "Then we'll stay here."

He was looking into her deep, deep eyes—far-off and mysterious as the starlit blackness, and yet very near, and timidly loving. Maggie sat perfectly still—perhaps for moments, perhaps for minutes—until the helpless trembling had ceased, and there was a warm glow on her cheek.

"The man is waiting—he has taken the cushions," she said. "Will you go and tell him?"

"What shall I tell him?" said Stephen, almost in a whisper. He was looking at the lips, now.

Maggie made no answer.

"Let us go," Stephen murmured entreatingly, rising and taking her hand to raise her, too. "We shall not be long together."

The general objection that Stephen is not good enough for Maggie to fall in love with is hardly valid, at least in this century. Taking into consideration Maggie's lack of social experience, her yearning for affection, and her passionate disposition, combined with the sense of excitement that she would feel at the realization that she actually does attract so eligible a young man, it is obvious that Stephen Guest is precisely the sort of man with whom she would fall in love. As the author said herself of these objections,

> The other chief point of criticism—Maggie's position towards Stephen—is too vital a part of my whole conception and purpose for me to be converted to the condemnation of it. If I am wrong there—if I really did not know what my heroine would do under the circumstances in which I deliberately placed her—I ought not to have written this book at all, but a quite different book, if any. If the ethics of art do not admit the truthful presentation of a character essentially noble, but liable to great error—error that is anguish to its own nobleness—then, it seems to me, the ethics of art are too narrow, and must be widened to correspond with a widening psychology.[34]

That Maggie would feel remorse for her conduct is equally believable, for "situation ethics" did not apply in 1859; she attains a kind of nobility and stature by her renunciation.

And there is so much else in the book that is both perfect and memorable, that the Stephen Guest involvement fades into oblivion by comparison. The tenderly drawn relationship between Maggie and Tom in their childhood, for example—the author draws Tom with a sure hand, and, though she sees his faults, she obviously loves and respects him. So must the reader. Tom represents the conventional view, and, despite the sense of outrage he provokes because of his treatment of Maggie, we recognize, as did George Eliot, that conventions and moral codes must be upheld. Maggie is the exception who must suffer for her individuality. Nowhere in *The Mill on the Floss* is there any suggestion that society's creed must be abrogated *in toto*.

Then, there are the marvelous Dodson sisters and their husbands. No one ever forgets Aunt Pullet's house, where the stair carpets are kept rolled up to save them, and there is an old mat and duster especially provided to polish the children's shoes: "Mrs. Pullet's front doormats were by no means intended to wipe shoes on; the very scraper had a deputy to do its dirty work." There is the unforgettable Aunt Glegg, who has "better lace laid by in her right-hand drawer of her wardrobe . . . than ever Mrs. Wooll of St. Ogg's had bought in her life, although Mrs. Wooll wore her lace before it was paid for," and who "economizes" by never wearing her curled front hair-piece before ten in the morning. Aunt Glegg is the most formidable of the Dodsons and the one whom Maggie most dislikes; yet it is Aunt Glegg, when Maggie returns after her renunciation of Stephen, who speaks her mind to Tom:

> Mrs. Glegg allowed that Maggie ought to be punished—
> she was not a woman to deny that—she knew what conduct
> was; but punished in proportion to the misdeeds proved
> against her, not to those cast upon her by people outside
> her own family, who might wish that their own kin were
> better.

And she is the only one who offers Maggie a home. Marian Evans drew upon her memories of her mother's sister, Mrs. Everard, in creating Aunt Glegg's domineering temper, but George Eliot recognized as sterling worth her ability to stand by her kin. Not until *Middlemarch* was she to present again such a remarkable study of family relationships. For, though *The Mill on the Floss* is Maggie's book, Maggie acquires a major part of her interest from her juxtaposition with her family and with that society of which her family is so integral a part.

Through the spring and summer of 1859, Marian Evans Lewes worked constantly at her novel. Once her identity as George Eliot was revealed, there was no longer any need to keep the reason for the hours spent at her desk a secret, and by June there was enough manuscript ready to send to John Blackwood, who declared himself delighted. In July, she broke off long enough to go to Switzerland with her husband; their trip was not only a holiday, but also provided the necessary occasion for Lewes to visit his sons at Hofwyl School and tell them about Marian and himself. In August, after their return to England, there was a pleasant, different diversion; her editor made her the gift of a handsome pug dog. "Pug is come!—come to fill up the void left by false and narrow-hearted friends," [35] she wrote appreciatively. "Pug" very quickly became a member of the family; "our very slow child," [36] Marian called him, but he had to be left at Wandsworth in September, while she and Lewes made a brief visit to Dorsetshire. She was in search of accurate information about mills, and found one at Weymouth that suited her purposes exactly. At the end of that month, they made a two-day trip to Gainsborough, to verify certain details about the tides of the river Trent.

Meanwhile, letters flew between Edinburgh and Holly Lodge. Charles Dickens had asked to publish "George Eliot's next novel" in his magazine *All The Year Round,* at what seemed to be more advantageous terms than Blackwood had offered. Marian, who felt that she must earn as much money as possible, was tempted, especially since she was aware that Blackwood had been under some pressure to discontinue publishing the work of a "woman of loose morals." [37] He had not, however, remotely contemplated taking her name from his list, and his assurances made her decide to continue with him. Besides, the idea of serializing her novel had not really appealed to her. The total impact of the book would be lost by division into "shilling numbers."

In January 1860, the final title of the book was chosen. Sections of the manuscript were sent off in batches, and Blackwood continued his encouraging letters. Harper Brothers contracted for the American rights on the basis of early proof sheets, and Marian received a welcome check for one hundred pounds for German translation rights, sight unseen. It was an exciting time as the book progressed to its tragic ending; the final chapters were in Blackwood's hands by the end of March. "No words of mine can ever convey any feeling of the greatness you have achieved," he wrote exuberantly. "The book is a greater triumph even than *Adam Bede*." [38]

Now that *The Mill on the Floss* was finished, she was, for the moment, free. She and Lewes had planned to spend two months in Italy, not only for a rest and change of scene, but also because Charles, Lewes's eldest son, would be finishing his education that summer and would be coming to live with them in England. Marian looked forward to this event, but she knew that the presence of an eighteen-year-old boy would, in a sense, restrict their activities and independence, and she had always wanted to see Rome. And she also wanted ". . . if possible, to feed my mind with fresh thoughts. . . ." [39] Certainly, she intended to write another novel. She did not foresee, however, that the Italian journey would lead her into a new, and, for her, unexplored area—the historical novel and *Romola*.

XIII

The Italian journey to which Marian had looked forward for many years did not have a very auspicious beginning. She found the ascent of Mont Cenis by diligence and sledge the most exciting event, especially when they actually crossed the famous pass in the "faint hint of morning in the starlight which showed us the vast sloping snow fields as we commenced the descent." [1] At Susa, she and Lewes boarded the train for Genoa. There was a stop midway at Turin where, in the railway station, she caught a glimpse of Count Cavour, who had just become the country's premier. At Genoa, they took ship for Leghorn, stopping long enough for a day's excursion to Pisa, and then continued on to Civitavecchia. Here, customs delayed them for an exasperating four hours under a broiling hot sun before they could take the train for Rome. They had left England on March 24th and arrived at their destination on April 1st. Nine days of constant travel with unusual delays and bad weather had interfered with sleep as well as with digestion, and their first impression of the Eternal City was not improved by the railway approach through some of the ugliest suburbs they had ever seen, nor by the fact that all the good hotels were full, because their arrival coincided with the beginning of Holy Week. "If I had written to you the first day we entered it (Sunday), I could have told you of no feeling other than disappointment," she wrote to John Blackwood.

> I thought my imagination had suffered a loss in coming to look at an ugly modern city, and losing forever the scene of varied unbroken grandeur I had always called up to myself at the mention of Rome.[2]

But, in a few days, this first unpleasant impression was entirely obliterated. Marian had been to visit the Capitol and the Colosseum, and had taken her first drive along the Appian Way, and Lewes had found a delightful apartment for them in a private home which they could lease at a very low rent for the month that they planned to stay. The city was in a state of great excitement over Garibaldi's anticipated attempt to liberate Sicily, though the "March of the Thousand" would not take place until June, and, as Marian wrote, "I feel some stirrings of the insurrectionary spirit myself, when I see the red pantaloons at every turn in the streets of Rome."[3] By the end of the first week, her pleasure was such that she wanted to stay until she knew Rome by heart.[4]

English travelers had always amused the natives, ever since the institution of the "Grand Tour," begun in the sixteenth century. Armed with their indispensable guidebooks, determined not to miss a single landmark, they traditionally approached sightseeing with a diligent singleness of purpose that frequently left the onlooker exhausted. Marian and George Henry Lewes were no exception. Every day had its scheduled program of monuments and museums, but, unlike many of their compatriots, the Leweses made repeated return visits to the places that most attracted them. The Forum, the Baths of Caracalla, the Vatican Library, St. Peter's, and certain of the churches impressed Marian deeply; and her Journal notes of these impressions make fascinating reading, not only for their intrinsic value as a nineteenth-century travel record, but also as indications of her own appreciation and critical sense. To quote a few of these impressions, Michelangelo's "Moses" "did not affect me agreeably";[5] the "Pietà" "has real tenderness in it";[6] the Guernico "Entombment of St. Petronilla" left her with the feeling that "it might as well have been left undone."[7] The illumination of St. Peter's in honor of Easter was "a thing so wondrous, so magically beautiful, that one can't find it in one's heart to say it is not worth doing."[8]

On some days, she and Lewes went on excursions to places of interest near by, such as the Villa Pamfili Doria, where they had a most beautiful view of Rome and the Campagna "before the snow had vanished from the mountains";[9] and they traveled by donkey to the ruins of Tusculum, which Marian greatly enjoyed "in spite of our loquacious guide, who exasperated George."[10] They visited Tivoli and "padded along the wet streets under umbrellas to look at the Temple of the Sibyl and to descend the ravine of the waterfalls." [11] And, of course, they visited the graves of Shelley and Keats in the Protestant Cemetery. They enjoyed many of the Eastertide processions, and, on one occasion, Marian "knelt down to receive the Pope's blessing, remembering what Pius VII had said to the soldier—'that he would never be the worse for the blessing of an old man.' " [12] The wonders of the city enchanted her. "I think Rome will at last chase away Maggie and the Mill from my thoughts," she wrote John Blackwood. "I hope it will, for she and her sorrows have clung to me painfully." [13]

They left Rome reluctantly at the end of April and went on to Naples, arriving there in the midst of a pouring rain. But almost at once the weather became brilliant, "showing us the blue sea, the purple mountains and bright city in which we had almost disbelieved when we saw them in the travel posters." [14] Naples did not offer the art and the architecture of Rome, but the possibilities for excursions were endless. Pozzuoli, Capo Miseno, Baia, Cumae, Capo di Monte where they visited the king's summer residence, St. Elmo, and the Herculaneum sculptures at the Musea Borbonico—all received delighted attention and detailed notes. The great Temple of Neptune at Paestum enthralled Marian; Amalfi surpassed "all imagination of a romantic site for a city that once made itself famous in the world." [15] They visited Sorrento and crossed the mountains on donkeyback for a glimpse of the Siren Isles. The most exciting event, however, was their visit to Pompeii, which they saw in the company ("unhappily," Marian noted in her Journal [16]) of two Russians whom they had met at the Hotel des Etrangers. Even that circumstance could not diminish the sensation she experienced from seeing the recently excavated city. "I hope I shall never forget the solemnity of our first entrance into that silent city. . . ." [17] Lewes was equally affected, though he did not approve of the obscene frescoes in the bedrooms of the principal houses.[18] Marian did not remark on these; perhaps her husband saw to it that her attention was directed elsewhere.

About the second week in May, they traveled to Leghorn by ship, then proceeded by train to Florence. Like Rome, Florence was in a state of great political excitement, but Marian wrote John Blackwood that

> "we are selfishly careless about dynasties just now, caring more for the doings of Giotto and Brunelleschi, than for those of Count Cavour. On a first journey to the greatest centre of art, one must be excused for letting one's public spirit go to sleep a little." [19]

Nevertheless, they could not help but be aware of the movement to reform the government of Tuscany, and this background must have given a special sense of immediacy to their own reading in Florentine history. They both were inveterate readers, who invariably prepared for visits to foreign cities by reading about them as much as possible before leaving England, and usually supplemented that preparation by books bought on the spot. Shortly after their arrival in Florence, Lewes was reading an account of Savonarola, the fiery Dominican preaching monk who had attempted to reform the city politically as well as religiously in the fifteenth century, and it was Lewes who, out of a clear sky one morning, suggested that Savonarola's life might be good material for an historical novel. Marian immediately and enthusiastically agreed. Not only were there political parallels between the fifteenth and the nineteenth centuries—Count Cavour had only recently sought the help of the French Emperor,

Napoleon III, just as Savonarola had depended on King Charles IX (and, in both instances, France had been a disappointment) —but the character of the Prior of San Marco, who had fervently believed that God spoke through him, fascinated her. At once she bought several biographies, copies of Savonarola's sermons and poems, and began to read. With Lewes she visited the monastery of San Marco; women were permitted to go no farther than the Chapter House where the great "Crucifixion" of Fra Angelico was displayed, but Lewes was conducted through the entire monastery and took notes. They bought prints of other Fra Angelico paintings, so that Marian, with the help of the notes, could visualize what Savonarola had actually seen, daily, within the cloister walls. Of course, they also visited all the museums and churches and took the usual drives into the surrounding countryside. But Savonarola was Marian's chief interest, as is evidenced from her letter to Major William Blackwood (her editor's brother and business associate) on May 27th:

"... Florence has aroused a keener interest in us even than Rome, and has stimulated me to entertain a rather ambitious project which I mean to be a secret from everyone but you and Mr. John Blackwood." [20]

They left Florence on the first of June and stopped at Bologna—"the ugly, painful towers of Bologna made me desire not to look at them a second time ..." [21] and at Padua, where they visited Giotto's chapel. They reached Venice "at ten o'clock on a moonlit night. What stillness! What beauty!" Marian wrote in her Journal. "Looking out from the high window of our hotel on the Grand Canal, I felt it was a pity to go to bed. Venice was more beautiful than romances had feigned." [22] For eight days, they toured all the landmarks, always by gondola, which Marian loved.

> Of all dreamy delights, that of floating in a gondola along the canals and out on the Lagoon is surely the greatest. We were out one night on the Lagoon when the sun was setting, and the wide waters were flushed with the reddened light. I should have liked it to last for hours: it is the sort of scene in which I could most readily forget my own existence, and feel melted into the general life.[23]

Some of this emotion was certainly recalled by George Eliot when she came to write the final chapters of *Romola*. Reading her Journal, one can almost see her attempting to put into words the atmosphere, the mystic quality, of the experience for future reference.

But the projected novel had to be delayed for the moment, because it was nearly time for Lewes's eldest son, Charles, to leave Hofwyl School. Marian was both excited and anxious about his coming back to England with them. "I hope my heart will be large enough for all the love that is required of me." [24] And from Venice she wrote Mrs. Bell, the housekeeper left in charge at Holly Lodge:

> Pray think of everything within reach that will make Charles's room look comfortable, and, if possible, pretty. Especially beg Martha to scrub away at the dirty paint, which is one of the dreariest things in a bedroom. Remember that the view of Scilly, over the drawing room door, was to be put in Charles's room.[25]

One could not say that Marian was naturally either domestic or especially maternal, but for Lewes's sake she was eager to do everything required of her, and more, to welcome his son, even though it meant hurrying through Verona, Milan, Brera—with time for only a glimpse of the Luini frescoes—and across the Splügen Pass in a torrential rain. They reached Zurich at the end of June, where they stopped for two days so that Lewes might confer with the eminent physiologist, Dr. Moleschott, then they went on to Hofwyl for Charles's graduation exercises. Here letters were waiting from John Blackwood, telling of the good sale of *The Mill on the Floss* and asking about the "great project" which Marian had mentioned in her letter to his brother. Marian answered at once:

> "I don't think I can venture to tell you what my great project is by letter, for I am anxious to keep it a secret. It will require a great deal of study and labour and I am athirst to begin." [26]

At the moment, however, she was fully occupied with Charles's graduation and with packing his boxes to be sent to London. Also, Lewes had decided that Thornton, his second son, needed a foundation in mathematics better than Hofwyl provided if he was to embark on a career in the Indian Civil Service, which was what he thought he wanted to do, so arrangements had to be made for him to follow his family to England as soon as a suitable school could be found. Then Marian could not resist the temptation to stop at Geneva, to see Monsieur and Madame D'Albert-Durade for the shortest of forty-eight-hour visits; much to her joy, Monsieur D'Albert had successfully translated *Adam Bede* into French, and she now assigned him the translation rights to *The Mill on the Floss,* as well.

The Leweses reached Holly Lodge on the first of July, where all operations were immediately directed to preparing Charles for his Civil Service examinations which he had to take in August. Neither Marian nor Charles's father was able to accomplish what they had hoped of their own work in that month, but they did not begrudge the lost time. Indeed, Marian was overjoyed to find that "their son," as she hereafter referred to Charles, was a delightful addition to the family; "it is very sweet as one gets old to have someone young about." [27] And no one could have been more pleased and proud than herself when he passed the examinations at the top of the list and was appointed to the Post Office Service as a clerk in the secretary's office, at a salary of eighty pounds a year. *"Magnificat anima mea!"* she wrote to Barbara Bodichon. "The dear lad is fairly launched in life, now." [28] For Charles's sake, she agreed that they must move into town so that he would be nearer his work. She and Lewes bought a house in Blandford Square, which meant all the chaos and upheaval of moving. Then Thornton's situation had to be settled; he needed both the advantages and the restraints of family life along with his schooling, and finally, through the help of John Blackwood, a family was found in Edinburgh whose home was, by Lewes's suggestion, "Episcopalian and gentlemanly," [29] who would gladly take on a teen-age boy for a reasonable fee, and were "willing and capable of looking after him in every respect." [30] Thornton was sent for, and spent a few days with his family before Lewes took him up to Scotland to enter the Edinburgh High School. In the midst of all this excitement, Marian was sitting for her portrait to Samuel Laurence, a noted artist in pastel chalk, whose portrait of Thackeray in that medium had been greatly admired.

Against the background of this general confusion, it is easy to interpret her letter to John Blackwood of August 28th:

I think I must tell you the secret, though I am distrusting my power to make it grow into a published fact. When we were in Florence, I was rather fired with the idea of writing an historical romance—scene, Florence; period, the close of the 15th century, which was marked by Savonarola's career and martyrdom. But just now I am quite without confidence in my future doings, and almost repent of having formed conceptions which will go on lashing me now until I have at least tried to fulfill them.[31]

Her natural diffidence and lack of confidence were always greater when extraneous, although willingly assumed, obligations interfered with her concentrating on her work, and certainly there had been and would continue to be innumerable distractions. Blackwood, however, was his usual encouraging self: "Your letter communicating the Great Secret is truly refreshing," he wrote four days later.

Savonarola and his times is a splendid subject for you, and you have such a power of imparting reality to everything you write that your Romance will not read like fiction. I expect that you will return the Historical Romance to its ancient popularity.[32]

Inspired by his confidence, Marian continued her researches into fifteenth-century Florentine life. But she also had another project in mind; she wanted to do an English story for anonymous publication in *Blackwood's Magazine*, the fact of her authorship to be withheld until it was published in book form. Though Blackwood was preparing a fourth edition for November, she felt that sales of *The Mill on the Floss* had been impaired because her *nom de plume* had been revealed. She still wanted desperately for her books to be judged fairly on their own merits, and not pre-judged on the basis of her personal life, though her obsessive concern for this was really completely unwarranted. *The Mill on the Floss* had been received enthusiastically. Even Queen Victoria had expressed her admiration of it.[33] And her personal life had been accepted, at least in her own immediate, professional circle, to the extent that when Charles Mudie, one of London's leading booksellers, opened a new establishment with a grand soiree, the invitation sent to Blandford Square was addressed to "Mr. and Mrs. Lewes." Anthony Trollope, too, one of the most respected and respectable of Victorian novelists, had become a very close friend, interesting himself in young Charles's progress at the Post Office and using his own personal connections there in his behalf. But still, Marian worried. She wanted to write something that would achieve a success comparable to that of *Adam Bede*. By November, she was at work.

> I am engaged now in writing a story—the idea of which came to me after our arrival in this house, and which has thrust itself between me and the other book I am writing. It is "Silas Marner, the Weaver of Ravelow." [34]

Silas Marner rightly deserves the praise it has received as being the most perfect—insofar as form is concerned —of all her works. Springing, as she told John Blackwood, from a "recollection of having once, in early childhood, seen a linen-weaver with a bag on his back . . ." [35] the story has a folk-tale quality, though the reality of it is as vivid and concrete as that found in *Adam Bede*. Characteristically, Marian doubted its success. "It seems that nobody will take any interest in it but myself, for it is extremely unlike the popular stories going. . . ." [36] But, despite many interruptions, she had two hundred thirty pages ready to send to Edinburgh by mid-February. John Blackwood wrote that he read them "with the greatest admiration," [37] and only tentatively voiced his feeling that there might be a few "brighter lights." Marian agreed that the story did *seem* somber, but added,

> . . . I hope you will not find it at all a sad story as a whole, since it sets—or is intended to set—in a strong light the remedial influences of pure, natural human relations.[38]

Perhaps this intention, so explicitly stated by the author, is the major reason why *Silas Marner*—a minor work—has achieved the status of a major classic. From the opening sentence—

> In the days when spinning wheels hummed busily in farm houses—and even great ladies clothed in silk and thread-lace had their toy spinning wheels of polished oak— there might be seen, in districts far away from the lanes, or deep in the bosom of the hills, certain pallid and undersized men, who, by the side of the brawny country-folk looked like remnants of a disinherited race.

the reader is aware of a special kind of magic at work, whereby actuality becomes almost indistinguishable from "once upon a time." It is easy to point out that the conversations between Silas Marner and William Dane about "The Assurance of Salvation" probably had their origin in Marian Evans's earnest colloquies with Maria Lewis; or that the New Year's Eve ball at the Red House was doubtless drawn from her memory of similar parties at Arbury Hall which she either attended herself or was told about. The marvelous scene at the Rainbow, the local pub, which was praised unanimously by all the reviewers, is drawn with so sure a hand that the reader can only wonder at it, while remembering that Robert Evans took his small daughter with him on his trips about Warwickshire, and that she listened without realizing what she had heard. Mr. Tookey, for example: "There's people set up their own ears for a standard and expect the whole choir to follow 'em." And Mr. Massey: "There's allays two 'pinions; there's the 'pinion a man has of hisen, and there's the 'pinion other folks have of him. There'd be two 'pinions about a cracked bell, if the bell could hear itself."

It is easy to say, too, that the background plot of *Silas Marner*—the secret marriage of Geoffrey Cass to a low-born drunkard, from which he is released in the nick of time to propose to Nancy Lammeter, only to have his wrong-doing exposed in the end, has been done time and again in fiction. It is certainly permissible to say that the discovery that Dunstan Cass was the thief who stole Silas's gold seems almost too "pat"; the providential draining of the pond really does come coincidentally, though George Eliot does succeed in making the reader believe it at the time of the reading. But any and all flaws in this novella can be explained and justified by the author's equal skill in creating a kind of allegory in which a poor weaver, damned and cast out by his fellows, is redeemed—not by religion, but by the demands made upon his sympathies by a little child who wanders into his cottage out of a snowstorm, and claims from him the love that he has resolutely refused to give to anyone else.

For, as George Eliot knew, it was the character of Silas Marner that was the key to the story's success or failure. The novella succeeds because Silas is what she made him. We see him alone in his cottage working at his loom, a source of fascination and dread to the village boys who peek in at his window to look at him, running from him in terror if his eyes happen to light on them. He is isolated from the world in bleak hatred of it; he has separated himself from his fellow humans because of the injuries that some of them have inflicted on him. We learn of his past, of the crime that he may—or may not—have committed, for he is subject to cataleptic trances in which he loses all memory of his actions; we are never certain whether he is guilty or not, and the most masterful stroke of the entire story is the moment when he returns to Lantern Yard with Eppie, only to discover that it and all his accusers are gone. He has been redeemed by the love of a child dependent on him, to whom he has given love, and his past is wiped out—erased—physically as well as spiritually. We see him in the throes of his miserliness, where his gold has no purpose except its own existence, and the sense of triumph its possession gives to him. When Dunstan Cass steals the gold, Silas comes to the Rainbow, "a pale thin figure . . . uttering no word, but looking round at the company with his strange, unearthly eyes." And then, he returns to his cottage that same New Year's Eve, to find a heap of gold on his hearth—the golden hair of a small girl who weeps when she wakens to find him bending over her.

> But there was a cry on the hearth: the child had awakened, and Marner stooped to lift it on his knee. It clung round his neck, and burst louder and louder into that inarticulate cry of "mammy," by which little children express the bewilderment of waking. Silas pressed it to him, and almost unconsciously uttered sounds of hushing tenderness, while he bethought himself that some of his porridge which had got warm by the dying fire, would do to feed the child with if it were only warmed up a little.

Silas's defenses have been breached. Assuming full responsibility for Eppie's upbringing, he, too, grows in grace and stature, until finally he literally rejoins the human race. The moment comes when Eppie's real father, Geoffrey Cass, wants her to acknowledge him; Silas's life is complete when she says that Silas is the only father she has ever known and that she will stay with him. The story ends in fairy-tale fashion with Eppie's marriage; Silas, the proud patriarch, is now loved by those who had once feared and despised him, and, more important, is now himself able to love and forgive.

Silas Marner was written quickly. By March 21, 1861, it was on the press, and it was published on April 2nd, not in the magazine, but in a single volume, for John Blackwood had decided that it was too choice a work for magazine publication. Six printings were called for by the end of May, and it was in its third edition by January of 1862. It was translated into French, German, Italian, and Dutch, and it was equally popular in America. Today, if high school seniors know no other of George Eliot's works, they may almost invariably have read *Silas Marner*—though its continued presence on "required readings" lists has often, regrettably, proved an obstacle to the enjoyment of the book for its own sake. That readers in 1861 enjoyed the book is certain; that George Eliot loved the writing of it is equally so.

After the last page of *Silas Marner* had been written, Marian took a two-week holiday at Hastings. While her husband collected molluscs for a new scientific work he was outlining, she walked along the beach, wrote letters to friends, and, in general, revived her flagging energies. Her Italian novel was beginning to nag at her. She had done little about it for several months; even the background research had been neglected. And she was discovering that her memories of Florence, though vivid, lacked the details necessary for her to do what had become one of the most characteristic qualities of her novels —the complete re-creation of a society. There was nothing for it; just as she had revisited Gainsborough-on-

Trent for *The Mill on the Floss,* she would have to return to Florence. Lewes was in instant accord with her wishes; he had an article on "Spontaneous Combustion" —the outcome of an argument with Charles Dickens over the disposition of the villain in *Bleak House* with which he unequivocally disagreed on scientific grounds—to complete for the *Westminster Review,* but the molluscs could wait. Almost overnight they packed their portmanteaux and reserved passage on the Channel steamer. On April 19th, having written only the briefest of farewell letters to very close friends, they left England for a two-month sojourn in Italy.

XIV

For many years, it has been fashionable to deprecate
Romola. Considered the worst of George Eliot's novels, it
has been criticized for the ponderous, minute, almost
archaeological reconstruction of fifteenth-century Florence; for the admittedly excessive stagey small talk among
the citizens in the early chapters which prevents the action from getting under way quickly, and for its very
melodramatic, involved plot. These faults have been generally considered the inevitable result of an author's
working in a medium wholly new; i.e., historical fiction;

but such a statement is not wholly accurate. In a sense, all George Eliot's novels are historical fiction except for *Daniel Deronda*. Generally, she preferred to place her stories in the England she had known as a child. We can agree, however, that *Romola* is the most remote of her books in point of time, and that she had to embark on the re-creation of its world from scratch, so to speak, without the advantages that her own memory and familiarity with the surroundings provided.

That *Romola* cost her untold effort is undoubted. Her often repeated comment, "I began it a young woman— I finished it an old woman," indicates only to a very slight degree the time, the strength, and the energy that went into its composition. Her Journal and letters between April of 1861 and July of 1863 give the fullest account of how she agonized over the book, and even these can but suggest the despair that occasionally assailed her. Her unwillingness to tell her publisher about the book as it formed in her mind seems to indicate her doubts, despite the fact that she wanted very much to write it.

> It may turn out I can't work freely and fully enough in the medium I have chosen, and in that case I must give it up: for I will never write anything to which my whole heart, mind, and conscience don't consent. . . .[1]

All authors experience anxiety when they begin a new book; the question might be asked, however, why George Eliot's doubts should have been so especially strong concerning *Romola*. There is one possible answer: *The Mill on the Floss* had exhausted her, both physically and emotionally, and *Silas Marner* had been written under conditions that had been trying, to say the least. And her grave concern over her husband's ill health during 1861 made sustained concentration almost impossible. It is not surprising, really, that she experienced not only initial, but also continuing, anxiety. It was not until April of 1862 that she could note in her Journal that she was at last "writing with enjoyment." [2]

It should be noted, too, that in April 1861, when she and Lewes set out for Florence to do the additional research that she felt was needed, she really was quite excited at the prospect of beginning *Romola*. Though she was ill with flu the entire first week they were in Italy, she wrote to John Blackwood in mid-May: "We have been industriously foraging in old streets and old books. I feel very brave just now, and enjoy the thought of work." [3] She followed a daily schedule of work at the Magliabecchian Library; Lewes always went with her and helped her to take notes. In her eagerness to capture the conversational idiom of fifteenth-century Florence, she copied phrases from novellas and plays, all written in the language of that time; to get a precise picture of the medieval city, she perused guidebooks and memoirs written by contemporaries of Lorenzo de' Medici. She read collections of manuscript letters, and consulted numerous histories, especially those of monastic orders. Savonarola's sermons and poems received special attention; long extracts were copied and translated for possible later quotation in the novel. She walked through the city streets, trying to reconstruct the crucial scenes—the Piazza del Duomo at the moment of Lorenzo de' Medici's death; the Piazza della Signoria and the Pyramid of Vanities; the Palazzo Vecchio and Savonarola's execution. "She is 'drinking in' Florence," Lewes wrote enthusiastically to John Blackwood,

> . . . and as far as the old past life can be restored, she will, I am certain, restore it, if only from that wonderful intui-

tion with which genius throws itself into all forms of life. As I often tell her, most of the scenes and characters of her books are quite as *historical* as to her direct personal experience, as the 15th century of Florence; and she knows infinitely more of Savonarola than she knew of Silas.[4]

It is interesting to speculate as to whether, at this point, she intended to make Savonarola the hero of her novel. If she did, this intention might have been one reason why the book was so difficult to begin, for it is well known that historical figures are almost impossible to use as fictional protagonists.

The Leweses had planned to leave Florence at the end of May, but their minds were changed for them by Thomas Adolphus Trollope. The brother of the novelist Anthony Trollope, Thomas Adolphus had been a long-time resident of the English colony in Florence; both he and his wife had called on Marian and her husband within a few days after their arrival. Now he persuaded them to stay in Italy a week longer, so that he might take them to visit the Camaldoli and La Verna monasteries in the Val d'Arno. Marian was delighted at the prospect; so was Lewes, even though he was suffering from a bad sore throat and a persistent cough. The journey was wearisome—Trollope's carriage brought them as far as Pratovecchio, where they had to leave it and go the rest of the way on foot. Marian was provided with a pony for herself and her portmanteau, though she insisted on walking occasionally while Lewes rode. The entire distance, according to Baedecker, could be walked in three and a half days—the carriage had hastened the trip for them, because they had not had to make overnight stops, but, even so, they did not reach Camaldoli until six-thirty in the evening, having left Florence before seven that morning.

At the monastery, they were most graciously received. Lewes was coughing violently, so the Father Apothecary was summoned to give him some medicine. They dined with the Guest Master, but Marian had to sleep in the cow barn, for only men were allowed inside the enclosure. However, as he had done at San Marco, Lewes took copious notes for her. The next day they climbed the steep mountain road to Sacro Ermeno, the mother house of the Calmaldulensian order, which had been little altered from the time when St. Romuald founded it in 1012. Again, Marian had to remain outside, but when the Abbot heard from Lewes and Trollope that there was a lady in the party, he came outside the walls to greet her and personally conducted her to a higher point on the mountain where she might look down at the monastery for a better and larger view. Then the trio started for Bibbiena; on the way, Marian's pony slipped and fell near the edge of a precipice, but fortunately she was not hurt.[5] The next day they walked and rode to La Verna, and saw the monastery built by St. Francis of Assisi. The heat was intense, the Lewes, especially, was exhausted. Marian, too, was exceedingly tired and glad to return to Florence. She had, however, seen the Casentino area outside the city; and when it came time to describe Romola's flight from Tito Melema, George Eliot would remember.

By June 19th, they were once again at Blandford Square, having made a brief stop at Hofwyl to visit Lewes's youngest son, Bertie, who was still in school there. Marian unpacked, and planned to spend the summer in concentrated work.

This morning, for the first time, I feel myself quietly settled at home. I am in excellent health, and long to work steadily and effectively. If it were possible that I should produce *better* work than I have yet done! [6]

She was still reading and taking notes, and corresponding with Thomas Adolphus Trollope about minute historical points and fifteenth-century Florentine slang; but her heart and mind were divided because her husband was still ailing. The sore throat and cough would not leave him, and she worried about him constantly. As a result, her work did not progress: "Read a little this morning —my mind dwelling with much depression on the improbability of achieving the work I wish to do," [7] she wrote in her Journal in July. By mid-August, she was in the depths of depression:

> Got into a state of so much wretchedness in attempting to concentrate my thoughts on the construction of my novel that I became desperate, and suddenly burst the bonds, saying I will not think of writing.[8]

A few days later, however, when Thornton descended upon them for a whirlwind visit en route to spending his vacation in Switzerland with Bertie, she recovered her spirits. "This morning I conceived of the plot of my novel with new distinctness," [9] she noted in her Journal on August 20th, and on the same date, Lewes wrote John Blackwood,

> "The Book" is slowly crystallizing into what will be a magnificent programme. Until quite lately, I thought she would relinquish altogether in despair, her singular diffidence being exaggerated in this case. But now I think it will be written. If only I could see the first chapter! [10]

But the first chapter was to be still longer delayed. Lewes's health grew worse, and he was finally advised to try the "water cure" at Malvern, which was noted for its hydropathic springs and bracing air. Marian took her books with her; she was reading Marchese's *Storia di San Marco,* a history of Savonarola's monastery, and she was also correcting proofs for a new edition of *Adam Bede.* When they returned to London in mid-September, Lewes was much better from "one week's packings, bathings, cold water draughts, and extensive walking," [11] and Marian, in addition, was cheered by a royalty check for one thousand pounds for *Silas Marner.* Since her husband was almost completely recovered, Marian could relax her vigilance over him a little and begin work with renewed hope on her novel. But *Romola* posed stubborn problems. "My mind still worried about my plot—and without any confidence in my ability to do what I want," [12] she confided to her Journal on October 4th. On the 7th, however, we find the firmly written entry, "Began the first chapter of my novel." [13] Then she caught a cold, which correspondingly affected her energy. "Not very well. Utterly desponding about my book," [14] she wrote on October 28th. On the 31st, "Still with an incapable head —trying to write, trying to construct, and unable." [15] And on November 6th, "So utterly dejected, that in walking with G. in the park, I almost resolved to give up my Italian novel." [16] Lewes, however, must have encouraged and protested to some effect, because four days later she wrote, "New sense of things to be done in my novel and more brightness in my thoughts . . . this morning the Italian scenes returned upon me with fresh attraction." [17] By December 8th, she had reached the point where she could share with Lewes a general outline of the book.

> G. had a headache, so we walked out in the morning sunshine. I told him my conception of the story and he expressed great delight. Shall I ever be able to carry out my ideas? Flashes of hope are succeeded by long intervals of dim distrust.[18]

Finally, on January 1, 1863, she wrote triumphantly, "I began again my novel of 'Romola.' " [19]

Once begun, she had hoped that the novel would proceed smoothly, but, as is always true with historical novels, there were countless details to be checked, and additional information to be secured, the need for which is never apparent until the book is under way.

> Detained from writing by the necessity of gathering particulars: 1st, about Lorenzo de' Medici's death; 2nd, about the possible retardation of Easter; 3rd, about Corpus Christi day; 4th, about Savonarola's preaching in the Quaresima of 1492.[20]

Small wonder that the Journal entry for February 17th reads, "I have written only the first two chapters of my novel besides the Proem, and I have an oppressive sense of the far-stretching task before me. . . ." [21] And a few days later comes the despairing question, "Will it ever be finished? Ever be worth anything?" [22]

It was not only the writing of the book that was difficult, but publication plans as well. Naturally, John Blackwood had expected to publish *Romola;* he had been in close touch with Marian about it for many months. But Lewes had just accepted the post of chief literary adviser to the *Cornhill Magazine,* and now George Smith, of Smith-Elder Publishers and editor of *Cornhill,* made an offer for *Romola* that so far exceeded anything that Blackwood could meet that Marian decided to accept it, even though the contract included serial publication in the magazine, which she disliked. Seven thousand pounds with a return of copyright after six years was an enormous sum, and she felt that she could not refuse it. She wrote Blackwood of her change of plans, and he replied with an understanding letter, wishing her and the book well.

His more private opinion, however, was expressed in a note to a close friend:

> The conduct of our friends at Blandford Square is certainly not pleasing, nor in the long run will they find it wise, however great the bribe may have been. It is too bad after all the kindness she has experienced but I am sure she would do it against her inclination. The going over to the enemy without giving me any warning and with a story on which from what they said I was fully intitled to calculate upon, sticks in my throat, but I shall not quarrel—quarrels, especially literary ones, are vulgar.[23]

He considered Lewes the "villain" of the episode, and was strongly inclined to believe that he had persuaded Marian to agree to his mercenary ideas. What Blackwood did not know was that Marian shared her husband's deep concern about his three sons. Charles was not rising as rapidly at the Post Office as had been expected. Thornton was preparing for the Indian Civil Service examinations, but they were known to be rigorous and there was no guarantee that he would pass them. Then there was Bertie, who was not as intellectually inclined as his brothers—some post would have to be found for him. And there was income which Lewes sent to his legal wife, which usually had to be augmented because she overspent. Marian's books were earning a good income, but the possibility of having to support three boys for an indefinite period, in addition to Agnes Lewes, made the offer of a really large sum of money—over twice as much as Blackwood's best offer—doubly tempting. Even though she would be hard pressed to finish *Romola* (she accepted George Smith's offer in May for publication in *Cornhill* beginning in July, and she was only half-way through Book I), financial considerations were probably uppermost in her mind at that moment. She did, how-

Mrs. Caroline Bray and Miss Sara Hennell, two of George Eliot's closest friends, in their old age.

4 Cheyne Walk, Chelsea, where George Eliot
died. From a drawing by W. W. Burgess.

ever, regret the coolness that had inevitably arisen between herself and John Blackwood. Their relationship would not be resumed on its old, cordial footing for several years.

All through the summer, autumn, and winter of 1862, and into the spring of 1863, Marian worked at *Romola*. There were diversions—Robert Browning paid his first visit in December of 1862, and became one of their devoted friends. Anthony Trollope came frequently; Isa Blagdon, Browning's good friend, came to tea. Marian attended the International Exhibition, and went occasionally to the theater and to the opera. Lewes suffered another bout of ill health, which worried her terribly, and this time she dared not take time to stop her work and accompany him when he went to "take the waters" at Spa, in Belgium. Serial deadlines were relentless in their demands. Not until June 9, 1863, could she write in her Journal, "Put the last stroke to Romola! *Ebenezer!*" [24] Exhausted, she sent the remaining manuscript to George Smith for publication in three volumes on July 6th, and left with Lewes for a much needed holiday on the Isle of Wight.

In view of this "saga of *Romola*" from first conception to final copy, one is disposed to consider the book a little more understandably than has been customary. The painful, slow writing of it, due in part to the author's determination to be accurate at all costs, and in part to external circumstances beyond her control, would naturally deprive it of that sense of immediacy which had made her previous books so brilliantly successful. Lewes put his finger on the first difficulty when he wrote to John Blackwood, "When you see her, mind your care is to discountenance the idea of a Romance being the product of an Encyclopedia." [25] An historical novel cannot be too well researched, but research must have time to become re-creation. The circumstances of *Romola*'s publication deprived George Eliot of any opportunity to "digest" her quantities of factual notes and transform them completely into fiction. The opening chapters, especially, are laboriously detailed. They read as though the author had grimly determined to include every detail of speech, dress, and architecutre she had derived from her studies, instead of selecting carefully those that would have established the era and the locale, while giving her main attention to the characters and their actions. Blackwood's comment is revealing, here:

> Her great difficulty seems to be that she, as she describes it, hears her characters talking, and there is a weight upon her mind as if Savonarola and his friends ought to be speaking Italian instead of English.[26]

And there are several passages that do read like a translation from the Italian. As a result of this "language barrier," the characterizations are not always in focus. George Eliot herself was conscious that she had not wholly succeeded in making the story of Romola, Savonarola, and Tito Melema come to life: ". . . my predominant feeling is this,—not that I have achieved anything, but—that great, great facts have struggled to find a voice through me, and have only been able to speak brokenly." [27]

Certainly, however, the book marks a signal advance in George Eliot's career as a novelist, because in it she consciously attempted to broaden her canvas and her point of view. *Adam Bede, The Mill on the Floss,* and *Silas Marner* had each been concerned with a single locale and a relatively homogeneous group of characters, but in *Romola* she attempted to depict an entire society, made up of all sorts and conditions of men. Nello the barber, Tessa the contadina, Spinni the soldier of fortune, Bardo the scholar, Piero de' Medici the aristocrat —monks, artists, shopkeepers, soldiers, beggars, bureaucrats—all appear, crossing and re-crossing the paths of the three principal characters, their lives interacting and precipitating crises until the final climactic moments of Tito's murder and Savonarola's execution. There is splendid pageantry in the Procession of the Pitying Mother, and the Pyramid of Vanities; suspense during the plot to force Savonarola to undergo the ordeal by fire; broad humor in the conversations in Nello's barbershop; and high excitement in the scene where Baldassare confronts Tito in the Rucellai Gardens. It is quite true that a book must be judged ultimately by its final effect, and *Romola* admittedly does fall short of greatness; but it is equally true that certain books must be examined in the light of the author's intention—*War and Peace* is a notable example—which, in a sense, fail because the author's vision was greater than words could convey. *Romola*, perhaps, falls into that category.

The plot, upon analysis, does have glaring faults. There are several rather bad coincidences: Baldassare, denied by his foster son Tito, takes refuge at the very house where Tessa, the first girl whom Tito has injured, is lodged; Romola recognizes Baldassare because the painter who has used him for a model for one of his pictures has also painted her portrait. Even worse is Romola's finding Tessa again by just happening to recognize Tessa's necklace (after one previous meeting) hanging from the corner of the peddler's basket to whom the pathetic contadina has sold it. But it must also be said that, while reading *Romola*, the author does persuade one to "willingly suspend his disbelief," and, since the book was written to be read and not analyzed, perhaps this is the supreme test. Despite the over-structured plot and the excessive detail, one does become involved with the story. And, since the initial premise is sound—that a clever and unscrupulous man with self-calculating charm, who thinks only of his own self-interest, can ruin the lives of all he touches—the reader becomes absorbed in his machinations, with the additional assurance of knowing —since George Eliot is George Eliot, and not Ernest Hemingway—that Tito Melema ultimately will receive his just deserts.

The book is fascinating, too, because of the way in which the motives of the three principal characters parallel each other on different levels. Fra Girolamo Savonarola—the beloved or hated Frate, depending on the point of view—is single-mindedly dedicated to the cause of reforming the corrupt government of Florence. His sermons move hundreds to join his cause, and for a time his slightest word is law. He has, at least at the beginning, a unique gift of prophecy; he knows what must be done for the city; he believes that he is the instrument chosen by God for the task. But he gradually reveals the flaw in his character that will be fatal: he cannot see beyond the course he is determined that he must follow. Human considerations, such as compassion, understanding, and personal involvement, are swept aside. He knows only duty, and, just as he follows duty's path as he sees its benefit to him, so must everyone else. On that basis alone, he orders Romola to return to the husband whom, with good reason, she has learned to despise.

"You assert your freedom proudly, my daughter. But who is so base as the debtor who thinks himself free? . . . And you are flying from your debts: the debt of a Florentine woman; the debt of a wife . . . You have no vocation such as your brother had. You are a wife. You seek to break your ties in self-will and anger, not because a higher life calls you to renounce them."

He tells her that she must find her happiness in performing her duties, and in sacrificing herself to the greatest good of her city where the help and strength of every man and woman will be needed for the dangerous days ahead.

Romola is persuaded. "Fra Girolamo's voice had wakened in her mind a reason for living apart from personal enjoyment and personal affection. . . ." She becomes one of his devoted followers and risks her life in nursing the victims of the great pestilence. And Savonarola, who thus speaks for the Florentines with his hypnotic and arrogant persuasion, made visible in the episode with Romola and implied with others, rises higher and higher until he becomes virtually the dictator of Florence. But, ironically, it is through Romola that the author shows how this power has corrupted him. Romola's godfather, along with four others high in Florentine affairs of state, is accused of treason; Bernardo del Nero is innocent, but the Council—at the subtle direction of Savonarola— sentences him to die with the others. Romola goes to the Frate to plead with him, begging him to intervene. To her shocked amazement, he will not use his power for mercy, because it will not add to his own prestige:

"The end I seek is one to which minor respects must be sacrificed. The death of five men—were they less guilty than these—is a light matter weighed against the withstanding of the vicious tyrannies which stifle the life of Italy and of God's kingdom on earth, the end for which I live and am willing myself to die!"

Romola flares back at him,

"Take care, father, lest your enemies have some reason when they say that in your visions of what will further God's kingdom, you see only what will strengthen your own party."

"And that is true!" said Savonarola with flashing eyes. Romola's voice had seemed to him in that moment the voice of his enemies. "The cause of my party *is* the cause of God's kingdom."

Political leaders of a later day have not, perhaps, expressed this sentiment with quite so much personal confidence, but it has a familiar ring! The remarkable portrayal of Savonarola, whom George Eliot certainly did know as well as she did Silas Marner, is one of the most powerful claims of *Romola* to excellence.

The character of the heroine is, at first glance, one of the novel's great weaknesses. The author herself recognized that Romola was "ideal," [28] and, for the twentieth century, she is a little too much so. But we must remember that the Victorians liked ideal heroines; Maggie Tulliver had distressed some readers because she was so recognizably human. And the unceasing devotion of the beautiful Romola to her blind father would have been heartily approved, as would her general goodness and gentleness. But this is not all of Romola; there are subtleties in her that are not readily apparent on a first reading of the novel. For instance, she has been raised by her father to be a scholar, to take her brother's place (after her brother joins the Dominicans) as his assistant in the writing of his masterpiece. She has been shut away in a library all her life and knows very little about the world except from books. Like Savonarola, she has created an image of herself before the world, an image which she is stubbornly determined to maintain. When she meets the dashing Tito Melema, he becomes the hero of a romance of which she, in her own eyes, is the heroine. She falls in love with him without the slightest reservation, refusing to heed even her dying brother's warning that Tito will cause her great sorrow. She does not see that Tito's willing agreeableness to live in her house after their marriage, and his false amiability about her continuing to give proper and filial attention to her father, cover a very calculating move on his part to serve his own interests. He is a stranger in Florence; to further his own ends he must have the respectability and the substantiality that her background provides, and through her friends he rises rapidly both politically and socially. He allows his wife the comfort of thinking that she will be able to continue her father's work, until a few weeks after the old grand signor's death; then, without warning, without so much as a word to anyone, he sells Bardi's great library and pockets the money.

Romola's first reaction to what she considers a terrible betrayal on her husband's part is shocked outrage. She immediately runs away. Savonarola meets her on the road outside the city and forces her to return, but the rosy haze in which she had permitted herself to live and believe is completely obliterated. Despite her willingness to serve the plague victims, it is long before she can forget herself and her own sorrow and humiliation. Wisdom comes slowly. It is not until, little by little, she learns that other people have received equal—if different—injustice at Tito's hands that she is able to view her own situation in perspective and to bring love and sympathy to Tessa, Baldassare, even Savonarola, who have special need of both. The Romola who flings her challenge at the Frate when he refuses to spare her godfather—"God's kingdom is something wider . . . else let me stand outside it with those I love . . ."—is not the outcry of a self-pitying, credulous girl who could think only of running away as the first remedy for hurt and sorrow. And when she leaves Florence again, and the drifting boat by chance brings her to a plague-stricken village, she gives her strength completely to helping the victims as a sufferer among the suffering. George Eliot intended this episode as a symbolical element in her story; [29] like Maggie Tulliver, Romola attains full stature as a person under the weight of adversity. Unlike Savonarola and Tito, she is able to learn from experience to open her heart; her suffering is great, but she is, in a very real sense, redeemed by it.

But the most interesting aspect of *Romola*—the one which really makes the book well worth several readings —is the remarkable characterization of the hero-villain, Tito Melema. This handsome Greek scholar turns up in Florence after a shipwreck with no money, but with a packet of valuable gems. He has survived the calamitous voyage, and he is quite certain that Baldassare, his foster father, who was swept overboard with him, has drowned. There is a remote possibility that Baldassare has survived, but Tito manages to rationalize it out of his mind. George Eliot here indicates her deep commitment to the philosophy of cause and effect; it is Tito's duty to search for his foster father, and from the very moment that he convinces himself that such a search would be disadvantageous to the career he envisions for himself in Florence, he has taken the first step toward corruption. He, too, has an image of himself, but a most contemptible one, for his is based solely and completely on selfish advancement. Savonarola thinks, at least, that he has the City of Florence and its greatness as his objective; Romola has her genuine love for her scholar-father and his work and her wish to continue everything as he would have wanted; but Tito is incapable of even a surface commitment to anything or anyone but himself.

And, as George Eliot skillfully demonstrates, Tito does possess qualities which, guided by discipline and true concern, could have made him a really great leader. Even after he sells the gems entrusted to him by Baldassare and manages to inveigle his way into Florentine society, fate provides him with several chances to redeem himself and fulfill his duty as a son. First, there is the letter he receives from Baldassare, saying that he was rescued and has been sold as a slave to the Turks. But Tito ignores the plea for ransom, again convincing himself that, because the letter is a year old, Baldassare must be dead. And then there is the terrible moment when Baldassare appears in Florence as a prisoner of war and confronts Tito—and Tito denies knowing him. From that moment on, Tito lives in terror of his life, for Baldassare becomes his special Nemesis, and that fear causes the gradual disintegration of all the prestige and status he has worked so long and deviously to acquire. An inevitable doom hangs over him which he uses every means to escape, but must ultimately face. As a fugitive from a mob bent on killing him as a member of Savonarola's party (it is not known that Tito has been a double agent and has worked secretly to destroy the Frate), he jumps into the Arno, only to climb onto the river bank and find Baldassare's iron hands about his throat. "Killed Tito in great excitement," [30] George Eliot wrote in her Journal on May 16, 1863. A century and some years later, that excitement is still communicated through the pages of *Romola*.

As a study of an individual who loves things and uses people, the character of Tito Melema has few rivals in fiction. He is the visible working out of the Machiavellian principle of the end justifying the means. He uses those who befriend him without conscience, letting them feel that he is doing them an honor in permitting themselves to be so used. His charm and his acknowledged abilities in literature would naturally open all doors to him in Florence, the cultural center of the fifteenth-century world, and his social ease and excellent manners seldom fail him. But, beneath this façade, he is a scoundrel. He allows himself to become involved with Tessa, the innocent little contadina, and even deceives her into believing that the carnival mock marriage performed over them is valid. At that very moment, he has set his eyes on higher game. It is Romola who will provide him with the means to achieve what he wants, so he marries her, and deceives her just as he has deceived Tessa, rationalizing whatever guilt he occasionally feels (and, at least at first, he is not so calloused as to be unable to feel guilt) by telling himself that Tessa, a common, ignorant peasant, should expect no better from himself, a grand signor. He finds, however, that one deception leads easily to another, and finally he does not even realize that he is a liar and a betrayer of trusts. He justifies everything he does on the grounds of his own safety; at the end of the novel, he is preparing to leave Florence, having gone as far as he possibly can there, before he is completely found out. Romola has left him, but even that does not concern him. Tessa and their two children are going with him, and the reader has the feeling that they, too, will soon be discarded. But in that moment on the river bank, when he lies at Baldassare's mercy, and the old man cries, "Ah, yes! You see me—you know me!", Tito recognizes not only his foster father, but also himself, and dies with the terrifying thought that eternity for him will be "this chill gloom with the face of a hideous past hanging over him forever."

When *Romola* was published in July 1863, the reviewers did not praise it in the same extravagant terms that had greeted *Adam Bede,* nor did the general public give it as overwhelming a reception. Robert Browning and the Trollope brothers praised it highly, and perhaps in their reaction we can find the clue as to what is really the major difficulty that any reader of *Romola* must be aware of and overcome. It is a "literary" novel, in the same sense that Browning's poem *Sordello* is a "literary" poem. It appealed in its own day, and does still, to those who are fascinated by studies in psychology and social history, and are sufficiently knowledgeable about Italian history in particular to appreciate the author's more than competence in re-creating medieval Florence with accuracy and verisimilitude down to the last detail. Such readers understand the reason for the drawn-out opening chapters; they recognize that these provide the basis and the background for the story. To quote George Eliot's own words,

> It is the habit of my imagination to strive after as full a vision of the medium in which a character moves as of the character itself. The psychological causes which prompted me to give such details of Florentine life and history as I have given, are precisely the same as those which determined me in giving the details of village life in "Silas Marner," or the "Dodson" life out of which were developed the destinies of Tom and Maggie.[31]

If it is against this intention that *Romola* is weighed and may be found wanting in some respects, the author was first to agree—especially in regard to the character of the heroine:

I can well believe that the many difficulties belonging to the treatment of such a character have not been overcome, and that I have failed to bring out my conception with adequate fulness.[32]

The important thing, however, is that George Eliot recognized the novel's deficiencies. Even so, she learned much from having written it, and readers learn much from having read it. We may not agree with the *Spectator*'s reviewer that *Romola* was "much the greatest [book] she has yet produced"; [33] our judgment may coincide with Henry James's evaluation: "More than any of her novels it was evolved from her moral consciousness encircled by a prodigious amount of literary research." [34] Nevertheless, *Romola* remains a definite landmark in George Eliot's career as a novelist, and, for that reason if no other, cannot be too lightly dismissed.

XV

Between autumn of 1863 and spring of 1865, Marian had little time for writing. She and Lewes had finally taken the momentous step of purchasing a house in London. They had discussed the possibility for several years because they had long felt the need of finally putting down roots in a home of their own instead of living under the uncertainties of a lease, and neither of them had really liked the house in Blandford Square. But, until August 1863, no suitable place within their means had come on the market. Then, quite unexpectedly, they found The

Priory, at 21 North Bank, on the edge of Regent's Park. It was "not at all like a London house with rooms piled one above the other like boxes," Marian wrote excitedly to Monsieur D'Albert-Durade. "It stands in a garden detached from all other houses, and the living rooms are all on one floor." [1] With the garden and the entire park at her front door, she anticipated all the pleasures she had enjoyed in the country without the expense and the responsibilities. It is interesting to note that Regent's Park was a most desirable residential location in 1863, and the fact that the Leweses were welcome to purchase property there is a definite indication that they were not now considered as detrimental to public morals. Of course, by this time all the world knew that Marian Evans Lewes was George Eliot, the famous, sought-after novelist; and, while some of the conservative matrons might continue to take their time about leaving cards at The Priory, they certainly would not dream of "cutting" her if they happened to meet walking in the park or shopping at the greengrocer's. Nine years had wrought a change; had not Queen Victoria herself spoken of George Eliot's books with approval, to say nothing of Mr. Tennyson, the Poet Laureate? So Marian had no fears about what her neighbors would say when she moved into The Priory. She appreciatively considered this a sign of approval, compared with that first year when she and Lewes had been required to change lodgings five times.

But buying a house in which she intended to live for the rest of her life involved many unforeseen problems. "*Now* I have a mind made up of old carpets in new places and new carpets suffering from accidents; chairs, tables, and prices; muslin curtains and down draughts in old chimneys." [2] Painting, decorating, and shopping fully occupied her time. "The Priory is all scaffolding and paint," she wrote Mrs. Bray on September 1st.

Nor was moving her sole anxiety: "we are still in a nightmare of uncertainty about our boys." [3] Thornton, "at once amiable and troublesome, easy and difficult to manage," [4] who seems to have inherited some of his own mother's unstable temperament, had failed the second examination for the Indian Civil Service, and he refused to study more law and Sanscrit to prepare for another attempt. He had decided to go to Poland and join the guerilla forces who were fighting the Russians. Lewes, with Marian's assistance, persuaded him with great difficulty that such an idea was preposterous, and made a quick trip to see Edward Bulwer-Lytton, then at his country seat at Knebworth, Hertfordshire, who knew considerable about opportunities in the colonies for ambitious young men. Bulwer-Lytton deprecated the idea of Vancouver Island, which had been Lewes's first thought, and suggested Africa. Armed with advice and information, Lewes returned to London and finally made arrangements for Thornton to go out to Natal as a trader in October. At the same time, Bertie's future had to be decided; a place was found for him on a farm in Scotland where he could learn agriculture. Marian shared her husband's anxiety completely; she actually felt a greater responsibility for these boys who called her "Mother" than if they had been her own flesh and blood.

The Priory was ready by the contracted time, and the Leweses moved in on November 5th. Books were on the shelves within a week, though not arranged; the drawing room paper which had been especially designed for them was ruined by an accident and brand new had to be made. Marian, thinking it would be safe there, left a purse in a dressing table drawer and one of the workmen stole it.[5] And, to make matters worse, she was suddenly taken ill with influenza, which brought everything to a standstill for several days. Miraculously, however, everything was in relative good order by November 24th, and the Leweses held a gala reception and musicale in honor of Charles's coming of age.

> You would have liked to hear Jansa play on his violin; and you would perhaps have been amused to see an affectionate but dowdy friend of yours, splendid in a grey moire antique —the consequence of a severe lecture from Owen Jones on her general neglect of personal adornment [6]

Marian wrote amusedly to her friend Mrs. Congreave, and added, almost with a sigh, "I am glad to have gotten over this crisis of maternal and housekeeping duty." [7]

Nothing was further from her mind than another novel. Lewes had received a discreet inquiry from John Blackwood during the autumn,[8] but Marian was thinking of nothing but recouping her strength. *Romola* had exhausted her, and that the book did not "catch on" very well did nothing to raise her spirits. So she read, rested, played the piano, and entertained. The weekly musical evenings and the Sunday "at homes" quickly became Priory institutions. She helped Lewes read proof for his new work, *Aristotle: A Chapter from the History of Science,* and for a revised edition of his biography of Goethe. Family matters among the older members absorbed her rather sadly. Her husband's stepfather, John Willim, died in February 1864, and they had to take complete responsibility for his aged, ailing mother. Then Marian received word of the death of her half-brother, Robert Evans, and, a month later, of her half-sister's husband, Henry Houghton. Marian, whose sense of kinship was as strong as Aunt Glegg's, grieved for her widowed sisters and wrote at once. She was comforted when they both replied warmly, if reticently, indicating that the family front against her had been breached, and she continued to be on the best of terms with her nieces and nephews. Only Isaac remained obdurate, and this was a constant source of pain to her. She still loved her brother dearly, and the ending of *The Mill on the Floss* must have drifted across her mind frequently during those early spring days. Must tragedy strike that household, too, before they would be reconciled?

Perhaps to distract her mind from dwelling too much on the past, Lewes, out of a clear sky one morning, suggested that she try her hand at a play. They were both great admirers of Helen Faucit, the Shakespearean actress, and Miss Faucit had liked *Adam Bede*. It occurred to Lewes that Miss Faucit might also like the idea of having a play especially written for her by George Eliot, and he even sketched out a scenario. Marian rather liked the idea herself, and Miss Faucit, when asked, declared that she was delighted. The Leweses went up to Glasgow late in February to see her and to attend her production of *Much Ado About Nothing,* but the project of a George Eliot play for her was not realized. The idea, however, was not abandoned. Marian tucked it into the back of her mind for future reference while she and her husband went abroad to spend April and May in Italy.

Returning to England in June, they discovered that Charles had great news for them: " 'Our boy' Charles has just become engaged, and it is very pretty to see the happiness of a pure first love filled with nothing but promise . . . Altogether, we rejoice." [9] Gertrude Hill was a charming young woman, four years older than her fiancé, which Marian thought an advantage; Charles needed steadying, and she was frankly amazed that so lovely a girl had fallen in love with their "amiable bit of crudity." [10] Lewes was "rather melancholy" [11] at first hearing of his son's engagement, but, upon consideration, decided that he, too, was delighted. Miss Hill came from a highly respected if "liberal" family (her sister was the reformer, Octavia Hill), and the lack of opposition on the part of her relatives to her choice of Charles Lee Lewes as a husband is further indication of the increasing social acceptance of the Leweses.

But, despite Marian's pleasure in Charles's approaching marriage, there is an undercurrent of restlessness in her letters and Journal during the summer of 1864. She had not done any writing for over a year. Her only publication was a short story, "Brother Jacob," which she contributed gratis to the *Cornhill Magazine* in July, because George Smith, the editor, had undertaken *Romola* and the book had not gone well. "Brother Jacob," a strange little tale about a small-town confectioner whose pretensions to grandeur are undone when his half-witted brother exposes him, had been written in 1860 and laid aside; apart from revising it for *Cornhill,* she had not put pen to paper since. "Horrible skepticism about all things paralysing my mind," she wrote in her Journal on July 17th. "Shall I ever be good for anything again? Ever do anything again?" [12] The author's familiar pangs were once again besetting her. Lewes's play scenario for Helen Faucit was in her desk; it was, she knew in all honesty, dreadful, but the idea of writing a play still had its attractions. At least, it started her to work again. "I am reading about Spain, and am trying a drama on a subject that has fascinated me—have written the Prologue and am beginning the First Act." [13] The drama was *The Spanish Gypsy.*

Marian worked at it intermittently during the autumn and winter of 1864, but there were many distractions. Lewes's post as editorial assistant for *Cornhill* was abolished because the magazine had been losing money, which meant that his yearly income was lessened. He was not in good health, either, and though he could have accepted several editorships of various periodicals, he was afraid that he would not be equal to the responsibility. Anthony Trollope and John Chapman had been discussing the possibility of starting a new magazine, and came often to The Priory to urge him to be its editor, but, tempting as the idea of a brand-new venture was, he still hesitated. Then Marian was taken strangely ill in November. "Ill, obliged to keep perfectly quiet," [14] she wrote in her Journal on the 18th. The doctor decided that she had acute dyspepsia and prescribed accordingly, but, judging from her complaints of general malaise and "constant dull pain," [15] it is more likely that this was a first attack of the severe renal disorder from which she was to suffer for the rest of her life. She was still trying to work on her play, but finally, in February 1865, she was forced to stop. "Ill with bilious headache and very miserable about my soul as well as my body. *George has taken my drama away from me.*" [16]

The enforced rest was evidently what she needed, though she rebelled against it, and she was well enough to attend Charles's wedding to Gertrude Hill on March 20th. On March 21st, Lewes, after several refusals, finally accepted the editorship of the new *Fortnightly Review*. Marian was delighted for him, though she was still concerned about his health. As for herself, "About myself I am in deep depression, feeling powerless. I have written nothing but beginnings. . . ." [17] But her husband's enthusiasm and excitement over his new position must have been contagious, because on March 29th she wrote in her Journal, *"I have begun a novel."* [18]

If *Romola* be considered George Eliot's worst novel, *Felix Holt, The Radical* must be known as the one least read. Perhaps one reason for this is its background: it is set against the great struggles caused by the Reform Bill of 1832, and a certain amount of historical and political knowledge is necessary to understand fully the political implications of Harold Transome's candidacy for the House of Commons, and the violent arguments, pro and con, about the merits of the pending legislation. Then there is the century-old law case which casts its ominous shadow on every character in the novel; the author consulted Frederic Harrison, an expert in the laws governing inheritance and also an authority on trial procedure, who read the manuscript as it was being written to make certain that every legal fact was correct. But the very intricacy of the Transome-Bycliffe suit, which had to be presented in great detail for Esther Lyon's claim to be understood, would probably lessen the book's interest for some twentieth-century readers, although those who enjoy really good detective yarns should find the quest for the missing heir as fascinating a tangle to unravel as did the readers of 1866. Finally, *Felix Holt* is so definitely of its time. The Parliamentary hearings which were to culminate in the Reform Bill of 1867 were already in progress during 1865 while George Eliot was writing her novel, and, when the book was published in 1866, John Blackwood remarked, "Her sayings would be invaluable in the present debate." [19] It has been erroneously supposed that, for this very reason, *Felix Holt* lacks that sense of universality of human emotion which permeates *Adam Bede*. A reading of the novel quickly dispels that impression, however, for Felix Holt the young workingman, and Harold Transome the wealthy landowner turned politician, have their counterparts today, a century later.

Felix Holt also marks an important stage in George Eliot's development as a novelist. It is the first of her books in which there are two completely distinct plots, each of which could almost stand alone as a separate entity, carefully linked together by the machinations of Matthew Jermyn, the unscrupulous lawyer, who is agent for Transome Court and the only person who knows that Esther Lyon, the supposed daughter of Rufus Lyon, the dissenting preacher, is actually heiress to that great estate. What may be called the "Felix Holt plot" involves the political activities of a young watchmaker, Felix Holt, who, though well educated, has deliberately renounced all thought of personal gain and thrown in his lot with the ordinary workingmen in their efforts to get a candidate elected to the House of Commons who will vote for the Reform Bill. Here we see George Eliot's favorite theme of renunciation; Felix Holt is somewhat like Romola and Dinah Morris in his dedication to the common good, except that there is no religious basis for his dedication. In fact, he is entirely non-doctrinaire, both religiously and politically; he sees the churches as part of the Establishment that crushes ordinary people into a passive acceptance of their lot, and the government as a machine for exploitation. But he is not a blind partisan. He is not influenced by anarchistic theories. He sees just as clearly that the securing of the vote of the common man will not, in and of itself, improve the common lot. As he says at the political rally,

> I want the working man to have power. I'm a working man myself, and I don't want anything else. But there are two

sorts of power. There's the power to do mischief—to undo what has been done with great expense and labour, to waste and destroy, to be cruel to the weak, to lie and quarrel, and to talk poisonous nonsense. That's the sort of power that ignorant numbers have. It never made a joint stool or planted a potato. Do you think it's likely to do much towards governing a great country, and making wise laws, and giving shelter, food, and clothes to millions of men? Ignorant power comes in the end to the same thing as wicked power; it makes misery . . . Suppose out of every hundred who had a vote, there were thirty who had some soberness, some sense to choose with, some good feeling to make them wish the right thing for all? And suppose there were seventy out of the hundred who were, half of them, not sober, who had no sense to choose one thing in politics more than another, and who had so little good feeling in them that they wasted on their own drinking the money that should have helped to feed and clothe their wives and children; and another half of them who, if they didn't drink, were too ignorant or stupid to see any good for themselves better than pocketing a five shilling piece when it was offered to them. Where would be the political power of the thirty sober men? The power would lie with the seventy drunken and stupid votes. . . .

Recalling how the author, as a child, accompanied her father on his errands about the district, and how she listened to his conversations with other men, is it too far beyond belief to say that these words, in spirit, at least, express the convictions of Robert Evans? Especially in the light of her comment to John Blackwood that her personal recollections played a strong part in the writing of *Felix Holt?* [20] Certainly she did considerable background research, but her reading, by her own admission, was "illuminated" by her memory,[21] and her memory is what gives the political arguments in pub and town square their liveliness and sense of reality.

Felix Holt, therefore, is not a "radical" in the sense that he wants to overturn the established order. He takes the word in its literal meaning, "pertaining to the roots"; he wants to begin at the heart of the problem which is, as he understands it, the workingmen's inability to look beyond their immediate comfort and security to a greater, better goal. In him we see the recollection of those earnest conversations at John Chapman's, when Joseph Parkes, Herbert Spencer, Barbara Bodichon, Bessie Parkes, and Marian Evans were among the guests. For them, education was the answer to the problem, and Felix Holt, like them, believes also that the man in the street must be educated to that nobility of spirit and sound sense of judgment which will prevent him from being too easily swayed by unscrupulous politicians like Johnson—a ward-heeler type who stoops to any form of bribery to get votes for his candidate—to shout for the man who will pay for their ale in return for their support. To this cause, Felix is committed heart and soul— then he meets Esther Lyon, and, without in the least wanting to, falls deeply in love with her.

For Esther, at least on the surface, is everything he despises in a woman. She is coquettish, frivolous, and not a little vain. She languishes over Byron and dreams of a romantic lover who will marry her and bring her to a great house where she will live in luxury for the rest of her life. In her fantasies, she is like Hetty Sorrel in *Adam Bede,* but, unlike Hetty, she has been well educated—her "father" has even sent her to France to study, and she gives French lessons to the young girls of Treby Magna, a genteel way to earn her living—and she is very intelligent. She is drawn to Felix from their first meeting because she recognizes his honesty and integrity, and she does not want him to despise her. When she discovers that she is heiress to Transome Court, and goes there to stay with old Mrs. Transome, she is strongly attracted by Harold, the matriarch's son, but she finds his gallant attentions do not mean as much to her as Felix's earnest and genuine concern. And when Felix becomes involved in an election day riot, and is arrested and imprisoned, she believes completely that he took over the leadership of the mob only to decoy the hysterical, drunken men into taking the road out of town into the open fields where they could do no harm. She also believes that the police constable really did succumb to a heart attack, and not from Felix's blow, and she goes into court where she insists upon being called as a character witness for him. Her plea does not move the jury to free him—a touch of reality which elevates this sequence out of the general run-of-mill Victorian romance—though his sentence is the comparatively light one of four years' imprisonment for manslaughter. Her courage does, however, win for him the sympathy of Treby Magna, and Sir Maximus Debarry, the leading magnate, uses his influence to obtain a pardon. As for Esther, following the trial she renounces her claim to Transome Court and returns to her stepfather's home to wait for Felix's release. The novel ends with their marriage.

The "Felix Holt plot" admittedly is little different from those of many social protest novels. It is George Eliot's special gift that makes it seem new and fresh, especially for the fascinating insights it provides into the political furors of the early nineteenth century, and for the stalwart but unidealized portrait of the radical watchmaker. But the most remarkable aspect of the novel, especially from the point of view of characterization, is to be found in the "Transome plot." This expertly delineated story of guilt and retribution is one of the finest that George Eliot ever wrote. We are introduced to it in the very first chapter, where Mrs. Transome is waiting for her son Harold's return after an absence of fifteen years. With a sure hand, the author portrays the old lady wandering restlessly about the house, in her worn black dress and "visibly mended" lace. Mrs. Transome has lived for this day. Her every thought, prayer, and action have been for Harold. To save Transome Court for him, she has allowed the unscrupulous Matthew Jermyn to direct her financial affairs, though she knows him to be dishonest, and she knows, too, that Harold will soon discover that dishonesty. What Harold does not know, and what she will never tell him, is that Jermyn is, in fact, his father.

> For there is seldom any wrong-doing which does not carry along with it some downfall of blindly climbing hopes, some hard entail of suffering, some quickly satiated desire that survives, with the life in death of old paralytic vice, to see it self-cursed by its woeful progeny—some tragic mark of kinship in one brief life to the far-stretching life that went before, and to the life that is to come after, such as raised the pity and terror of men since they began to discern between will and destiny.

Thus George Eliot sets forth the theme of Mrs. Transome's story in the Introduction to *Felix Holt*. The author's deep belief in the law of consequences—that every action, good or evil, must inevitably affect the future—is movingly exemplified in the old lady who futilely tries to stave off the evil day when Harold must learn the truth. In some respects, the "Transome plot" resembles Anthony Trollope's *Orley Farm*, which George Eliot had read and thoroughly enjoyed before she began writing her novel. In *Orley Farm*, Lady Mason forges a codicil to her husband's will to preserve her son's inheritance, but Mrs. Transome's situation is far more tragic than hers.

She is not young, or beautiful, or marriageable. Her husband is still alive in a state of pathetic senility; her elder son, Durfey, has recently died as the result of a feckless, dissipated life. Harold is all she has left, and Harold is not a true-born Transome. With great compassion, George Eliot shows how Mrs. Transome came to yield herself to Matthew Jermyn in a moment of weakness, and strongly implies that her sin, too, was a consequence of a century-old wrong which generations of Transomes have tried to conceal. Had it not been for the Bycliffe claim, Mrs. Transome might not have transgressed. Having transgressed, she hopes only that, when Harold takes control of the estate, somehow things will be righted.

But Harold's return only speeds the inexorable Nemesis. He has been a successful merchant in Smyrna, and he is all business. Two things are uppermost in his mind: to put Transome Court in order, and to win the coming election to the House of Commons as a candidate for the Radical Party. Both these objectives bring him into direct collision with Matthew Jermyn, and collusion as well, for Jermyn is the only person he knows in Treby Magna who is capable of conducting an election campaign. Like Stephen Guest, Harold is young, handsome, and spoiled. But he is very quick-witted and shrewd, "and still quicker at translating other men's generalities into his own special and immediate purposes, . . ." and he knows what he wants. There is a ruthless streak in Harold which is not likable; the election means so much to him that he acquiesces to Jermyn's scheme of gaining the Sproxton men's support by plying them with free drink, even though he knows that riots can spring from such tactics. When he discovers that Esther is the Bycliffe heiress and can claim Transome Court, he quite calmly and practically decides to marry her.

He saw a mode of reconciling all the difficulties which looked pleasanter to him the longer he looked at Esther. When she had hardly been a week in the house, he had made up his mind to marry her; and it never entered into that mind that the decision did not rest entirely with his inclination . . . To be deeply in love was a catastrophe not likely to happen to him, but he was readily amorous.

Mrs. Transome, however, much as she would like the marriage, from the depths of her own experience sees matters quite differently:

"I wish he were in love with her, so that she could master him, and make him do what she pleased . . . No woman ever will. He will make her fond of him and afraid of him . . . A woman's love is always freezing into fear. She wants everything, she is secure of nothing. This girl has a fine spirit—plenty of fire and pride and wit. Men like such captives, as they like horses that champ the bit and paw the ground: they feel more triumph in their mastery. What is the use of woman's will?—if she tries, she doesn't get it, and she ceases to be loved."

Her words reveal the bitterness of a wife and mother who has lost all illusions. She has learned what her cherished son really is, and that all her dreams and sacrifices have not achieved the one thing she has wanted above everything—his unquestioning love, which would more than compensate for all the unhappiness and guilt she has suffered.

It remains only for Harold to learn the truth about himself, and this is inevitable from the moment he begins to investigate Jermyn's custody of Transome Court. The lawyer's dishonesty infuriates him; Jermyn has grown rich on money fraudulently obtained by juggled accounts and by secret sales of Transome land. Harold determines to take legal action, and he has every justification for doing so. He cannot understand his mother's insistence that he must not provoke Jermyn, and he laughs at her fears. George Eliot skillfully keeps the reader in suspense until almost the end of the novel, waiting to learn precisely what hold Jermyn has over Mrs. Transome. At last the two are brought together, face to face, and the lawyer, to her stunned dismay, blames *her* for his shady tactics in concealing the identity of Esther Lyon's real father, whom they both thought to be the last of the Bycliffes.

"I stretched my conscience a good deal in that affair of Bycliffe, as you know perfectly well. I told you everything at the time. I told you I was very uneasy about those witnesses; and about getting him thrown into prison. I know it's about the blackest thing anyone could charge me with, if they knew my life from beginning to end; and I should never have done it, if I had not been under an infatuation such as makes a man do anything. What did it signify to me about the loss of the lawsuit? I was a young bachelor. I had the world before me."

"Yes," said Mrs. Transome in a low tone. "It was a pity you didn't make another choice."

"What would have become of you?" said Jermyn, carried along a climax, like other self-justifiers. "I had to think of you. You would not have liked me to make another choice then."

"Clearly," said Mrs. Transome, with concentrated bitterness, but still quietly, "the greater mistake was mine."

He reminds her of his family, and of the respected position he holds in Treby Magna. Then he tells her that Harold will not dare to press his suit, if he is told the truth about his birth. At this, Mrs. Transome is finally roused from her apathy.

"Don't speak!" Mrs. Transome said peremptorily. "Don't open your lips again. You have said enough; I will speak now. I have made sacrifices, too, but it was when I saw that your tenderness had turned to calculation—after I saw that you cared for yourself only and not for me. I heard your explanations—of your duty in life—of our mutual reputation—of a virtuous young lady attached to you. I bore it; I let everything go; I shut my eyes; I might almost have let myself starve rather than have scenes or quarrel with the man I loved, in which I must accuse him of turning my love into a good bargain . . . And I have caused you to strain your conscience, have I? It is I who have sullied your purity . . . If I sinned, my judgment went beforehand—that I should sin for a man like you."

This scene is one answer to those who maintain that Victorian novelists were too prudish to mention anything unpleasant.

The moment comes when Jermyn and Harold must meet. The author, for maximum dramatic effect, puts this meeting in the local pub after the election, when there would naturally be the greatest number of witnesses present. Jermyn insists that the lawsuit must be abandoned: "You must repent else—for your mother's sake," he hisses, and Harold, furious at the mention of his mother in such surroundings, strikes him across the face with his riding whip. Jermyn leaps at Harold's throat.

"Let go of me, you scoundrel!" said Harold fiercely, "or I'll be the death of you."

"Do," said Jermyn in a grating voice. *"I am your father."*

Admittedly there is melodrama here, but there is only stark tragedy when Harold confronts his mother afterward at Transome Court.

He looked at his mother as he entered, and her eyes followed him as he moved, till he came and stood in front of her, she looked up at him with white lips.

"Mother," he said with distinct slowness, in strange contrast to his habitual manner, "tell me the truth, that I may know how to act."

He paused a moment, and then said, "Who is my father?"

She was mute: her lips only trembled. Harold stood silent for a few moments as if waiting. Then he spoke again.

"*He* has said—said it before others—that *he* is my father."

He looked still at his mother. She seemed as if age were striking her with a sudden wand—as if her trembling face were getting haggard before him. She was mute. But her eyes had not fallen; they looked up in helpless misery at her son.

Mrs. Transome's world has been utterly destroyed; there is left only the final heartbreak of Harold's rejection.

What a dreary future, after this dreary past? She, too, looked out into the dim night; but the black boundary of trees and the long line of the river seemed only part of the loneliness and monotony of her life.

Fortunately, Harold is reconciled with his mother through Esther Lyon's gentle persuasion; it would be quite unbearable if he were not, because George Eliot evokes such sympathy for Mrs. Transome. She in herself makes *Felix Holt* worth the reading, for there are few more brilliant studies in literature of the ravages of sin and the cancer of secret guilt.

Work on the novel proceeded slowly, due very largely to the amount of time that the author spent in working out the exact details of the Transome-Bycliffe lawsuit. She began the book in March 1865, and by October she had written only seventy-four pages. By early December she had finished Chapter X, but on the day before Christmas she was "sticking in the mud from doubt." [22] January was taken up with correspondence with Frederic Harrison about the legal details, and, from then on, writing progressed at a swifter pace. Volume II was finished by the 21st of April, and on May 31st she wrote triumphantly in her Journal, "Finished 'Felix Holt'!" [23] She had completed the manuscript in "a state of nervous excitement that had been making my head throb and my heart palpitate all the week before," [24] and had inscribed it to Lewes: "From George Eliot to her dear Husband, this thirteenth year of their united life, in which the deepening sense of her own imperfectness has the consolation of their deepening love." [25]

Felix Holt did not have as quick a critical success as either *Adam Bede* or *The Mill on the Floss;* political tempers were too hot in mid-July of 1866 for reviewers to give it an altogether unprejudiced appraisal. But it brought George Eliot great personal good fortune, in that it was published by Blackwood's. She had submitted part of the manuscript to George Smith, the publisher of *Romola,* but he had declined it on the ground that "it would not be a profitable venture." [26] Lewes thereupon undertook to write John Blackwood, who, despite any previous unpleasantness, responded quickly and generously: "I am delighted to hear that Mrs. Lewes has so nearly finished her Novel, and also much pleased that she should think in the first instance of her old friend . . . ;" [27] He read the first two manuscript volumes almost at one sitting—they reached Edinburgh on April 22nd, and his formal offer was in the mail on April 24th, before Volume III was even completed. The relationship which had meant so much to both author and editor was quickly re-established, on an even firmer basis of friendship than in the past. With Blackwood's assurance that *Felix Holt* would be an even greater popular success than *The Mill on the Floss* had been, Marian and Lewis left on June 7th for their annual summer holiday on the Continent.

XVI

The six-week visit to Holland, Belgium, and Germany was designed as a complete vacation and rest. Marian was suffering from her usual exhaustion after completing a novel, and Lewes was in a similar state from the launching of the *Fortnightly Review*. Their ultimate destination was the German health resorts of Schwalbach and Schlagenbad; they stayed about ten days at each spa, hoping that the peaceful routine of rest, promenades, and "taking the waters" would revive them. But bad weather and recurrent bilious attacks did not contribute much to

Pencil drawing of George Eliot done from life by Lady Alma Tadema in 1877.

The Priory, 21 North Bank, on the edge of Regent's Park. It was to this house that George Eliot came with George Henry Lewes in 1864, and it remained her home until her marriage with John Cross in 1880.

their improvement, and, also, they found themselves in the middle of the "Seven Weeks War" between Prussia and Austria. The places they visited were not too much affected—as Marian wrote to Mrs. Congreave from Schwalbach, "A few soldiers are quartered here . . . they are the only suggestion of war that meets our eyes." [1] Later, however, she wrote to John Blackwood, "We left Schlagenbad just early enough to be able to go down the Rhine to Bonn by the Dutch steamer, and soon after we were on board, we saw the Prussian troops marching to take Eltville, which we had quitted ten minutes before." [2] However, the journey had provided two memorable experiences. They had seen the Oberammergau Passion Play at Antwerp— ". . . the Christ was, without exaggeration, beautiful," [3] and, in tribute to Spinoza, had attended a service at the Portuguese synagogue at Amsterdam. Marian wrote to Sara Hennell

> The chanting and the swaying about of bodies—almost a wriggling—are not beautiful to the sense; but I fairly cried at witnessing this faint symbolism of sublime, far-off memories. [4]

They were both glad to get back to The Priory in August, where letters were waiting for them, many being congratulatory notes about *Felix Holt,* which was selling very well. One letter, however, was exceptionally welcome and very important because it provided the impetus for George Eliot's next work. Frederic Harrison, the lawyer who had helped her with the legal aspects of *Felix Holt,* began by remarking that he had re-read the novel some four or five times—always delightful news to an author's ear—and added that he had experienced some of the same feeling that came to him when he read Tennyson or Browning. Then he asked:

Are you sure that your destiny is not to produce a poem —not a poem in prose, but in measure—a drama? Is it possible that there is not yet one existing, or does it lie like the statue in the marble block? I am no fortune teller but I believe it is in the Stars.[5]

And he went on to suggest that she investigate the Positivist doctrines, which he felt sure would be of interest to her and might provide the framework for such a poem. In fact, he insisted that Positivism could be more readily disseminated by a work of art than by the most zealous direct proselytizing, adding, "There is not anyone, there has never been anyone but yourself to whom we could look for this." [6]

Marian was intrigued. Through her husband's interest in Auguste Comte's work, she had become thoroughly familiar with the general outline of Positivist thought. Also, through her growing friendship with the Congreaves, whom she had met for the first time when she was living at Holly Lodge, she had been persuaded to study Comte herself. When Dr. Congreave organized the Positivist Society in London in 1867, she would be present at his lectures and pledge an annual subscription for its work, for there was much in this "religion of humanity" that appealed to her. Unlike the violent diatribes of Karl Marx, Comte's work appealed to man's reason and sense of order as a means to achieve social betterment. His system could not be made the basis of political upheaval; it required the serious application of the intellect. Comte's statement—"Love, then, is our principle; Order our basis; and Progress our end" [7]—was in precise agreement with her own philosophy of life, and she also liked Comte's views concerning women:

With women, the "consecration of the rational and imaginative faculties to the service of feeling has always existed spontaneously," and now that the subordination of intellect to heart has become the grand ruling principle, women will assume their rightful place of honour and veneration, lending their incomparable influence over private life to the support of the priestly educators.[8]

She approved the idea of a humanity-centered religion —for Comte, humanity was the Supreme Being to be worshiped—with women representing its sympathy, compassion, and empathy. Such a religion coincided with her belief in "truth of feeling," though she could not abandon her intellectual faculties completely, as Comte felt that women should.

Neither could she agree with Frederick Harrison's proposal that any work of hers should become a medium of propaganda. In a letter dated August 15, 1866, she concurred that ". . . aesthetic teaching is the highest teaching, because it deals with life in its highest complexity." [9] But, she said firmly, "if it ceases to be purely aesthetic— if it lapses anywhere from the picture to the diagram—it becomes the most offensive of all teaching." [10] A poem, a novel, a play, "must lay hold on the emotions as human experience— . . . 'flash' conviction on the world by means of aroused sympathy." [11] Nevertheless, she added that such a work as he suggested could—indeed, should —be written:

> . . . my whole soul goes with your desire that it should be done; and I shall at least keep the great possibility (or impossibility) perpetually in my mind, as something towards which I must strive, though it may be that I can do so only in a fragmentary manner.[12]

On August 20th, she noted in her Journal, "I have taken up the idea of my Spanish drama, 'The Spanish Gypsy,' again." [13]

Literary critics of the twentieth century usually pass over George Eliot's poetry very quickly, if they do not ignore it altogether. Honesty compels the most lenient reader to admit that *The Spanish Gypsy*, "Jubal," "How Lisa Loved the King," "Armgart," and "A Minor Prophet"—all of which occupied her from August 1866 until July 1869, when she returned to fiction and *Middlemarch* —have deservedly passed into oblivion. The "Brother and Sister Sonnets" are better; despite some very lame lines, they have the merit of being honest reflections of her own personal emotion. And "Oh, may I join the choir invisible," written in Dresden in August 1867, has a solemnity and dignity that derive from her utter sincerity. It could be considered an accidentally first-class work of a competent minor poet. But, apart from this single poem, the poetry of George Eliot is, quite simply, a disaster. Obviously, it is greatly influenced by Wordsworth:

Old Agatha, whose cousins Kate and Nell
Are housed by her in Love and Duty's name,
They being feeble, with small withered wits,
And she believing that the highest gift
Was given to be shared.

("Old Agatha")

is a typical passage. That Old Agatha's "highest gift" is the grace of intercessory prayer for the entire village is praiseworthy—it also fits neatly with the Positivist teaching that "In prayer we identify ourselves more and more with the Being [i.e. Humanity] that we adore." [14] But the poem certainly justifies Swinburne's comment to the effect that Tennyson did the same things very much better!

Lapses of taste are frequent. The following lines from

"The Legend of Jubal," make one sigh for Mrs. Poyser's dairy.

> Now Jabal learned to tame the lowing kine
> And from their udders drew the snow white wine,
> That stirs the innocent joy and makes the stream
> of elemental life with fulness teem.

Then, there is "Armgart," a playlet about an operatic soprano, who is convinced that her voice is a gift from God which must be shared with humanity. A nobleman seeks her hand in marriage, but says that she must give up her career. She rejects him:

> "I will not take for husband one who deems
> The thing my soul acknowledges as good—
> The thing I hold worth striving, suffering for,
> To be a thing dispensed with easily,
> Or else the suffering of a mind infirm."

Pride, however, goes before a fall. Armgart loses her voice soon after she loses the Graf, but there is always Leo, her impressario, waiting in the wings. He saves her from despair by telling her that she must henceforth dedicate her life to helping others: ". . . learn to love/ Another's living child." A sentiment of which Comte would thoroughly have approved, though one wonders if George Eliot would have been quite as receptive to such advice if she had been told that she could write no longer. (The character of Armgart is interesting, however, as a preliminary sketch for the Princess Halm-Eberstein, Daniel Deronda's mother.)

But *The Spanish Gypsy* does deserve a little more respectful treatment, if for no other reason than for the enormous amount of preparation and work expended upon it, plus the fact that six editions of it were published during the author's lifetime. Longfellow and James Russell Lowell were both enthusiastic about it; [15]

it was dramatized by Garrita Barry Nash, and it was suggested to the composer Arthur Thomas that he turn it into an opera.[16] Eight thousand, five hundred copies were sold in America during its first year of publication. English sales were slower, but most of the critics praised it. The *Spectator* said that it was superior to Elizabeth Barrett Browning's *Aurora Leigh*.[17] But the main reason why a consideration of *The Spanish Gypsy* must be included in any biography of George Eliot is found in her letter to Monsieur D'Albert-Durade of July 1868: "I seem to have gained a new organ, a new medium that my nature has languished for." [18] One might wonder why her spirit especially craved poetic expression; it is interesting to note that Robert Browning, who had become a good friend and a "Priory regular," had begun work on his novel in blank verse, *The Ring and the Book*, during 1866. Sunday afternoon conversations almost certainly touched on literature and works in progress. George Eliot may have been inspired in that way to attempt a new literary medium, as well as by Frederic Harrison's letter.

Research occupied her during the entire autumn and early winter of 1866. There was some family excitement when Bertie left to join Thornton in Natal in October; Thornton had bought a three thousand acre farm and he wanted his younger brother's assistance in running it. There was tragedy, too; Charles's wife had miscarried, and her infant, the Leweses' first grandchild, had been born dead. And there was grave anxiety over Lewes's health; in December he became so desperately ill that Marian finally prevailed upon him to give up his editorship of the *Fortnightly Review*. The doctors advised a warmer climate, and suggested that they take a trip south. Marian, by now immersed in Part I of *The Spanish*

Gypsy, saw in the doctor's orders an opportunity to go to Spain, an idea with which her husband enthusiastically concurred. *The Spanish Gypsy* was especially dear to his heart, since it had grown out of his original suggestion that she attempt a poetic drama, and he knew that Marian was the kind of writer who needed to see the actual locale about which she wrote.

They left England on December 27th, stopping for a few days in Paris where Marian renewed her acquaintance with Madame Julius Mohl, the wife of the famous Orientalist, who had called upon her some years earlier with Florence Nightingale. Madame Mohl's salon on the Rue de Bac was one of the most interesting in Paris, and she immediately invited the Leweses to a breakfast party, at which Ernest Renan was to be one of the guests. Marian knew Renan's work thoroughly, though she was dubious about his *La Vie de Jésus,*[19] and she described him as "something between the Catholic priest and the dissenting minister." [20] Evidently he did not quite live up to her expectations; "his talk [was] pleasant, but not distinguished." [21]

On New Year's Day of 1867, they were on their way to Biarritz, where they rested for about a week in the sun before continuing through Aragon to Saragossa. By this time, Lewes's health was so greatly improved that they decided to extend their tour to include Granada. The old Moorish city under its red towers was everything they had dreamed; they climbed up into the mountains and actually met a gypsy tribe, including the "captain," who left his blacksmith's forge and called upon his entire family to entertain the English *busnos.*[82] (This fortunate occasion may be one reason why the scenes in the gypsy encampment in *The Spanish Gypsy* carry some sense of verisimilitude. Certainly Zarca, the gypsy leader, is the best realized character in the work.) Marian wrote to John Blackwood that Granada had been worth "a very long, long journey." [23] Since it had included a sixteen-hour trek over the mountains in a mule-drawn diligence, the journey did not lack discomfort, though they found excellent lodgings in the Alhambra Palace gardens at the end of it.

They returned to England, via Cordova and Madrid, in March, and Marian, under the impetus of fresh inspiration, settled down to work at once. On June 5th, John Blackwood came down from Edinburgh, and she read what she had finished of Part I aloud to him. Her Journal records that "He showed great delight." [24] She had hoped to continue working steadily, but, unfortunately, her husband once again succumbed to tortuous headaches and the doctors again advised a change of scene. They paid a brief visit to Niton on the Isle of Wight, but Marian knew that the only way Lewes would recover his natural energy was to be removed from the distractions of London, so, at the end of July, they went to Germany for the summer. "Mr. Lewes is regenerated by the breath of pine forests," she wrote to Oscar Browning, history master at Eton, who had recently joined their circle of friends,

". . . and by the end of September I hope he will be able to enter on a Winter Campaign in London with the prospect of keeping well for three or four months. I am not sanguine enough to expect that he will not gradually 'run down,' and require another journey in the spring." [25]

Nevertheless, he was well enough for her to continue with *The Spanish Gypsy,* and by October, when they once more returned to The Priory, she had made considerable progress.

There was one literary interruption. John Blackwood

asked her to write a special article for the magazine, addressed to the workingmen of England, reminding them of their responsibilities now that the new Reform Bill of 1867 had given them the vote. Very cleverly she wrote it as a speech given by Felix Holt, expressing that character's sentiments only more directly than in the novel, and it was published in the January 1868 issue of *Blackwood's Magazine*. Then, finally, she could devote herself exclusively to *The Spanish Gypsy*, and on April 29th it was finished. Blackwood graciously set up the manuscript pages in type as she finished the various sections so that she could see how they looked; in consequence, there was little delay in publication. It appeared in the bookstores on May 25, 1868.

If it was George Eliot's intention in writing *The Spanish Gypsy* to break fresh ground, it must be admitted that she succeeded. Her novels contain melodramatic elements, but never had she attempted sheer melodrama. The plot of *The Spanish Gypsy* is reminiscent of Lewes's play, *The Noble Heart,* in its theme of star-crossed lovers, except that the ending is not happy. Young Don Silva

> . . . A goodly knight,
> A noble caballero, broad of chest
> And long of limb.

is the governor of Bedamár. His task is to guard the frontier against El Zagal, the Moor. He is in love with and is planning to marry Fedalma, an orphan girl of unknown parentage, whom his mother has raised and educated. His intention brings him into conflict with Father Isidore, Prior of San Domingo and Grand Inquisitor, who is quite certain that Fedalma, despite her Christian upbringing, is a heretic. By a convenient coincidence, gypsy prisoners are being held in the castle dungeons as punishment for their collaborations with El Zagal; among them is their king, Zarca. On the very night that Don Silva tells Fedalma that they must marry early the following morning—only in this way can he protect her against the intrigues of Father Isidore and the Inquisition—Zarca escapes from prison, finds Fedalma, and tells her that she is his daughter. He reminds her that she is a gypsy princess by birth, and insists that she must forsake Silva in order to assume her responsibilities and obligations to her people.

> "You belong
> Not to the petty round of circumstance
> That makes a woman's lot, but to your tribe,
> Who trust in me and in my blood with trust
> That men call blind. . . ."

Fedalma agrees—almost too quickly!—to help him and the other prisoners leave the fortress by a secret passage, and she goes with them into the mountains.

Don Silva, discovering that she is gone, follows her. She refuses to return to Bedamár with him, saying that it is her duty to remain with the gypsies. Silva then decides to become a gypsy himself. He does not know that Zarca has intrigued with El Zagal and the Moorish army to sack and pillage Bedamár; he returns to the city which he formerly governed, with the gypsies, after the battle is over, to find that many of his family and friends are dead. He also discovers that the gypsies have decided that Father Isidore must die by fire. His blood and heritage reassert themselves; he berates Zarca, and, when the gypsy reminds him of his blood oath by which he forsook Spain, in a burst of rage he stabs him with his dagger. With his dying breath, Zarca enjoins Fedalma to remember her duty to become queen of her people, and to lead them to the lands in Africa which El Zagal has promised them. At the end of the play, Silva and Fedalma part forever, he to go on a pilgrimage to Rome in penance for his sins, she to fulfill her father's last command. George Eliot had originally intended to have Fedalma and Silva die along with Zarca; Lewes persuaded her to use a less tragic ending, which, nonetheless, contains one of the most incredible "last farewells" ever written. Fedalma speaks:

> Our marriage rite
> Is our resolve that we will each be true
> To high allegiance, higher than our love.
> Our dear young love—its breath was happiness!
> But it had grown upon a larger life
> Which tore its roots asunder. We rebelled—
> The larger life subdued us. Yet we are wed;
> For we shall carry each the pressure deep
> Of the other's soul.

George Eliot's intentions for *The Spanish Gypsy* were of the highest. The inspiration for the story came to her one day in Venice, when she saw a painting of the Annunciation at the Scuola di San Rocco:

> It occurred to me that here was a great dramatic motive of the same class as those used by the Greek dramatists, yet specifically differing from them. A young maiden, believing herself to be on the eve of the chief event of her life— marriage—about to share in the ordinary lot of women, full of young hope, has suddenly announced to her that she is chosen to fulfil a great destiny, entailing a terribly different experience from that of ordinary womanhood. She is chosen, not by any momentary arbitrariness, but as a result of foregoing hereditary conditions: she obeys. "Behold the handmaid of the Lord." [26]

It is the same theme that Paul Claudel used so magnificently in *L'Annonce Faite À Marie*. Of course, as might be expected, George Eliot interposes her own personal ideas regarding duty:

> We cannot be utterly blind to the results of duty, since that cannot be duty which is not already judged to be for human good . . . In Silva is presented the claim of fidelity to social pledges; in Fedalma, the claim constituted by an hereditary lot less consciously shared.[27]

Heredity and obligation—these are the twin elements of duty. Tragedy comes of rebellion.

> Silva presents the tragedy of entire rebellion: Fedalma of a grand submission, which is rendered vain by the effects of Silva's rebellion: Zarca, the struggle for a great end, rendered vain by the surrounding conditions of life.[28]

A grand design indeed, one which would have been treated in the grand manner had George Eliot been either Shakespeare or Browning, which is to say had her ability as a poet equaled her genius as a novelist. But she was neither Shakespeare nor Browning, and the kindest criticism one can make of *The Spanish Gypsy* is to offer it as an example of what can happen when a writer strays too far afield from his *métier*. Blank verse was definitely not George Eliot's forte, and, even as closet drama, *The Spanish Gypsy* lacks the power of Browning's *A Blot in the 'Scutcheon*, or even Tennyson's *Becket*. Also, she was obviously too immersed in Positivism. Despite her insistence to Frederic Harrison that art and propaganda are two separate and distinct things, the shadow of Auguste Comte falls across every page. There are some good aphorisms, supplied by Zarca:

> . . . no great deed is done
> By falterers who ask for certainty.

No good is certain, but the steadfast mind,
The undivided will to seek the good.

Or—

The worst of misery
Is when a nature framed for noblest things
Condemns itself in youth to petty joys,
And, sore athirst for air, breathes scanty life
Gasping from the shallows. You are saved
From such poor doubleness. The life we choose
Breathes high, and sees a full arched firmament.
Our deeds shall speak like rock-hewn messages,
Teaching great purpose to the distant time.

Such polished platform eloquence from an untutored gypsy does, however, strain one's credulity. And the pedestrian uninspired narrative sections—for example:

Silva had doffed his mail, and with it all
The heavy harness of his warlike cares.
He had not seen Fedalma.

serve only to make the "dramatic" sections seem more bombastic.

The Spanish Gypsy, however, is also proof that no writing done by a good writer is without its use, no matter how inferior to his best it may be. George Eliot had achieved her purpose in the poem—she had tried her hand at a totally different literary form, and, among her own contemporaries, received great acclaim for it, even though some of the praise may have been given in the spirit of Dr. Samuel Johnson's comment about the dog dancing on its hind legs. And the poem afforded her a technical advantage, as well as personal satisfaction. The sheer discipline of fitting ideas and words into iambic pentameter would direct her attention very closely to language, as a medium, to the ultimate benefit of her prose.

On November 22, 1868, Marian Evans Lewes wrote in her Journal,

> The return of this St. Cecilia's Day finds me in better health than usual with me in these last six months. But I am not yet engaged in any work that makes a higher life for me—a life that is young and grows—though in my other life I am getting old and decaying. It is a day for resolves and determinations.[29]

It was her forty-ninth birthday, and she felt that she had reached a kind of crossroads. Definitely she was an established writer now and, for the first time in many years, she was free from financial anxieties. Her books were selling well on both sides of the Atlantic. But she knew that she must write again; she could not rest on her laurels, for much was expected of her. Any new book would be judged, not only on its own merits, but also according to her reputation. The Christmas season passed without any notations regarding future work, only her usual end-of-year summary of achievements, thanksgivings, and hopes. But by January 1, 1869, she had reached a decision. "I have set myself many tasks for the year—I wonder how many will be accomplished?" [30] Poems were among these tasks, but the most important, from the point of view of her own profession and the history of literature, is stated in the simplest of lines:

"A novel called *Middlemarch*." [31]

XVII

The necessary part of great intellectual powers in such a success as *Middlemarch* is obvious. The subtitle of the book is *A Study of Provincial Life,* and it is no idle pretension. The sheer informedness about society, its mechanism, the ways in which people of different classes live and (if they have to) earn their livelihoods, impresses us with its range, and it is real knowledge; that is, it is knowledge alive with understanding. George Eliot had said in *Felix Holt,* by way of apology for the space she devoted to "social changes" and "public matters": "there is no private life which has not been determined by a wider public life." The aim implicit in this remark is magnificently achieved in *Middlemarch*, and it is achieved by a novelist whose genius manifests itself in a profound analysis of the individual.[1]

Any commentary on *Middlemarch* must begin with the unequivocal statement that it is, by every criterion of the novel and all canons of criticism, a masterpiece. It was received with the greatest acclaim in its own time, and appreciation for it seems only to grow with the years. Virginia Woolf pronounced it "one of the few English novels really written for grown up people," [2] and, indeed, it falls into the category of such works as Browning's *The Ring and the Book,* which Henry James described as being like a great Gothic cathedral "that, with any first approach, we but walk vaguely and slowly, rather bewilderedly, round and round it. . . ." [3] *Middlemarch* is not as exalted as a cathedral, but it bears a strong resemblance to those sturdy enduring parish churches of Warwickshire and East Anglia which have stood for centuries, symbols of continuity in the land which they survey. For in *Middlemarch* George Eliot set herself the task of depicting not just individuals, but an entire society, whose roots run deep into the past, which—like the churches— remains basically the same, no matter what conflicts disturb the surface. More than that, she transcended the limitations of her own time; her account of human experience in this novel is as true today as it was in 1871 when it was published.

That *Middlemarch* took much time to write is not surprising. It would be amazing if the contrary were true, and the novel would certainly have been less than it is. The author's knowledge of her locale and characters required, literally, saturation in both; and it was not until

August 1869, seven months after that New Year's Day entry in her Journal, that she actually began to write. Even then, only the Fred Vincy–Featherstone section, with a doctor as one of the characters, was clearly in her mind. On September 11th, she wrote with her characteristic anxiety, "I do not feel very confident that I shall ever make anything satisfactory of 'Middlemarch.' " [4] On December 31, *1870*, over a year later, she noted, "I have written only 100 pages—good printed pages—of a story which I began about the opening of November, and at present mean to call 'Miss Brooke.' " [5] She was referring to the Dorothea Brooke–Edward Casaubon section, which she was eventually to merge with the Vincy–Featherstone story. It is not until March of 1871 that the words "my novel" can definitely be interpreted as *Middlemarch* as we now know it.

Behind this long gestation period of experimentation and blocking, in addition to the author's inner trepidations about her ability to write the book she wished to write, were an additional series of calamities and griefs. Illness and a "leaden pressure" [6] plagued her during the early months of 1869, and in March she was advised to get out of the damp English weather. She and Lewes went to Italy, traveling this time by way of the Riviera and the Grande Corniche, but it rained incessantly, and even the comforts of Thomas Adolphus Trollope's villa just outside Florence brought no ease to her general sense of malaise. A dreadful sore throat and chronic headache added to her miseries. Naples was a little better, and Marian recovered sufficiently to enjoy the week at Rome. It was there, on April 18, 1869, that she first met John Cross. Lewes was already acquainted with the Cross family through Herbert Spencer, and Elizabeth Cross, John's sister, had been one of the first ladies to call on Marian

Lewes at The Priory. When John Cross and his mother arrived in Rome, hearing that the Leweses were at the Hotel Minerva, he went immediately to leave their cards. He was a great admirer of George Eliot's novels, especially *Romola*, and he was delighted at this fortuitous opportunity to meet the celebrated author. Fifteen years later, after her death, when he was writing her biography, he recalled the afternoon when he and his mother called upon her, and put down his first impression of the lady who was later to become his wife:

> I have a very vivid recollection of George Eliot sitting on the sofa with my mother by her side, entirely engrossed with her . . . And through the dimness of these fifteen years, and all that has happened in them, I still seem to hear, as I first heard then, the low, earnest, deep musical tones of her voice: I still seem to see the fine brows with the abundant auburn-brown hair framing them, the long head broadening at the back, the gray-blue eyes, constantly changing in expression, but always with a very loving, almost deprecating, look at my mother, the finely formed, thin, transparent hands, and a whole *Wesen* that seemed in complete harmony with everything one expected to find in the author of "Romola." [7]

The Leweses returned to The Priory on May 5th, but any good the journey might have done them was quickly dissipated, for, three days later, Thornton Lewes arrived in England from Natal. His father had received a letter from him in January, telling of various ailments, and he had advised his son to come home as quickly as possible; but neither he nor Marian had had the remotest idea of how serious their son's condition was. Thornton had contracted a spinal disease, the result of an injury received when wrestling, and he was in constant, agonizing pain. Morphine was the only medication then known to relieve such suffering, and it had to be administered at regular intervals almost around the clock. Marian was trying to begin her novel, and also to help Lewes to nurse Thornton, whom she dearly loved. That the young man was only twenty-five years old made the situation doubly tragic; Marian wept at his patience and courage, for, in the rare intervals when pain left him, he could still enjoy music, and his conversation had all his father's spirited charm. These brief flashes of what he once had been grieved her almost as much as the shrieks of pain which, without morphine, he could scarcely control.

The illness dragged on for months. There were occasional respites, when Thornton could rest on an iron bedstead on The Priory lawn,[8] alternating with violent relapses which made him nearly hysterical. In August he suffered an attack of paraplegia, which paralyzed him from the waist down. Miraculously, he recovered the use of his legs, but his strength and powers of resistance had been lowered substantially. Marian suffered excruciatingly with and for him, to the point where she nearly collapsed under the strain. "I have such a horror of a mental breakdown, like old Mrs. Trollope's, for example," she wrote to Sara Hennell. "Her body was as strong as iron; but, for years before she died, she had totally lost her memory." [9] In late September there was a brief improvement, though "His face has more than ever of that wizened look that has come instead of its old beauty, and that pains me to see; I cannot shake off the impression it creates in me of a slow withering." [10] Marian's fears were prophetic. On October 9th, Thornton died in her arms. She was heartbroken. "This death seems to me the beginning of our own." [11]

Lewes, alarmed at how frail and ill she looked, and fearing that indeed she might break down completely, took her to Limpsfield in Surrey, to the home of friends, where she could be assured of quiet and solitude. Though his own grief was great, he had been more prepared for his son's death—his medical knowledge had made it impossible for him to anticipate any other outcome. Now his concern was all for Marian. He did not permit her either to read or to answer letters, or even to do very much writing. Gradually, she became calmer and more reconciled; she would never have wanted to see Thornton in a state of utter dependency for the most fundamental physical care. Slowly, her health and strength returned under Lewes's watchful and tender eyes. Back at The Priory in mid-November, she was fully ready to begin work on her novel.

But now Lewes became ill. He had given prodigally beyond the measure of his strength to Thornton, and then had drawn upon it even more to care for his wife, without giving himself any time at all to recover from his own grief. Prolonged headaches, fainting spells, and numbness in his hands and feet were alarming symptoms, and finally, in March 1870, with Marian's insistence added to the doctor's, he agreed that he needed a rest. His wife breathed a sigh of relief: "An interesting journey in which we shall see many acquaintances and be within reach of amusements will be the best thing for him," she wrote John Blackwood. "He *looks* better than usual, but he is conscious of a marked diminution in his power of brain-work, and I observe, in everything he undertakes, that while there is the same intensity as of old, he is quickly fatigued." [12] But, of course, there had to be a reason for travel; Lewes was not one to feel that rest included idleness. Fortunately, a reason lay at hand— he had embarked upon an enormous psychological study called *Problems of the Life and Mind,* and he was deeply interested in the diagnosis and treatment of mental illness. Some very important work in that field was being done in Germany. Accordingly, to Germany they would go.

Berlin was their first stop, where Lewes immediately plunged into a round of visits to hospitals and lunatic asylums, conferring with professors and doctors. He was elated at being seated in the section reserved for dignitaries at the University festival,[13] and he and Marian were invited to a formal dinner at the American Embassy, where their host, Ambassador George Bancroft, saw to it that they met some of the most important people in Berlin. Prince Frederick of Schleswig-Holstein was especially cordial; he even invited them to be his house guests. The season was a brilliant one musically and theatrically; Anton Rubinstein, Hans von Bülow, and Clara Schumann were all giving concerts, and at the opera the Leweses heard *The Marriage of Figaro* and *Tannhäuser*. After a week of festivity, they went on to Vienna, stopping briefly at Prague en route, where another round of entertainment had been planned for them. Their activities had to be curtailed, however, because Marian—who had been fighting a cold in Berlin—now succumbed to an ulcerated throat. She had to spend most of her time at the hotel, while Lewes pursued his scientific investigations and attended such social functions as he could be persuaded to attend without her. She recovered sufficiently to enjoy Salzburg and Munich, and Lewes, too, seemed completely over the alarming symptoms that had assailed him in England. Certainly his eagerness to begin on his new book was at peak. Marian, however, was still not too well when they returned home in May. "I am languid and my novel languishes, too," she wrote in her Journal. "But tomorrow may be better than today." [14]

The end of May was taken up with a three-day visit to Oxford, where they were the guests of Mark Pattison, rector of Lincoln College, and his wife. Entertainment was the order of the day for the distinguished visitors; among the people invited to meet them was Mary Augusta Arnold, niece of the poet Matthew Arnold, who would later become the novelist Mrs. Humphry Ward. Benjamin Jowett, Master of Balliol College, came to supper, and so did a young tutor named Walter Pater, who had made quite an impression with his articles on the Pre-Raphaelite painters. Since Marian had recently made the acquaintance of Dante Gabriel Rossetti and Edward Burne-Jones, Pater's conversation interested her greatly. But the Oxford visit, though exciting, was exhausting, and when she and Lewes returned to London, she noted in her Journal that they were "delighted to be under their own roof again." [15] She looked forward to a good two months of uninterrupted work, before paying a return visit to Limpsfield in August.

Lewes, however, again became suddenly and violently ill. The doctor prescribed sea air, a favorite nineteenth-century panacea for untreatable ailments, so they arranged to go to Cromer, a watering place on the Yorkshire coast. "To me, the most desirable thing just now seems to have one home, and stay there," Marian wrote to Barbara Bodichon. "I get more and more disinclined to the perpetual makeshifts of a migratory life, and care more and more for the order and habitual objects of home." [16] During their month away, they also visited Whitby, where Mrs. Burne-Jones was vacationing with her children. The month of August was spent at Limpsfield, where Lewes continued to improve, much to Marian's relief, and in September they were once more back at The Priory, rested, refreshed, and finally in what might be called good health. Lewes was busy revising his *Biographical History of Philosophy* for the fourth edition and was re-reading all his sources, and Marian was at her desk. Though the world was saddened by the bitter Franco-Prussian War, which found Marian's sympathies divided between the two antagonists—"Thoughts about war are not sanitary, and they urge themselves through every other subject" [17]—she was happy that her husband was well and that she was in better spirits than she had been for over a year; and, above all, that she was able to *work*.

Once the story of "Miss Brooke" merged with the story of Fred Vincy's expectations, the writing evidently went smoothly enough during the winter of 1870 and the early spring of 1871. On March 19, 1871, Marian wrote in her Journal, "I have written about 236 pages (print) of my novel which I want to get off my hands by next November. My present fear is that I have too much matter—too many *momenti*." [18] She was also involved in a very active social life; the guest list for Sunday afternoons at The Priory had greatly expanded and frequently close friends were invited to luncheon before the general "at home." At one such luncheon late in April of 1871, Robert Browning and Anthony Trollope were entertained, along with the Russian novelist Ivan Turgenev, whom Lewes had known in Berlin twenty-three years before. The lists of other guests at the receptions and musicals included an increasing number of women—Mrs. Clough, the widow of Arthur Hugh Clough the poet, Lady Colville, whose husband was a member of the Privy Council, and Lady Castletown. "Society" had indeed accepted the Leweses, and, if any other indication were needed, an invitation to them both to participate in the Scott Centenary Festival at Edinburgh that August proves that they were no longer regarded askance.

The Priory was in need of extensive alterations and repairs that spring, and Marian continued to suffer severe headaches and general lassitude, so Lewes went in search of a country retreat. He found a charming house at Shottermill in Surrey—interestingly enough, it was owned by Mrs. Alexander Gilchrist, whose husband had been the first biographer of William Blake, so its literary associations as well as its quiet location immediately appealed to Marian. They moved in—bags, baggage, and *Middlemarch*—on the second of May. On the thirty-first, John Blackwood came down to see them, and carried away the completed manuscript of Book I, "Miss Brooke." For Marian, by this time, had decided what would be the grand design of the novel: there would be eight "books," each one focused on episodes involving separate sets of characters, subtly and intricately connected by the simple fact that they all lived in the town of Middlemarch. The final intermeshing of these lives would not become fully apparent until the end of the novel, and the conclusion would not be so much a climax as a resolution to the several situations, with the underlying feeling that the story told had been only one of many—that the people whom George Eliot had come to know so well and had presented so vividly would continue to live their lives, even though no author's or reader's eye would be upon them.

George Eliot's all-consuming desire to present as complete a picture as possible—almost a photographic reproduction as far as external details were concerned—led to the unusual length of the novel, which ultimately was published in four volumes instead of the standard three.

The length worried the author; it also worried John Blackwood, who made tentative, tactful inquiries as to whether all the details included were really necessary. He was delighted as portions of the manuscript reached him in Edinburgh during the summer of 1871; Shottermill had turned out to be an ideal retreat for the Leweses, for there were no interruptions except welcome ones, like the call the Tennysons paid on them in August. Still, Blackwood was mystified by the fact that Book II, "Old and Young," seemed to begin as though George Eliot were starting a totally new novel, instead of continuing the action of Book I. It was a quite daring approach, one which, her editor warned, might be criticized, but he added that "this does not matter where all is so fresh and true to life." [19] The author replied with her customary directness:

> . . . I hope there is nothing that will seem to be irrelevant to my design, which is to show the gradual action of ordinary causes, rather than exceptional, and to show this in some directions which have not been from time immemorial the beaten path.[20]

After this frank statement, Blackwood had nothing but praise, and willingly acceded to Lewes's suggestion that the novel be published first in half-volume parts at two-month intervals, a procedure that Victor Hugo had followed successfully with *Les Misérables* in 1862, reserving the four-volume edition for later publication. Accordingly, the first number of *Middlemarch* appeared in the bookstores on December 1, 1871. The novel was not yet finished, but its plan was fixed so firmly in George Eliot's mind that, this time, working only a few months in advance of publication, even interrupted by a trip to Germany in the autumn of 1872 for Lewes to take the waters at Homburg, does not seem to have been any trial to her. And she was constantly encouraged by critical praise as the successive parts appeared: as she noted in her Journal in May 1872, "The reception of the book hitherto has been quite beyond what I could have believed beforehand, people exalting it quite above anything else I have written." [21] Book VII was finished on November 4th, in time for December publication, and the entire novel was issued in four volumes for the Christmas trade. Through all these months, her husband was her devoted "encourager." It was at this time that he became, in effect, her manager and secretary; it was he who wrote her letters, both business and personal, and it is to him that the world owes the delightful description of George Eliot in the throes of composition:

> She is writing—writing—writing!—to parody Garrick's admirer I will say—"Why Sir, *away* from her desk she is a perfect woman, but *at* the desk—oh!—my!!—God!!!" [22]

Nevertheless, he kept her *at* the desk. His intense pride in her, both as a woman and as an author, made him want to spare her every conceivable intrusion on her time, so that she could devote all her energies to what he knew would be a masterpiece.

To *Middlemarch* at fifty-two, George Eliot brought the full strength of her maturity, the result of over forty years of reading, study, observation, thought, and experience. Everything she herself had become, and every literary technique she had learned, went into the novel's creation. Every character is the complete realization of those scattered throughout her earlier novels, and the four separate story lines are also culminations of earlier themes. It is impossible to summarize the plot of *Middlemarch* without doing it grave injustice; the novel must be read *in toto* from beginning to end for one to receive its full impact. It is possible, however, to consider the four stories, bearing in mind that these are so carefully linked together that they cannot really be seen in isolation.

The two primary plots revolve around two marriages, those of Dorothea Brooke and Edward Casaubon, and Tertius Lydgate and Rosamond Vincy. The marriage relationship had been of interest to George Eliot in *Romola,* but Tito's and Romola's marriage seems shallow set beside the incisive delineation of Dorothea's unhappiness with her scholar husband who is twenty-seven years her senior. Like Romola, Dorothea is led to accept Casaubon's proposal under a cloud of illusion—the illusion that she can somehow be of help to a man whom she considers the epitome of wisdom and intellectual brilliance. Like Maggie Tulliver—and Marian Evans—she has considerable intellectual capacity of her own, but Middlemarch has offered her little or no scope for fulfilling her ardent longings. The only way she can see to accomplish any of the things she dreams of so constantly is by marriage to a man who will allow her to live in the luster of *his* attainments.

> She felt sure that she would have accepted the judicious Hooker if she had been born in time to save him from that wretched mistake that he had made in matrimony, or John Milton when his blindness came on; or any of the other great men whose odd habits would have been a glorious piety to endure . . . The really delightful marriage must be that where your husband was a sort of father and could teach you even Hebrew if you wished it.

Yet she is no blue-stocking spinster; she is young, ardent, and beautiful. She is courted by Sir James Chettam, whom her family urges her to marry, but she cannot envision life with him as anything better than the usual routine of Middlemarch, which, delightful as it is, does not satisfy her deep yearning after something—anything —that will make high demands of her. George Eliot compares her to St. Teresa of Ávila:

> Here and there is born a Saint Theresa [*sic*] foundress of nothing, whose loving heartbeats and sobs after an unattained goodness tremble off and are dispersed among hindrances instead of centering in some long-recognizable deed.

Dorothea, too, wants to do good for the world. "I have a belief of my own, and it comforts me," she tells her husband's cousin, Will Ladislaw.

> "That by desiring what is perfectly good, even when we do not quite know what it is and cannot do what we would, we are part of the Divine power against evil—widening the skirts of light and making the struggles with darkness narrower."

Then Edward Casaubon comes into her life. To most observers, he is an elderly, unattractive man—Celia, Dorothea's sister, comments quite frankly on his two white moles with hairs in them—whose life's work, a book to be called *A Key To All Mythologies*, which after thirty years is still in the note-taking stage, is more of a joke than anything else. But Dorothea feels only "reverential gratitude" at the thought of his deigning to marry her, and, during their short engagement, she willingly works to turn herself into the kind of wife who will be worthy of such a man. She will make no changes in his house despite its gloominess; there will be no piano in the drawing room because music fatigues Mr. Casaubon. She starts to learn Greek; it is more difficult than she had anticipated (the author's irony is delightful, here), and she quickly discovers that her husband is only annoyed by her diffident offer to help him classify his quantities of notes so that he may, finally, begin to write his book. Their wedding trip to Rome is a disaster. George Eliot does not give a clinical account of their complete lack of physical compatibility, nor is it needed. The picture of Dorothea sobbing her heart out in their luxurious hotel suite, while Mr. Casaubon is spending yet another day rummaging for manuscripts in the Vatican Library, is all that is necessary for a perceptive reader to understand that no communication exists on any level in this marriage.

The dreadful moment comes when Dorothea is forced to recognize that her husband is a fraud, that his great book will never be written; and, even if it is, it will not be the magnificent contribution to scholarship which he had led her to expect. Casaubon has collected material for too long; other scholars have already written and published work far in advance of his. She shrinks from this knowledge in revulsion; yet she pities the man intensely, for, if he has been blind, so has she. When he asks her to promise to carry on his work after his death (which neither of them realizes is so imminent), she is torn between compassion for him and her own honest recognition that the work is worthless:

> . . . his heart was bound up in his work only: that was the end for which his failing life was to be eked out by hers . . . [But] if she were to say "No! If you die, I will put no finger to your work"—it seemed as though she would be crushing that bruised heart.

Duty, not affection, makes her decide to do as he wishes, but he dies before she can give her answer. And even after his death, she is not free of him; his will gives her all his fortune provided she does not marry Will Ladislaw, his attractive artist cousin, of whose attentiveness to Dorothea he has been—without the slightest reason—almost pathologically jealous. At this point, however, Dorothea courageously refuses to be bound any longer. Even before her poignant words to Ladislaw, "I will learn what everything costs," she has learned the lesson that everything *does* cost something, in strength, emotion, and love, if not in coin of the realm.

We sympathize with Dorothea in her struggle for self-realization, and also, strange to say, we are made to sympathize with Casaubon. Nothing is more pitiful than that individual who has overrated his intellectual powers; Casaubon is comparable to George Tesman in Ibsen's *Hedda Gabler,* though he lacks Tesman's comic overtones. Not that Casaubon does not provoke laughter, but it is impatient, ironic laughter. His letter of proposal is a masterstroke of characterization; such phrases as, "Our conversations have, I think, made sufficiently clear to you the tenor of my life and purposes: a tenor unsuited, I am aware, to the commoner order of minds," and, "I await the expression of your sentiments with an anxiety which it would be the better part of wisdom (were it possible) to divert by a more arduous labour than usual," indicate that pride in himself and his own attainments which will be his downfall. If Casaubon was indeed modeled on Dr. Rufus Brabant, one can only stand in awe of a writer who could transmute so deep a personal humiliation into such superb fiction. George Eliot might have drawn him with bitterness, made him a villain. But Casaubon emerges as a pitiable, but nonetheless recognizable, human being. Though he willingly poses as a model for a painting of St. Thomas Aquinas (sly irony is here) , inwardly he knows that he is not the great scholar that he thinks he has made the world believe. And he, too, has entered marriage with high hopes and illusions, only to be devastated by its inevitable realities:

> . . . the young creature who had worshipped him with perfect trust had quickly turned into a critical wife, and early instances of criticism and resentment had made an impression which no tenderness and submission afterwards could remove. To his suspicious interpretation, Dorothea's silence was now a suppressed rebellion; a remark from her which he had not in any way anticipated was an assurance of conscious superiority; her gentle answers had an irritating cautiousness in them; and when she acquiesced, it was a self-approved effort at forebearance. The tenacity with which he strove to hide this inward drama made it the more vivid for him, as we hear with more keenness what we wish others not to hear.

Locked in his own self-imposed isolation, knowing that he is old and ill, unwilling to accept Dorothea's slightest overture, he is corroded within by suspicion and jealousy that drive him to compose the infamous will, which, in turn, leads his wife to do the one thing he does not wish —the one thing he fears: to marry a younger, more attractive man. He misreads Dorothea completely, in trying to make her accept her future financial security on his terms, and he is condemned for it after his death by the very people he had held most in contempt. In her penetrating analysis of the Casaubon marriage, George Eliot presents the tragedy created by ignorance and self-delusion on the part of both husband and wife.

Another kind of tragic marriage is that of Tertius Lydgate and Rosamond Vincy. Like Dorothea and Casaubon, they carry within them the seeds of their own destruction (a favorite George Eliot theme) which, combined with the social pressures of Middlemarch, lead to disaster—a different kind of disaster, of course, for these two are compelled to go on living together, even after they have learned the full truth about each other. Also, in this marriage, George Eliot delineates fully the effect that outside forces have in directing and shaping human destiny. Dorothea and Casaubon are county gentry, and thus, in a sense, are removed from the immediate atmosphere of the town. But Lydgate is a doctor, and he is dependent on the good will of Middlemarch for his living. Rosamond is the daughter of one of the town's leading manufacturers, but she has no personal income and is completely dependent on her husband's fortunes. That she does not realize this is perhaps not greatly to her discredit, at least at first, for Victorian wives were kept in ignorance of their husbands' business affairs. But her continuing self-indulgence, when Lydgate tells her in so many words that they must economize or face bankruptcy, indicates her basic selfishness, as does her refusal to stand by her husband when misfortune finally strikes. She is beautiful, and she knows it, but she is also devious, and willing to go to any lengths to get what she wants. The scene where she agrees to follow Lydgate's wishes, all the time knowing full well that she has already done the exact opposite, is merciless in its exposure of her as a shallow little coquette. John Blackwood, after reading this section, wrote that Lydgate was to be commended for not beating her! [23] One wonders just how much of Agnes Lewes went into the creation of Rosamond Vincy. Her deliberate inveigling of Ladislaw to visit her in her husband's absence is contemptible—not that Ladislaw should be censured less for going, but it is plainly Rosamond who is pulling the strings. Only when Dorothea manages to speak with her does she come to her senses. Dorothea's gentle words,

"Marriage is so unlike everything else. There is something even awful in the nearness it brings. Even if we loved someone else better than those we were married to, it would be no use . . . I mean, marriage drinks up all our power of giving or getting any blessedness from that sort of love. I know it may be very dear, but it murders our marriage, and then the marriage stays with us like a murder, and everything else is gone. And then our husband —if he loved and trusted us, and we have not helped him, but made a curse in his life—"

shame Rosamond into an even greater self-realization, for she knows, as does all Middlemarch, that Edward Casaubon neither loved nor trusted his wife as Lydgate does her.

But in this marriage, the husband is also at fault. Lydgate is no knight in shining armor, though he begins with high ideals and aspirations. As a doctor, he is eager to cure the sick, and he has many plans for improving the local hospital. He has studied at Edinburgh and Paris and is proud of his knowledge, which, in his opinion, makes him a cut above the average run of the medical profession. Naturally, he runs into opposition; the local doctors are perfectly content with the status quo. His first mistake is when he accepts the assistance of Bulstrode, one of the local magnates, whom he dislikes but thinks he can use. When he votes with Bulstrode for the Reverend Mr. Tyke as chaplain for the hospital, and against Mr. Farebrother, for whom he has a sincere liking but in whom he finds no possible help for his own self-advancement, he takes the first step on the downward path. His second error is when he becomes involved with Rosamond Vincy. Had he possessed a modicum of common sense, he would have realized that Dorothea Brooke was the proper girl for him; but Dorothea does not fit his notion of what a wife should be:

To a man under such circumstances, taking a wife is something more than a question of adornment, however highly he may rate this; and Lydgate was disposed to give it first

275

place among wifely functions. To his taste, guided by a single conversation, here was the point upon which Miss Brooke would be found wanting, notwithstanding her undeniable beauty. She did not look at things from the proper feminine angle. The society of such a woman was about as relaxing as going from your work to teach the second form, instead of reclining in a paradise with sweet laughs for birdnotes and blue eyes for a heaven.

So he is easily trapped into marriage by Rosamond Vincy: "In half an hour he left the house an engaged man, whose soul was not his own, but the woman's to whom he had bound himself." Because of Rosamond, he is forced to make one compromise after another, until he finally accepts money from Bulstrode under circumstances which make Middlemarch believe that he, too, is as dishonest as his "benefactor" has been revealed to be. True to form, Rosamond turns on him; only with Dorothea's help is he able to ride out the storm. In the end, he and his wife must leave Middlemarch. He prospers as a doctor, but he has been stripped of his ideals and hopes, for Rosamond and Middlemarch between them have effectively ruined him—and he cannot leave Rosamond. "He had chosen this fragile creature and had taken the burden of her life upon his arms. He must walk as he could, carrying that burden pitifully."

Running parallel to these two marriages is the courtship of Fred Vincy and Mary Garth. This was the first section of the novel to be written, and involves Rosamond's brother, Fred, whose entire life has been governed by his expectations of inheriting his Uncle Featherstone's property. Not that he is in the slightest avid about this, but thanks to the continual assurances of his family and friends, and what he takes to be assurances from his uncle, he has never really applied himself to any useful work. His father wants him to be a clergyman (here George Eliot incisively scores the wrong kind of parental ambition), but it is to Fred's credit that he realizes his complete lack of vocation to the ministry. It is also to his credit that he is steadfastly in love with as fine a girl as Mary Garth, though her family is not quite so high in the social scale as the Vincys because her father is an estate agent, and not a wealthy manufacturer. Fred's charm and rather feckless disposition recall both Stephen Guest and Arthur Donithorne, but he is far more likable than either of them. And when his uncle finally dies, and the will reveals that the estate has been left to a remote cousin, Fred pulls himself together with a vengeance. Defying his father—and, paradoxically, earning his respect—he goes to Caleb Garth, Mary's father, to learn how to manage land. In the end, he is rewarded; he is given Stone Court, the property he had hoped to inherit, to manage, with option to buy when he earns enough money. Mary, assured that he has finally settled down, marries him, to the general approval of Middlemarch—including the Vincys.

Binding these three plots together is the story of Nicholas Bulstrode, whose activities as the town's leading banker naturally lead to his having a finger in most of the pies. Like Matthew Jermyn in *Felix Holt*, he is a powerful man, and he exults in his power. By his *yea* or *nay*, he can alter any course of events at will, and he is rather more pleased than not that he is feared, instead of liked. Respectability envelops him, and he takes a sanctimonious pride in the fact that God's will and his own are remarkably similar. It is not until very near the end of the story that his own closely guarded secret guilt is revealed—that his great wealth began when he worked as a clerk for a receiver of stolen goods, and that, though he had known his first wife's daughter was living at the time of their marriage (his first wife had been the wealthy Widow Dunkirk, many years his senior), he had concealed this information from her so that he might eventually inherit her fortune. One other man, Raffles, had known that Mary Dunkirk was alive; he had been paid for his silence, and Bulstrode had presumed that he was dead. He had moved to Middlemarch and had lived there in complacent safety for many years. Then the disreputable Raffles reappears and begins to blackmail him. Bulstrode's desperation grows as the demands increase:

> It was not that he was in danger of legal punishment or beggary; he was in danger only of seeing disclosed to the judgment of his neighbors and the mournful perception of his wife certain facts of his past life which would render him an object of scorn and an opprobrium of the religion with which he had diligently associated himself.

When chance delivers Raffles into his hands, ill and on the point of death, Bulstrode's struggle with his conscience is appalling, but he is too tangled in the web of lies he has created about himself to resist temptation. He does not kill Raffles outright, but he lets the housekeeper watch by the man's bedside at night and does not tell her when the doses of opium—which Lydgate has prescribed —should be stopped. Thus, when Raffles dies, Bulstrode has drawn Lydgate into his web, and, when the facts are ultimately disclosed, the doctor, too, suffers from the town's censure.

Bulstrode's "fatal secret" could be considered the one weakness of *Middlemarch*. It is a variation of the "missing heir" theme, and that Will Ladislaw turns out to be that missing heir to the Dunkirk fortune is almost too convenient. (The character of Ladislaw, too, is disappointing; he is not nearly so believable or fully realized as the rest. Whether or not he was added merely to provide the possibility of a happy ending for Dorothea is difficult to say. If he was modeled on George Henry Lewes, this might explain the author's lack of perspective in presenting him.) Fortunately, however, the attention is not focused on the action of concealment, as is done in *Felix Holt*, but on the remorse of Nicholas Bulstrode, "this unhappy man who had longed for years to be better than he was," who has tried to conceal and rationalize his wrong-doing, and finally has to face far worse consequences than might have been his, had he at once admitted his guilt. Like Casaubon, he evokes pity, for his essential weakness is all too human. There is no more poignant scene in *Middlemarch* than the one where Mrs. Bulstrode, her eyes opened at last to the true character of the man she had married in such blind trust, comes to stand by him.

> A movement of new compassion and old tenderness went through her like a great wave, and putting one hand on his which rested on the arm of the chair and the other on his shoulder, she said solemnly but kindly, "Look up, Nicholas."
>
> He raised his eyes with a little start and looked at her half amazed for a moment . . . His confession was silent, and her promise of faithfulness was silent. Open-minded as she was, she nevertheless shrank from the words which would have expressed their mutual consciousness as she shrank from flakes of fire. She could not say, "How much is only slander and false suspicion?" And he did not say, "I am innocent."

The characters of *Middlemarch* alone make the book a memorable one, and George Eliot's remarkable gift for creating living, believable people is not confined to the leads. The Reverend Mr. Farebrother, who lives with his mother and her sister, is a splendid study of a small-town vicar striving to rise above the limitations of his society. Mr. Brooke, Dorothea's uncle, is delightful with his counsels of moderation—he had tried doing research himself, once, but discovered that "it wouldn't do"—and his bewilderment at feminine attitudes. Caleb Garth is a direct descendant of Adam Bede, but he has lived longer and seen more than Adam, so that his homely, practical common sense is tempered with wisdom. There is Mrs. Cadwallader, wife of one of the district clergy, with her sharp tongue and kind heart, and the doctors, each one carefully individualized, though they appear intermittently and briefly. Through them the context of Middlemarch is revealed; we are never unconscious of the fact that Dorothea, Lydgate, Casaubon, *et al.* are living within a well-defined social framework.

Nor is this society static, for George Eliot chose to set her novel in the period of the 1830's, the era of the Reform Bill, when tremendous social, political, and economic changes were sweeping across England. Every character in the novel is touched by the implications of the Reform Bill, from shopkeepers to landowners; Dorothea's interest in model cottages for Sir James Chettam's tenants is only one aspect of it. Another is the conversation in the pubs—again recollected from Marian Evans's childhood, but more finely honed and delineated, even, than those of *Felix Holt*. The political repercussions are centered on Mr. Brooke's candidacy for the House of Commons, which gives rise to some of the most amusing passages in the book. Mr. Brooke is a political innocent, whose canvassing for votes always ends in his being hoodwinked by his hoped-for constituents, and his speech on the hustings concludes in a shower of rotten eggs. Those interested in the social history of early nineteenth-century England will find a mine of information in *Middlemarch*.

That *Middlemarch* is George Eliot's finest novel, there is no doubt. To quote John Blackwood, "You are like a giant walking among us and fixing everyone you meet on canvas." [24] Her intention when she began to write was to give the world its world to study, and this she triumphantly realized. That she had done so was immediately recognized in her own time, but the most important opinion recorded about *Middlemarch* was, perhaps, her own. On November 4, 1872, she wrote in her Journal,

> I have finished my book and am thoroughly at peace about it—not because I am convinced of its perfection, but because I have tried to give out what was in me to give, and have not been hindered by illness or death from making my work a whole, such as it is.[25]

In a word, she knew that she had done well.

XVIII

Every creative artist, whatever his medium, hopes to attain that point in his professional development where it can be said that he has reached the heights. For an actor, this may be his performance as Hamlet; for a dramatic soprano, the rôle of Wagner's Isolde. For a composer, it may be a symphony which somehow distills and synthesizes those ideas, impressions, and emotions experienced in his lifetime and presents them all as an entity, complete and entire in itself; for a poet, it will be that poem which does not *mean*, but *is*. For George

Eliot, by her own admission, that height had been achieved in *Middlemarch;* it was not only a work unique for her, but it was also a landmark in literature. No novel written after 1872 could be quite the same as it would have been prior to *Middlemarch*—and that this distinction applied to her own work, as well, she was well aware. It is not surprising at all that she should feel even more strongly that familiar sense of "despair that I can ever produce anything else worth giving to the world"; [1] or that she should write very soberly to John Blackwood, "it is a bold thing to write another book after 'Middlemarch.' " [2] After Everest, what remains to climb? And since she never put pen to paper until she felt the "germ of some new work grow into imperious activity" [3] within her, for nearly eighteen months George Eliot remained away from the desk, and Marian Evans Lewes presided in The Priory drawing room.

For the first time, she allowed herself to enjoy being a celebrity. Courted, sought after, quoted—a volume entitled *Wise, Witty, and Tender Sayings of George Eliot* had been published early in 1872—she was *the* novelist of the hour, and she loved every moment of it. The winter and spring months of 1872–1873 marked the transformation of the informal Sunday receptions at The Priory to the nearest thing to a salon that London provided. Invitations there were coveted. The Leweses did not issue them indiscriminately; as Marian wrote in answer to a request for an invitation for a friend of a friend,

> I was very glad to see Mr. Jebb, for I had a pre-established respect for him and should willingly have invited him. In general, as you divine, we are averse to the enlargement of our circle by the hasty introduction of "friends," seeing

that very charming people are capable of having decidedly uncharming friends.[4]

In other words, throngs of curious people were not encouraged at The Priory, nor was idle chitchat. Marian preferred small groups, where conversation could be interesting and general enough to include everyone; the one taboo subject was the work of George Eliot. She usually sat in a large armchair beside the fire, where, dressed in handsome black silk or velvet, a lace mantilla over her gray-streaked hair, she was an arresting, imposing figure. Lewes played the role of host superbly; he was a delightful raconteur, and he always knew the precise moment to change a subject, or to interrupt a guest (usually a friend of a friend) who was prolonging a *tête-a-tête* with Marian to the exclusion of another guest. The guest list on these occasions read like a list of "Who's Who in Literature of the Seventies," and names such as Lord Arthur Russell and Sir Henry Holland indicate that "society" enjoyed frequenting The Priory receptions as well. There were also small evening parties during the week for very intimate friends; one of the most exciting of these was given in honor of Tennyson, when the Poet Laureate provided the entertainment by reading from his own works.

The Leweses were also in great demand as guests at dinner parties, and there were concerts, art exhibits, opera, and the theater. In December 1873, their social activity had reached the point where they bought a horse and carriage. "Keeping one's own carriage" was quite a Victorian status symbol; the Leweses had arrived indeed, socially as well as financially. They were also looking for a country house where they could have some restful seclusion during the summer months, for London was hectic during "the season" and Marian's health required occasional rest and escape from city smoke and fog. She and her husband were both fast reaching the point where they were wearied by summers in Europe, or making the circuit of English watering places, though they greatly enjoyed their visit to Cambridge in May 1873. Despite the cold weather, which put a damper on the boat races, Hallam Tennyson, the Laureate's son, was a delightful and thoughtful host. Later that year, they had a marvelous weekend as guests of Benjamin Jowett, Master of Balliol, a visit which they found so delightful that it became an annual event.

But Marian was not completely idle that year, as far as writing was concerned. Lewes was finally getting the first volume of his gigantic *Problems of the Life and Mind* (known jokingly in the family circle as his "Key to All Psychologies") ready for publication, and she spent the spring months helping him with the proofs. Evidently she was giving considerable thought to her own work, as well. At the end of June, they went abroad, having been unsuccessful in finding a small country house even to rent for the summer, and at Fontainebleu they walked through the park, discussing her new novel. At Frankfurt, on July 30th, Lewes bought "books on Jewish subjects," [5] and they also attended a Friday evening service at a synagogue. By November, she was writing to John Blackwood, "I am slowly simmering towards another big book . . ." [6] which, judging from her usual pattern of work, can be interpreted as meaning that she was compiling background material and perhaps even drawing up a preliminary outline. She and Lewes spent Christmas at Weybridge with John Cross and his mother; the Crosses had become close friends since their first acquaintance in Rome, and "Nephew Johnnie" had become a "Priory regular." Back at The Priory on January 1, 1874, Marian recorded in her Journal that "Nothing is wanting to my happiness but the uninterruped power of *work*." [7] And Lewes's letter to John Blackwood, dated January 7th, strikes a familiar chord:

> I am hard at work and wish she were; but she simmers and simmers, despairs and despairs, believes she can never do anything again worth doing, etc. etc. A word from you may give her momentary confidence. Once let her *begin*, and on she will go of her own impulse.[8]

Clearly, George Eliot had gone back to her desk. She was planning *Daniel Deronda*.

The writing of this, her last, novel took two and one-half years. There were the usual social distractions, family difficulties, and one tragedy—Bertie Lewes died in Natal in June of 1875, and word did not reach his parents until several months later. Lewes was not very well, and while he continued to work doggedly on *Problems of the Life and Mind*, more and more he had to devote himself to looking after Marian. Her health was very frail. She suffered four acute renal attacks while she was writing *Daniel Deronda*, and the excruciating pain she endured from them left her exhausted for weeks at a time. Her physical condition was undoubtedly one reason why the book went so slowly. It was not until May of 1875 that Volume I was ready for John Blackwood's perusal, but even his enthusiasm over it could not persuade her to hurry. In October of 1875, she finished the second volume, and it was decided to publish the book in monthly parts, as was done with *Middlemarch*. Blackwood wanted to begin publication in January 1876; Marian insisted that it be delayed until February.

I can't say that I am at all satisfied with the book, or that I have a comfortable sense of doing in it what I want to do; but Mr. Lewes is satisfied with it, and insists that since he is as anxious as possible for it to be fine, I ought to accept his impressions as trustworthy. So I resign myself.[9]

A comment more resembling the author of *Scenes from Clerical Life* than of *Middlemarch,* but in it lies the clue as to the major difficulty with *Daniel Deronda,* which has exasperated critics almost from its publication because of its unevenness and lack of cohesiveness, as compared with its immediate predecessor. The book did not fulfill the author's intention, but, in order to discuss the book intelligently, some attention should be given to what that intention was.

The first observation that a reading of *Daniel Deronda* provokes is that George Eliot is breaking new and different ground. The most obvious indication of this is that the setting and the background of the story represent the author's own contemporary world—the England of the 1870's. Even more important, her characters are drawn, not from small-town society or the country people, but from the county aristocracy who live on vast estates and spend their holidays at German watering places or aboard their yachts, for whom loss of money is a catastrophe far greater than loss of character. George Eliot is as merciless as were her American contemporaries Mark Twain or William Dean Howells, in *The Gilded Age* and *The Rise of Silas Lapham,* though she is more compassionate than either—or than Henry James, whose *Portrait of a Lady* appeared three years after *Daniel Deronda* and was greatly influenced by it—in exposing the shallow lives of those who have too much money and too little sense of duty. The reader, as might be expected, senses the author's personal disapproval of a man like Henleigh Grandcourt, as the exact antithesis of—indeed, an affront to—a man like Adam Bede, or her own father. Like Charles Dickens, George Eliot did not really approve of aristocratic society, but her view of it is less distorted than his because she never had cause to be jealous or scornful thereof. While she fully understood the value of—and the need for—money, her desire to acquire it had not been engendered by grinding poverty or debtor's prison; and she had never felt the slightest obligation to cater to the very rich, at the same time despising them. Thus, even her portrait of Henleigh Grandcourt, certainly the most insufferable and subtly cruel of that particular breed of Englishman (he is described on one occasion as looking "as neutral as an alligator"), is tempered with ironic insight and understanding. Grandcourt certainly deserves to have a miserable marriage, but he is the product of his *ambiance,* as well as of his own personality and self-determination. Had he been obliged to earn his living, instead of being permitted to live in expectation of becoming his uncle's heir, or marrying into wealth, he might have been a different kind of person.

A second new factor in *Daniel Deronda* is its definite emphasis on a particular theme, to the point where it almost becomes a *pièce à thèse.* George Eliot's reason for writing the novel as she did is given in the following passage from a letter dated October 29, 1876, to Harriet Beecher Stowe. (The two authors had become good friends through correspondence and greatly admired each other's books.)

> But precisely because I felt that the usual attitude of Christians towards Jews is—I hardly know whether to say more impious or more stupid, when viewed in the light

of their professed principles, I therefore felt urged to treat Jews with as much sympathy and understanding as my nature and knowledge could attain to . . . There is nothing I should care more to do than to rouse the imagination of men and women to a vision of human claims in those races of their fellowmen who must differ from them in customs and beliefs.[10]

She had sufficient material at hand to exemplify fully the English attitude toward Jews—Jews had not been able to run for public office until the Repeal of the Jewish Disabilities Act in 1864, and not until 1872, with the repeal of the Test Acts, were they permitted to enter Oxford or Cambridge. A particular instance of this kind of ruling which distressed her enough to mention it in one of her letters [11] was that of James Joseph Sylvester, recognized as a brilliant mathematician, who had taught at the University of Virginia and was first professor of mathematics at Johns Hopkins, but could not teach in his native country because he could not receive the requisite English degree. Added to the current general interest in the matter of Jews receiving certain legal rights was her own deep interest in Jewish history and religious thought dating back to her translation of Strauss in the 1840's, and back still farther to the King James version of the Scriptures on which she had been raised. To the end of her life, she especially loved to read aloud from the *Psalms* and the prophetic passages from *Isaiah* and *Jeremiah*. Long before the twentieth century popularized the concept of Judaeo-Christian relations, Marian Evans was aware of them, and in *Daniel Deronda* deliberately sought to give them a sympathetic, understanding presentation.

It is against this background that what she called the "Jewish elements" of the novel must be considered. For many readers and critics, these have proved a most irritating hodgepodge of sentimentality and propaganda, beginning with the character of the hero. Daniel Deronda, described as a "seraphic boy," is at times almost too handsome, courtly, noble-hearted, and generous. He is the ward (but not the heir) of Sir Hugo Mallinger and has been raised in the height of luxury. Eton, Cambridge, the grand tour—all have provided him with the requisites for making him a perfect "English gentleman." But, like Romola whom he closely resembles, there is more to Deronda than meets the eye. The reader's interest in him does not slacken because of his awareness that he does not wholly belong to the wealthy society that surrounds him at Diplow, his guardian's estate. This sense of being an outsider provides an element of mystery which is not solved until the book is near its end, and is all the more interesting because the solution is not dependent on any external agency like a missing will.

There are two separate plots in *Daniel Deronda;* the hero in his search for his identity functions as the link between them. One plot may be called the Deronda–Mirah–Mordecai story, and it is this part of the book that has been harshly criticized for its similarity to so many contrived, run-of-the-mill "sensation novels," in which a wealthy young man falls in love with a poverty-stricken girl, and love conquers all. It must be admitted that Deronda's appearance in a rowboat at the very moment when Mirah Lapidoth is about to throw herself into the Thames seems very opportune; however, this episode would have been considered more "realistic" in the 1870's than today, for those young girls in London who were faced with the grim alternatives of the river or the streets. And the "Jewish elements" do give a new twist to an old story. Mirah is the first Jewess that

Deronda has ever met; he has all the prejudices of his class against the Jews, but he cannot feel anything but compassion for Mirah. The fact that she has run away from a scheming father, who wants her to pursue a singing career as "protégée" of a wealthy patron of his choice, only to line his own pockets, arouses Deronda's indignation; that she is searching for her mother and brother from whom she has been separated is a bond between them, for all his life he has longed to know who his mother is. He takes Mirah to the home of Mrs. Meyrick, the mother of one of his college friends, who cares for her. Discovering that she has an exquisite voice, he arranges to have her sing at several social functions where influential people will hear her and find pupils for her to teach.

But he does more than this. He embarks on a search for Mirah's mother and brother, and, indirectly, this search leads him to the resolution of his own dilemma. He meets Mordecai, who asks him if he is a Jew. Deronda recoils from the question, but not from the man. Compelled by some strange attraction that he feels for the elderly clock-maker, he goes again to visit him. Long before he discovers that Mordecai is Mirah's brother, he has already subconsciously identified himself with the Messianic leader of the old man's dream:

"You must not be only a hand to me, but a soul—believing my belief—being moved by my reasons—hoping my hope —seeing the vision I point to—beholding a glory where I behold it!" Mordecai had taken a step nearer as he spoke, and now laid his hand on Deronda's arm with a tight grasp; his face little more than a foot off had something like a pale flame in it—an intensity of reliance that acted as a peremptory claim, while he went on.—"You shall take life; it will be planted afresh; it will grow. You shall take the inheritance; it has been gathering for ages. The generations are crowding on my narrow life as a bridge; what has been and what is to be are meeting there; and the bridge is breaking. But I have found you. You have come in time. You will take the inheritance that the base son refuses because of the tombs which the plough and harrow may not pass over or the gold-seeker disturb: you will take the sacred inheritance of the Jew."

When, finally, at his guardian's behest, he goes to Genoa to meet his mother, and learns from her own lips the truth of his birth—that he is a Jew—he is not only willing but eager to accept his destiny:

> "I consider it my duty—it is the impulse of my feeling—to identify myself, as far as possible, with my hereditary people, and if I can see any work to be done for them that I can give my soul and hand to I shall choose to do it."

There is now no obstacle to his proposing to Mirah; at the end of the novel, he and his bride are on their way to Israel. Mordecai has died, but Deronda will carry on his mission—the re-establishment of a homeland for his people. It is fascinating to find in this novel, published in 1876, an almost prophetic foreshadowing of the Zionist movement which was inaugurated twenty years later.

Though the Deronda–Mirah–Mordecai plot may seem incredible, viewed in retrospect, nevertheless George Eliot once more persuades the reader into suspending his disbelief. The character of Mirah is, perhaps, something of a stumbling-block, because she is so completely and wholly good, and she is not so vividly and compellingly realized as Dinah Morris. She is reminiscent of Caterina Sarti in "Mr. Gilfil's Love Story," in her ability to charm an audience with her beautiful voice, but she is more idealized than Caterina. It is impossible to imagine Mirah's being attracted by Captain Wybrow. George Eliot, however, gave her this special nobility of character simply because Mirah *is* a Jewess and is the embodiment of the author's special feeling about the Jewish people. There is a "lost princess" quality about her, too, and her presence in the novel creates the same kind of fairy-tale atmosphere so predominant in *Silas Marner*. We know positively, without question, that Mirah will find her brother, and that ultimately she will marry the man she loves. Although Mirah, with Deronda and Mordecai, lives and moves in a very real world, she also exists in a special dimension of her own, and her story is believable, as romance is believable, because it creates its own rules and standards of credibility.

And for all its "happy ever after" conclusion, implicit in this plot is the ever-present conviction that destiny cannot be thwarted, a conviction which gives the romance a strain of steel reality. The Princess Halm-Eberstein, Deronda's mother, truly a tragic figure, has not only forsaken her Jewish background but has also avoided her responsibilities as a mother because she believes that her magnificent voice sets her apart from the rules governing ordinary women's existence. Unlike Mirah, she has refused to accept the customs and the traditions of her people; now, slowly dying of cancer, she can no longer deny these ties of blood and heritage. She must see her son once more, even though she cannot acknowledge him before the world and dares admit to no one but him that she is a Jewess. She has allowed Sir Hugo Mallinger to adopt him so that he may escape the stigma of his people, but her well-intentioned attempt to alter his life has failed, for Deronda feels an innate kinship for the very people he has been taught to regard as wholly separate from himself. Once more George Eliot plays on the theme of illusion versus reality; Deronda, Mirah, and Mordecai all live with illusions, but because they have no illusions about themselves—they are not playing roles—they live in accordance with the best they know—they are given the grace of turning some of their dreams into reality. In contrast to them is the lonely, self-deluded princess, who must face the grief of having lost every illusion she possessed, and can do nothing but mourn the loss of her dreams.

The princess's fate is made more explicit in the lives of the characters in the second plot of *Daniel Deronda,* which can almost stand by itself as a remarkably modern story of a marriage doomed to failure because a husband and wife—Henleigh Grandcourt and Gwendolyn Harleth —are deliberately living lies. Of the two, Henleigh Grandcourt is the more contemptible, because there is not a single action in his entire life that has not been calculated toward a single end: the acquisition of power over other people. He wants to feel that his wife is "his to do as he liked with, and to make her feel it also." He is attracted by Gwendolyn Harleth because she is beautiful and high-spirited, and possessed of a fastidious disdain for the commonplace which wins his languid approval. She is the kind of girl who will be an asset as the wife of a man due to inherit a title and a considerable estate; she will wear the Grandcourt diamonds with elegance and grace. The fact that he is bound by his solemn word of honor to marry Lydia Glasher, who, some ten years previously, had left her husband to run away with him and has borne him four children, does not deter him for a moment, even though Lydia's husband has recently died and he could fulfill his promise. He arrogantly marries Gwendolyn, knowing that she is fully aware of Lydia's existence, and feeling the contempt for his bride—though he is far too clever to show it—that such men invariably feel for women they think have not followed the highest dictates of their consciences.

> He knew quite well that she had not married—had not overcome her repugnance to certain facts—out of love to him personally; he had won her by the rank and luxuries he had to give her, and these she had got: he had fulfilled his side of the contract.

As return payment, he dictates what she shall wear, her choice of friends, and her means of amusement, and gives voice to his cold jealousy of any courtesy that Daniel Deronda shows to her. That Gwendolyn becomes more and more frightened of him is, in his opinion, all to the good.

> . . . his soul was garrisoned against presentiments and fears: he had the courage and confidence that belong to domination, and he was at that moment feeling perfectly satisfied that he held his wife with bit and bridle. By the time they had been married a year, she would cease to be restive.

The implications in this revelation of Grandcourt's secret thoughts are all the more sinister because of the faultless mask he wears in public as the solicitous, if reticent, husband, and he knows he can depend on Gwendolyn's decency and good breeding to give no indication that she is, actually, terrified of his incredibly horrifying possessiveness.

> For their behaviour to each other scandalized no observer—not even the foreign maid warranted against seasickness; nor Grandcourt's own experienced valet; still less the picturesque crew, who regarded them as a model couple in high life. Their companionship consisted chiefly in well-bred silence. Grandcourt had no humorous observa-

tions at which Gwendolyn could refuse to smile, no chit-chat to make small occasions of dispute. He was perfectly polite in arranging an additional garment over her when needful, and in handing her any object that he perceived her to need, and she could not fall into the vulgarity of accepting or rejecting such politeness rudely . . . A lady was obliged to respond to these things suitably; and even if she had not shrunk from quarreling on other grounds, quarrelling with Grandcourt was impossible; she might as well have made angry sounds to a dangerous serpent coiled in her cabin without invitation. And what sort of dispute could a woman of any pride and dignity begin on a yacht?

Grandcourt had an intense satisfaction in leading his wife captive after this fashion: it gave their life on a small scale a royal representation and publicity in which everything familiar was got rid of, and everybody must do what was expected of them whatever may be their private protest—the protest (kept strictly private) adding to the piquancy of despotism.

George Eliot's brilliant insight into such a marriage may have been equaled, but surely never surpassed.

But the most remarkable character of *Daniel Deronda* —indeed, it might be said of all George Eliot's novels—is that of Gwendolyn Harleth, the author's example *par excellence* of how the immutable law of consequences operates to almost destroy a human being with the increasing corrosion of guilt and remorse. We see Gwendolyn first in a gambling room at a German watering place; the author was drawing on actual experience, here. In Homburg, in 1872, she had watched Byron's grandniece losing money at roulette; "it made me cry to see her fresh face among the hags and brutally stupid men around her." [12] Gwendolyn is the cynosure of all eyes, Daniel Deronda's among them, as she wins a huge amount and just as quickly loses it all. When friends commiserate with her, she says loftily that she cares only for the excitement of the play, that gambling is an antidote to her perpetual state of boredom. She looks upon herself as a "princess in exile," who will one day find her place in the world, and direct her destiny—and everyone else's—with a firm, graceful hand.

All this, however, is so much surface bravado. The reader quickly discovers that Gwendolyn Harleth is terrified about her future. Even as she stands at the roulette table, there is a letter in her purse from her mother, telling her that the family fortune has been lost in an unfortunate stock speculation and that she must come home at once. She has been gambling in hope of winning a large sum of money. When she loses, she secretly pawns her one good piece of jewelry, a turquoise necklace, to give her a starting stake. When it is mysteriously returned to her at the hotel, she guesses at once that Deronda— whom she does not know, but whom she has noticed watching her in the gambling room—has repurchased it, and she is so humiliated that she returns at once to England without trying her luck again. This episode serves to establish Gwendolyn Harleth as an individual always eager to make the grand gesture, and extremely sensitive to others' opinions. She is too proud to run the risk of meeting Deronda, lest she feel compelled to explain her reason for gambling to him; she refuses to explain her motives and would rather be completely misunderstood than, in her estimation, lower herself by confiding her difficulties to anyone.

Her pride in her ability to manage her life without advice or assistance leads to her tragic solution of a very real dilemma. Returning to England, she discovers that her mother has not exaggerated the situation in the slightest. They must leave Offendene, their lovely home, and live in a small, crowded cottage. Faced with the necessity of becoming a governess, Gwendolyn refuses to accept such a fate. She thinks first of going on the stage, but, assured by Herr Klemser, the music master, that she has no talent whatever, she turns to the second string on her bow. She knows that she has attracted Henleigh Grandcourt at the archery contest—that he had been on the verge of proposing to her before she went to Germany. She had left England almost in flight because she had met Lydia Glasher and her children, and had determined never to marry a man responsible for another woman's misery. Now, faced with poverty, and knowing that marriage to Grandcourt will ensure a comfortable life for her mother and sisters, as well as for herself, she accepts his suit.

The consequences of this action are soon brought home to her. Lydia Glasher sends her the Grandcourt diamonds, with a vindictive note prophesying that the wife of Grandcourt will be as miserable as the mistress. Gwendolyn, who had thought herself completely removed from any connection with Mrs. Glasher, because no one in their circle knows about that unhappy woman —or, at least, no one has mentioned her, which for Gwendolyn is the same thing—finds herself devoured by feelings of guilt. She, who had once prided herself on being able to manage Grandcourt to her satisfaction, now answers every flick of his rein. Guilt leads to self-hatred, which, inevitably, leads to intense loathing of her husband. To her increasing horror, she finds herself longing for Grandcourt's death:

And the intensest form of hatred is that rooted in fear, which compels to silence and drives vehemence into a constructive vindictiveness, an imaginary annihilation of the detested object, something like the hidden rites of vengeance with which the persecuted have made a dark vent for their rage, and soothed their sufferings into dumbness. Such hidden rites went on in the secrecy of Gwendolyn's mind, but not with soothing effect—rather with the effect of struggling terror. Side by side with the dread of her husband had grown the self-dread which urged her to flee from the pursuing images wrought up by her pent-up impulses . . . her vision of what she had to dread took more decidedly than ever the form of some fiercely impulsive deed, committed as in a dream that she would instantaneously wake from to find the effects real though the images had been false: to find death under her hands, but instead of darkness, daylight; instead of satisfied hatred, the dismay of guilt; instead of freedom, the palsy of a new terror—a white, dead face from which she was forever trying to flee and forever held back.

It is this dread that impels her to seek help from Daniel Deronda. Deronda, who has watched her gamble, finds her something less than admirable, and Gwendolyn, ever since that episode, has longed for his approval. For once in her life, she is driven to explain her actions, and he, recognizing that he can have misjudged her, urges her— as Savonarola does Romola—to interest herself in a world "beyond the small drama of personal desires."

> "The refuge you are needing from personal trouble is the higher, the religious life, which holds an enthusiasm for something more than our appetites and vanities. The few may find themselves in it simply by an elevation of feeling; but for those of us who have to struggle for our wisdom, the higher life must be a region in which the affections are clad with knowledge."

Gwendolyn's reply is tragic in its simplicity: "You said affection was the best thing, and I have hardly any—none about me." The admission is made. Gwendolyn Harleth is unable—has never learned—to really bestow love. And she is married to a man equally incapable of it. Like the couple in T. S. Eliot's "A Game of Chess," communication has ceased, as they silently, inexorably, continue to destroy each other.

But Gwendolyn is redeemable. Though she wishes for Grandcourt's death, she struggles desperately against that temptation. Like Caterina Sarti, she goes so far as to find a knife; she secretes it in a locked drawer of her dressing case, then throws it over the railing of the yacht into the sea. When her husband takes her for a sail in a little boat off the coast of Genoa, she does not want to go with him because she is afraid of what she may do. Her worst fears are realized: Grandcourt, while turning the sail to return to port, is suddenly struck by a heavy gust of wind and is swept overboard. "I did kill him in my thoughts," she admits brokenly to Deronda, when he is able to come to her.

> "I saw him sink and my heart gave a leap as if it were going out of me. I think I did not move. I kept my hands tight. It was long enough for me to be glad, and yet to think it was no use—he would come up again. And he *was* come—farther off—the boat had moved. It was all like lightning. "The rope!" he called out in a voice—not his own—I hear it now—and I stooped for the rope—I felt I must—I felt sure he could swim and he would come back whether or not and I dreaded him. That was in my mind—he would come back. But he was gone down again, and I had the rope in my hand—no, there he was again —his face above the water—and he cried again—and I held my hand, and my heart said, "Die!"—and he sank; and I felt "It is done—I am wicked—I am lost!"—and I had the rope in my hand—I don't know what I thought —I was leaping away from myself—I would have saved

him then. I was leaping from my crime and there it was —close to me as I fell—there was the dead face—dead, dead. It can never be altered. That was what happened. That was what I did. You know it all. It can never be altered."

"It can never be altered." Gwendolyn's despairing cry is one well known to the human heart. But George Eliot, by the time she came to write *Daniel Deronda,* had grown beyond the cold, inexorable inevitability of cause and effect that had been so deeply ingrained in her by Maria Lewis. Perhaps during her journey to Spain she had heard the proverb, "God writes straight with crooked lines," or perhaps she had absorbed some of Robert Browning's philosophy that good can arise out of the most sordid situation, if those involved in it wholeheartedly desire good. Gwendolyn does. "I believe that you may become worthier than you yet have been," Deronda tells her. "No evil dooms us hopelessly except the evil we love and desire to continue in, and make no effort to escape from." He assures her that her failure to throw the rope to Grandcourt was due to genuine momentary paralysis, rather than to any real desire to murder him, and that no matter how quickly she had moved, her husband would have drowned. He reminds her that she jumped into the water to try to save him. She does not believe him easily; at the end of the novel, she is still a prey to remorse born of guilt, and she is not convinced that she can alter her life in any way. But she is at least willing to try. As a beginning, she accepts the final humiliation that her husband had prepared for her, when his will reveals that he has made little provision for her and has left the bulk of his estate to his illegitimate son by Lydia Glasher. She returns to live at Offendene with her mother and sisters, to "piece back her life to that time when they first went there, and when everything was happiness about it, only she did not know it." Like all George Eliot heroines, Gwendolyn grows in stature under adversity, and the fact that her adversity is caused by herself—she could have chosen not to marry Grandcourt—makes her more fascinating. In some ways, Gwendolyn Harleth is more complex and interesting even than Dorothea Brooke; she is so totally unlike—so far as can be ascertained—anyone in her creator's experience, yet she is always vividly and humanly real.

Daniel Deronda was finished in June 1876, and the Leweses went abroad for the remainder of the summer. Upon their return to England in September, the search for a country house once more occupied them in earnest. Finally one was found—The Heights, Whitley, in Surrey. At last they had their longed-for retreat, where they could find healthful air, restful surroundings, and few distractions. (Visitors who came were enjoined to choose those days in the week when the London train brought in fresh fish!) Now the Leweses could happily enjoy quiet summers in expectation of gay London seasons, and that they took great pleasure in being celebrities while they were in London is undoubted. In May of 1877 they were invited to a dinner party to meet Queen Victoria's daughter, Princess Louise, and her Scots husband, the Marquis of Lorne, at the princess's special request. In November of that same year, Lewes's name was proposed among those being considered for the rectorship of St. Andrew's University in Glasgow. In February of 1878 they attended the marriage of Lionel Tennyson, the Laureate's younger son, to Eleanor Locker at Westminster Abbey. And in May 1878, the Leweses were presented to the Princess Royal and her husband, the Crown Prince of Germany. Marian described that eventful occasion to Mrs. Bray:

The royalties did themselves much credit. The Crown Prince is really a grand looking man, whose name you would ask for with expectation if you imagined him no royalty. He is like a grand antique bust—cordial and simple in manners withal, shaking hands and insisting that I should let him know when we next came to Berlin . . . *She* is less distinguished in physique, but equally good-natured and unpretending, liking best to talk of nursing soldiers and of what her Father's taste was in literature. She opened the talk by saying, "You knew my sister Louise . . ." [13]

But illness plagued them both, and Lewes, especially, was in very bad health. Rheumatic gout afflicted him periodically during 1877 and 1878, plus his usual head-aches, and what the doctors euphemistically called "stomach cramps." The summers at Whitley, with long walks and rest, helped to allieviate the chronic pain. He seemed as spirited and ebullient as ever, but, when they returned to The Priory in mid-November of 1878, he became alarmingly ill. He rallied on the twenty-first long enough to write to John Blackwood, telling him that *The Impressions of Theophrastus Such,* George Eliot's newest book, was on its way. Then he insisted on going into town to tend to some business, and caught a feverish cold.

From that moment on, he grew steadily worse. "Mr. Lewes continues sadly ill, and I am absorbed in nursing him," [14] Marian wrote to John Blackwood on the 25th of November. The doctors were determinedly hopeful, but his wife, who had cherished him in sickness and in health for twenty-four years, could not shake off a dreaded premonition— ". . . I have a deep sense of change within. . . ." [15]

George Henry Lewes died on the evening of November 30, 1878. He was buried in Highgate Cemetery on a bleak

December day, and Marian returned to The Priory alone. Her desk was abandoned; countless letters remained unanswered. Their son Charles was the only person she could see, and only for the most necessary business affairs that required her personal attention. Ordinarily, her Journal entry for New Year's Day was filled with thankgivings for past blessings and plans for the coming year; but the entry of January 1, 1879, was one brief, poignant line: "Here I and sorrow sit." [16]

XIX

Just as it is impossible to underestimate the influence of George Henry Lewes on George Eliot's life, so it is impossible to overestimate the depth of Marian's grief and loneliness during those first months of 1879. She had not only lost a devoted husband, who had completely reciprocated the love she gave him; Lewes had also been her critical guide and mentor, and, since genius always needs some outside force to keep its energies directed toward specific goals, it was he who had kept her "at the desk." He had been her shield against the annoyances and distractions and importunities which constantly presented themselves, and which, had she been required to deal with them herself, would have eaten into her time and energy, leaving less of both for the gifts that God gave her to use in other ways. And he had never been jealous of her success. On the contrary, his delighted, visible pride in her set the tone for others' reception of her work. The perfect rapport that had existed between them had been the secure anchor of her life for nearly a quarter-century. That she should feel more desolate than the average woman, having suffered such a loss, is quite understandable—if for no other reason than because she was not an average woman, and her marriage to Lewes had not been a "satisfactory relationship."

Nor could she emulate her sovereign and, like Queen Victoria following the Prince Consort's death, retire completely from the world. Though she desperately desired solitude, there was still work that she had to do. She wanted to do "certain things for his sake," [1] as she wrote John Cross on January 30th. First and foremost was the revision of Volume V of her husband's *Problems of the Life and Mind*, containing a tremendously complicated section on "Mind as a Function of the Organism." That she was able to bring *her* mind to concentrate on it at all at such a time is indicative not only of her dedication, but also of her complete understanding of what Lewes would have wished. Then, there was her own book, *The Impressions of Theophrastus Such*, scheduled for publication in the spring. This work, a collection of essays purportedly written by a Mr. Such, containing his observations on the general state of the world, was one which Lewes had enthusiastically urged her to write. Like *The Spanish Gypsy*, another of Lewes's enthusiasms, it is a disappointment. Actually, it is a return to the kind of writing found in "Poetry and Prose from the Notebook of an Eccentric"; but Theophrastus Such lacks the eccentric's humor and lightness of touch. Marian did not like the book when she had finished it, and proposed to suppress it completely.[2] Usually, authors are not the best judges of their own work, but, in this instance, George Eliot's opinion should probably have been heeded. *Theophrastus Such* is well written, but adds nothing to its author's reputation.

Gradually, however, her self-imposed isolation and seclusion began to tell upon her; and, knowing that her husband would never have wished her to become a recluse, she began to see a few very close friends. John Walter Cross was one of the first to call at The Priory— he came in a dual capacity, as Marian's "dearest nephew" and as her financial adviser, for Lewes had trusted him with all their investments. Mrs. Congreave and Mrs. Burne-Jones also came in March. Another caller was Henry Sidgewick, one of Lewes's friends, whom Marian wished to consult about setting up a scholarship at Cambridge in her husband's memory. By late spring, she had regained sufficient strength and serenity of spirit to take charge once more of her personal correspondence and to attempt to cope with her business affairs.

The latter, however, caused her considerable travail and weariness of spirit. Taxes were an unfathomable mystery that Lewes had always handled, without so much as a word to her. Then, there were the charities. Marian had always given generously to charity, but there were certain personal concerns about which the rest of the world knew nothing. Chief among them was—still— Agnes Lewes, and she had begun sending money to Agnes's children by Thornton Hunt after Hunt's death in 1873. Lewes's nephew, Vivian, also began to importune her for assistance; Bertie's wife, Eliza, came from Natal, fleeing with her two children from an impending Kaffir invasion, and she was almost totally dependent on her mother-in-law. Marian also sent gifts to her own nieces and nephews—her brother's and sister's children, and a regular sum to her old teacher, Maria Lewis, who was living in straitened circumstances at Leamington. Charles' children (Marian's and Lewes's grandchildren) were also recipients of her generosity. And, then, there were the friends who wanted to borrow money, always for the best of causes, whom Marian found very difficult to refuse. Though she had a remarkable business sense, she was feminine enough to be susceptible to a plea for help, and she knew perfectly well that, like most women, she could not always distinguish between the genuine need and the random demand. She did not want to be mean-spirited, but neither did she want to be weakly indulgent.

In this respect, she had to admit that she indeed was not fit to stand alone. Lewes had always taken care of these matters, and she shrank from revealing them—especially the question of Agnes's income—to an outsider. It would have been logical for her to have put all these financial concerns into Charles Lewes's hands, but she had to admit in all honesty that, dear as Charles was to her, he was not at his best when coping with a bank balance. So she finally turned to the one friend in her immediate circle who could be depended on for honest, sensible, sound advice, and whose friendship for both Lewes and herself would make him discreet—John Walter Cross. On April 22, 1879, she wrote to him; "I am in dreadful need of your counsel. Please come to me when you can—morning, afternoon, or evening." [3] He came to The Priory the next evening, and, to quote his own words, "From this time forward I saw George Eliot constantly." [4]

When Marian Evans Lewes and John Walter Cross were married at St. George's, Hanover Square, on May 6, 1880, her family and friends were as astounded as they had been when she had gone to Germany with Lewes in 1854. Most of them knew, and liked, Cross; he was a very personable man, a graduate of Rugby, who had entered his family's firm of Deniston, Cross and Company, and had been for a short time in charge of the New York office. Returning to England in 1869, he had almost immediately risen to the highest position in the London office; it was in that same year that he had met Marian for the first time in Rome. That August, the Leweses had come to the Cross home at Weybridge for lunch, and "A day did the work of years." [5] The Leweses also spent several Christmases at Weybridge, and when they bought The Heights, "nephew Johnnie" had been a frequent visitor, as well as being a "Priory regular" in London. In 1879, when he received Marian's urgent summons, he was nearly forty years old and possessed of a maturity and a stability that a man half again his age might have envied. He, too, had known tragedy and grave responsibility; he had been head of the Cross household since his father's death, and he had lost his mother a few weeks after Lewes died. So there was an immediate and unusual bond of sympathy between Marian and himself, that overcame completely the gap in their ages.

The transition in Marian's letters from "nephew Johnnie" to "Best loved and loving one" [6] came swiftly between April and October of 1879. Marian herself admitted at the time of her marriage that she was doing "what not very long ago I should myself have pronounced impossible for me." [7] But in John Cross she found not only the same kind of devoted affection that Lewes had given her, but also an amazingly similar meeting of minds. Their courtship began when they started reading Dante together in the original and discussing philosophy. In May, Cross finally persuaded her to open the piano again and play for him. He came to see her once or twice a week while she was at The Heights during the summer; when she returned to The Priory in the autumn, they saw each other constantly. It was Cross to whom she turned for comfort when her beloved editor, John Blackwood, died suddenly on October 29th. It is interesting to speculate whether she would have considered marriage—despite her acknowledgment of affection —to a man twenty years her junior, had not this one more link with the past been severed, though it must be remembered that in 1880 a man nearing forty was considered a full-grown man, old enough to cope with the world. In January and February they were seen frequently together in public, at art exhibits and concerts, and in March, his sisters—Eleanor, Mary, and Florence —invited Marian to Weybridge for a short visit. Back in London on the 9th of April, Marian recorded in her Journal, "My marriage decided." [8] Her own feelings about this momentous decision are best conveyed in her letter to Eleanor Cross: ". . . I cherish the thought that the family life will be the richer and not the poorer, through your brother's great gift of love to me." [9]

That she and John Cross truly loved each other cannot be doubted, but she was well aware that there would be criticism. Letters had to be written, explaining what to many seemed inexplicable—that she could consider marrying anyone after the perfect happiness she had known with Lewes. Some individuals even remarked maliciously that for her to marry at this late date represented a belated, rather indecent, bid for respectability. Her Positivist friends, the Congreaves and Frederic Harrison, were disturbed at first because Positivism forbade second marriages, but they also agreed that they wanted Marian to be happy, and sincerely wished her well. As for her very close friends, they were wholehearted in their joy for her, as was Cross's immediate family, and, most surprising of all, as was Charles Lewes, who affectionately and approvingly gave her in marriage. As for Marian, she seems to have been more than a little dazed. Chided by one old friend for not having notified her until after the event, she wrote quite honestly,

> Do not reproach me for not telling you of my marriage beforehand. It is difficult to speak of what surprises ourselves, and the decision was sudden, though not the friendship which led to the decision.[10]

None of them, however, seemed to realize the terrible loneliness such a perfect union would, of course, assuage as well. In one household, however, there was unequivocal approval, and perhaps there was understanding there. It was Isaac Evans who took pen in hand:

> My dear Sister,
>   I have much pleasure in availing myself of the present opportunity to break the long silence which has existed between us, by offering our united and sincere congratulations to you and Mr. Cross, upon the happy event . . . My wife joins me in sincerely hoping that it will afford you much happiness and comfort. She and the younger branches unite with me in kind love and every good wish. Believe me
>
> > Your affectionate brother,
> > Isaac P. Evans.[11]

A rather "Isaac-ish" letter, but Marian responded to it with her customary generosity: ". . . it was a great joy for me to have your kind words . . . for our long silence has never broken the affection for you which began when we were little ones." [12] Her joy at that moment must have been profound.

The wedding journey to Italy was delightful. Cross noted later that he had never seen Marian in better health, that she was able to walk for hours without the slightest fatigue, and did not even succumb to the digestive complaint which was rampant in Venice, though he himself did. When they returned to England at the end of July, they went to The Heights for a few weeks, then to Lincolnshire and Cambridge to visit Cross's two married sisters, who welcomed the bride and groom with open arms. Repairs and decorating of the very beautiful house which Cross had purchased for them at 4 Cheyne Walk in London were not yet complete, so they returned to The Heights after the family visits, to wait with great impatience and anticipation. They were eager to be settled in London, not only because it was difficult for Cross to commute to his office, but also because there were so many friends they wanted to see, and so many interesting plays and concerts to attend. They were also happily planning for receptions, dinners, and musicales at 4 Cheyne Walk.

Then, without warning, late in September, Marian succumbed to the most severe renal disorder she had yet experienced. On September 29th, there being some improvement, her anxious husband took her to Brighton for a week, but the sea air did not have its usual effect. On the 17th of October, she suffered an even worse attack, and only opiates could deaden the pain. For several weeks she was desperately ill; then, gradually, her strong constitution reasserted itself and her strength began to return. Fortunately it was a cool, clear autumn, with good weather far into November, so that she could take the walks and drives which the doctor prescribed for her, on which she was dependent for her good health. She was well enough on November 22nd, her birthday, to help with packing the book boxes.

On December 4th, they moved into 4 Cheyne Walk, where they very quickly settled into London's quickened pace as the city approached the Christmas season. Concerts, plays, paying and receiving visits, plus getting the house completely in order and putting on the finishing touches filled Marian's happy letters to family and friends. On December 18th, the Crosses attended the regular Saturday afternoon Pop Concert at St. James's Hall. It was a very cold day, and Marian was wearing her fur cloak. But the hall was overheated, so she let the cloak slip off her shoulders over the back of her chair, despite her husband's warning that there was a nasty draft and that she was sensitive to drafts. The next morning she did have a scratchy throat, but she came down to breakfast as usual, and in the afternoon saw several visitors, among them Herbert Spencer. On Monday morning, her throat was sore enough for her to be willing to see a doctor, but her temperature and pulse were normal, so there seemed to be no cause for alarm. By Wednesday, December 22nd, however, there was a sudden change for the worse. As the doctors were examining her, she whispered to her husband, "Tell them I have a great pain in my left side." [13] Immediately after saying this, she slipped into unconsciousness and never revived. Her illness during the autumn had weakened her powers of resistance more severely than had been realized, and the sore throat, doubtless due to a streptococcic infection more virulent than the current state of medical knowledge could diagnose, had affected her heart.

Marian Evans Cross, "George Eliot," was buried beside George Henry Lewes in Highgate Cemetery on December, 29, 1880. Despite the snow and sleet, the chapel was crowded to hear Dr. Saddler, minister of the Unitarian Church of Hampstead, give the brief eulogy. Robert Browning, Thomas H. Huxley, and Leslie Stephen were among those present; William Blackwood, nephew of George Eliot's editor, came down from Edinburgh. And standing beside the grief-stricken John Cross was the equally grieved Isaac Evans. As the procession emerged from the chapel, it was joined by hundreds of other people, some of whom had waited patiently for over an hour; and many of them carried flowers—the bright colors lightening the somberness of the day—in tribute to the great author, but, even more, to the great woman whom they loved, even though they had never known her.

For, despite the fact that her own age definitely recognized her as a writer of genius, it was George Eliot's essential womanliness that especially appealed to nineteenth-century readers and critics. In the weeks and months that followed, commemorations in the major magazines and periodicals without exception stressed this quality. For example, *Blackwood's Magazine* for February 1881:

Not merely a great writer, but a great woman has passed away. In addition to the spell which bound the world to her genius, she had a personal power of drawing to herself in ties of sympathy and kindly feeling all who came under her influence.

314

or the same issue of *Cornhill:*

> . . . however we may differ from George Eliot's teaching
> on many points, we feel her to be one who, in the midst
> of great perplexities, has brought great intellectual powers
> to setting before us a lofty moral ideal, and, in spite of
> manifest shortcomings, has shown certain aspects of a
> vanishing social phase with a power and delicacy unsur-
> passed in her own sphere.

These tributes, however, genuine as they are, were written
in and for an age when for a woman to write at all was
remarkable, and rather miss the mark. George Eliot did
not consider herself a "woman writer," or a "literary
lady," or, worst of all terms, an "authoress." She was an
author, a professional, and she wished her work to be
judged by the highest possible standards. That adverse
criticism had a depressing effect on her is merely one of
those interesting paradoxes of feminine human nature;
there is not the slightest indication in her letters, Journal,
or recorded conversation that she demanded any special
indulgence because she was, first, a woman. Quite the
contrary, as her deliberate choice of a masculine pseudonym proved.

It is by the highest critical standards of the twentieth
century that she would wish her work to be judged as well;
and it must be admitted that her books, for the most part,
have stood well the test of time. There was a period when
she shared the common opprobrium of all Victorian writers, because, in the eyes of rather shallow critics, all Victorians lacked realism; and her stern statement, "The art
which leaves the soul in despair is laming to the soul and
is denounced by the healthy sentiment of an active community," [14] fell on deaf ears, if it was heard at all. But
recently she has once more come into her own. Certainly

Adam Bede and *Middlemarch* give her a secure claim to greatness, though critical opinion which seeks to dismiss all the rest of her work with a shrug does so at its own intellectual and critical risk. She cannot be read in bits and pieces. Her vision was of life in its entirety, and it is this entirety that she tried to present in every book she wrote. But one of the fascinations in reading her novels is to watch the growth of her own thought, the increased depth of her perception, and the ever-widening boundaries of her vision of life. It was her firm belief

> . . . that life on earth is being shaped
> To glorious ends, that order, justice, love
> Mean man's completeness. . . .
>   ("A Minor Prophet")

and John Cross once said of her, "It was often in her mind and on her lips that the only worthy end of all learning, of all science, of all life, in fact, is, that human beings should love one another better." [15]

It was in this spirit that her books were written, with the fervent hope that the knowledge, experience, understanding, and whatever wisdom she had gained, might be a source of comfort and help to those who read them. It was in this way that she strove to fulfill her own ardent wish—

> Oh, may I join the choir invisible
> Of those immortal dead who live again
> In minds made better by their presences: live
> In pulses stirred to generosity,
> In deeds of daring rectitude, in scorn
> For miserable aims that end with self,
> In thoughts sublime that pierce the night like stars,
> And with their mild persistence urge man's search
> To vaster issues. . . .

                              May I reach
        That purest heaven, be to other souls
        The cup of strength in some great agony,
        Enkindle generous ardor, good pure love,
        Beget the smiles that have no cruelty—
        Be the sweet presence of a good diffused,
        And in diffusion ever more intense.
        So shall I join the choir invisible
        Whose music is the gladness of the world.

No one who knew George Eliot doubted for a moment
that her wish was granted. No one today who reads her
novels can doubt that their conviction was justified.

REFERENCES

CHAPTER 1:

1. Cross, 7.
2. *Middlemarch,* Chapter LVII.
3. Cross, 294.
4. Letters, I, 41.

CHAPTER 2:

1. "Janet's Repentance," Chapter II.
2. *Ibid.*
3. *Ibid.*
4. Letters, VII, 324.
5. Cross, 80.
6. Cf. John Bennett, *Letters to a Young Lady,* Philadelphia: Grigg, Elliot & Co., 1849, Title Page.
7. Cross, 13.

CHAPTER 3:

1. Letters, I, 47.
2. Cross, 21.
3. *Ibid.,* 24.
4. Letters, I, 31–2.
5. Cross, 24.
6. *Ibid.,* 20.
7. *Ibid.*
8. Letters, I, 7.
9. Cross, 20.
10. *Ibid.,* 27.

11. *Ibid.*, 28.
12. *Ibid.*, 30.
13. *Ibid.*, 31.
14. Letters, I, 46–47.
15. Cross, 33.
16. *Ibid.*
17. Letters, I, 51.
18. Cross, 34.
19. *Ibid.*, 41.
20. Letters, I, 83.

CHAPTER 4:

1. Letters, I, 93.
2. Deakin, 53.
3. Cross, 529.
4. Quoted in Deakin, 53.
5. Cross, 44–45.
6. *Ibid.*, 52.
7. Letters, I, 54.
8. Cross, 62.
9. *Ibid.*, 53–54.
10. *Ibid.*, 54.
11. *Ibid.*
12. *Ibid.*, 56.
13. *The Mill on the Floss,* Book V, Chapter 3.
14. Cross, 531.
15. *Ibid.*
16. *Ibid.*, 55.
17. Letters, I, 128.
18. *Ibid.*
19. Cf. Letters, I, 129.
20. Cf. *ibid.*, 132.
21. *Ibid.*, 137.
22. Cross, 56.
23. *Ibid.*, 52.
24. Letters, I.

CHAPTER 5:

1. Cf. Letters, I, 156.
2. *Ibid.*, 165.
3. Quoted in Walter Ernest Allen, *George Eliot,* New York: Macmillan, 1964, p. 47.
4. Letters, I, 225.
5. Quoted in Allen, 48.
6. Cf. Edward Zeller, David Friedrich Strauss in his life and writings, London: Smith Elder, 1874, Vol. I, pp. 1–2.
7. *Ibid.*, Vol. II, 437.
8. Cross, 63.
9. The fund for publication was raised under the aegis of Joseph Parkes, one of the most vocal Radicals of the day, and a fervent supporter of the Reform Bill of 1832. His daughter, Bessie, later became one of Mary Ann's best friends, and their warm relationship continued even after Mary Ann's "elopement" with Lewes. Bessie Parkes married Louis Belloc in 1867; one of her children was the essayist and poet Hilaire Belloc, and her daughter was known to literature as Mrs. Belloc Lowndes.
10. Cross, 65.
11. Letters, I, 179.
12. Allen, 45.
13. Cross, 64–65.
14. *Ibid.*, 66.
15. Letters, I, 184.
16. *Ibid.*, 185–186.
17. *Ibid.*, 189.
18. Cross, 66.
19. Letters, I, 194.
20. Cross, 68.
21. *Ibid.*, 70.
22. *Ibid.*, 76.
23. *Early Essays by George Eliot,* Westminster Press, 1919 (privately printed), p. 44.
24. *Ibid.*, 45.
25. *Ibid.*
26. *Ibid.*, 47.
27. *Ibid.*, 48.
28. Cross, 83.
29. Cf. Letters, I, 272.
30. Emerson's comment is interesting about her, especially considering the circumstances. He said, "That young lady has a calm, clear spirit." Deakin, 56.

31. Cross, 98.
32. *Ibid.*, 103.
33. Letters, I, 233–234.
34. Cross, 104.

CHAPTER 6:

1. Cross, 91.
2. Letters, I, 254.
3. *Ibid.*, 291.
4. Cross, 106.
5. *Ibid.*
6. *Ibid.*, 107.
7. *Ibid.*
8. *Ibid.*, 110.
9. *Ibid.*
10. Letters, I, 301.
11. Cross, 119.
12. Letters, I, 321.
13. Cross, 117.
14. *Ibid.*, 122.
15. *Ibid.*
16. *Ibid.*, 120.
17. *Ibid.*, 125–126.
18. Letters, I, 334.
19. *Ibid.*, 335.
20. *Ibid.*, 336.

CHAPTER 7:

1. Cf. *George Eliot and John Chapman*, 16.
2. *Ibid.*, 21.
3. *Ibid.*, 22.
4. Letters, I, 348.
5. *Ibid.*, 349.
6. *George Eliot and John Chapman*, 172.
7. Cross, 132.
8. Letters, I, 364.
9. *Ibid.*, 367.
10. Cross, 133.
11. Cf. Herbert Spencer, *An Autobiography*, New York: Appleton, 1904, p. 550.
12. Cross, 141.
13. Letters, II, 22.
14. *Ibid.*, 130–133.
15. *Ibid.*, 97.

16. *Ibid.*, 75.
17. Cross, 153.
18. Quoted in *George Eliot and John Chapman*, 67.
19. Cross, 157.

CHAPTER 8:

1. Dr. Burney was the grandson of Samuel Johnson's famous friend.
2. *George Lewes and George Eliot*, 10.
3. Deakin, 89.
4. *George Lewes and George Eliot*, 42.
5. *Ibid.*, 99.
6. *Ibid.*, 102.
7. *Ibid.*, 106.
8. *Ibid.*, 111.
9. *Ibid.*, 122–123.
10. Letters, I, lxix.
11. Cross, 164.
12. *Ibid.*
13. *Ibid.*, 165.
14. *Ibid.*, 166.

CHAPTER 9:

1. Letters, II, 169.
2. *Ibid.*, 171.
3. *Ibid.*, 173.
4. "Three months in Weimar," *Fraser's Magazine*, LI (June 1855).
5. *Ibid.*
6. Letters, II, 171.
7. Cross, 177.
8. *Ibid.*, 175.
9. *Ibid.*, 172.
10. "Liszt, Wagner, and Weimar," *Fraser's Magazine*, LII (July 1855).
11. *Ibid.*, 104.
12. Letters, II, 176.
13. *Ibid.*, 178–179.
14. *Ibid.*, 179.
15. *Ibid.*
16. *Ibid.*, 181.

17. *Ibid.*, 182.
18. *Ibid.*, 186.
19. Cross, 167.
20. Letters, II, 214.
21. *Ibid.*, 232.
22. *Ibid.*, 241.
23. Cross, 207.
24. *Ibid.*, 211.
25. "Silly Novels by Lady Novelists," *Westminster Review*, LXVI (October 1856).
26. Cross, 211.
27. *Ibid.*
28. *Ibid.*, 212.
29. Cross, 212.
30. *Ibid.*, 213.

CHAPTER 10:

1. Cf. Letters, III, 58.
2. Blind, 163.
3. Cross, 214.
4. *Ibid.*, 218.
5. *Ibid.*, 219.
6. Letters, II, 294–295.
7. *Ibid.*, 297.
8. Cross, 220.
9. *Ibid.*
10. Letters, II, 301.
11. *Ibid.*, 354.
12. *Ibid.*, 355.
13. Cross, 223.
14. *Ibid.*, 228.
15. Letters, II, 344.
16. Cross, 233.
17. Letters, II, 375.
18. Cross, 235.
19. *Ibid.*, 234.
20. *Ibid.*, 236.
21. Letters, II, 387.
22. Cross, 237.
23. *Ibid.*, 239.

CHAPTER 11:

1. Cross, 297.
2. *Ibid.*, 281.
3. *Ibid.*, 252.

4. *Ibid.*, 249
5. *Ibid.*, 254.
6. Letters, II, 449.
7. *Ibid.*, 450.
8. Cross, 281.
9. *Ibid.*, 282.
10. *Ibid.*
11. April 12, 1859.
12. Cross, 295.
13. *Ibid.*
14. Blind, 155.
15. Cf. Letters, III, 98.
16. Cross, 296.
17. *Ibid.*, 284.
18. *Ibid.*, 286.

CHAPTER 12:

1. Cross, 288.
2. Letters, III, 19.
3. Cross, 292–293.
4. *Ibid.*, 293.
5. *Ibid.*, 295.
6. *Ibid.*, 298.
7. Letters, III, 41.
8. *Ibid.*, 67.
9. *Ibid.*, 74.
10. Cf. *ibid.*, 13.
11. *Ibid.*, 56.
12. Koko's Song, Act I, *The Mikado.*
13. Letters, II, 506.
14. Cross, 301.
15. *Ibid.*, 296.
16. *Ibid.*
17. *Ibid.*, 297.
18. Letters, III, 66.
19. Cf. *ibid.*, 73.
20. *Ibid.*, 75.
21. *Ibid.*, 78.
22. Cross, 313.
23. Letters, III, 87.
24. Cross, 304.
25. Cf. Letters, III, 93.
26. *Ibid.*, 101–102.
27. *Ibid.*, 106.
28. July 2, 1859.
29. Cross, 298.
30. Cf. Blanch Colton Williams,

George Eliot, New York: Macmillan, 1936, pp. 165ff.
31. Cross, 76.
32. *Ibid.*, 398.
33. Cf. Letters, III, 269.
34. Cross, 385.
35. *Ibid.*, 309.
36. Letters, III, 304.
37. *Ibid.*, 221.
38. *Ibid.*, 277.
39. Cross, 330.

CHAPTER 13:

1. Cross, 236.
2. Letters, III, 284.
3. Cross, 351.
4. Cf. Letters, III, 284.
5. Cross, 345.
6. *Ibid.*
7. *Ibid.*, 348.
8. *Ibid.*, 344.
9. *Ibid.*
10. *Ibid.*, 347.
11. *Ibid.*, 348.
12. *Ibid.*, 351.
13. Letters, III, 285.
14. Cross, 353.
15. *Ibid.*, 358.
16. *Ibid.*, 355.
17. *Ibid.*
18. Cf. Letters, III, 291.
19. Cross, 368.
20. *Ibid.*, 369.
21. *Ibid.*, 370.
22. *Ibid.*, 371–372.
23. *Ibid.*, 375.
24. *Ibid.*, 327.
25. Letters, III, 304.
26. *Ibid.*, 301.
27. Cross, 386.
28. Letters, III, 332.
29. *Ibid.*, 327.
30. *Ibid.*
31. Cross, 394.
32. Letters, III, 340.
33. Cross, 394.
34. *Ibid.*
35. *Ibid.*, 401.

36. *Ibid.*, 397.
37. Letters, III, 380.
38. Cross, 401.

CHAPTER 14:

1. Cross, 407.
2. *Ibid.*, 426.
3. *Ibid.*, 407.
4. Letters, III, 424.
5. Cf. *Ibid.*
6. Cross, 409.
7. *Ibid.*, 411.
8. *Ibid.*, 412.
9. *Ibid.*
10. Letters, III, 446.
11. *Ibid.*, 452.
12. Cross, 414.
13. *Ibid.*, 415.
14. *Ibid.*, 416.
15. *Ibid.*
16. *Ibid.*, 416.
17. *Ibid.*
18. *Ibid.*, 418.
19. *Ibid.*, 420.
20. *Ibid.*, 422.
21. *Ibid.*, 424.
22. *Ibid.*, 425.
23. Letters, IV, 38.
24. Cross, 435.
25. Letters, III, 474.
26. *Ibid.*, 327.
27. Cross, 441.
28. Letters, IV, 103.
29. Cf. *Ibid.*
30. Cross, 435.
31. *Ibid.*, 440.
32. *Ibid.*, 440–441.
33. *Spectator*, July 18, 1863.
34. Cf. Henry James, *Partial Portraits*, London: Macmillan, 1894, p. 55.

CHAPTER 15:

1. Letters, IV, 117.
2. Cross, 444.
3. *Ibid.*, 442.
4. Letters, IV, 117.

5. Cf. *Ibid.*, 112.
6. Cross, 444.
7. *Ibid.*
8. Cf. Letters, IV, 113.
9. Cross, 452.
10. Letters, IV, 154.
11. *Ibid.*
12. Cross, 458.
13. *Ibid.*, 454.
14. Letters, IV, 168.
15. Cross, 459.
16. *Ibid.*
17. *Ibid.*, 460–461.
18. *Ibid.*, 461.
19. Letters, IV, 247.
20. Cross, 475–476.
21. *Ibid.*
22. *Ibid.*, 469.
23. *Ibid.*, 477.
24. *Ibid.*
25. *Ibid.*
26. Letters, IV, 240.
27. *Ibid.*

CHAPTER 16:

1. Cross, 479.
2. Letters, IV, 291.
3. Cross, 481.
4. *Ibid.*
5. Letters, IV, 286.
6. *Ibid.*
7. Basil Willey, *Nineteenth Century Studies*, Harper Torchback, 1966, p. 195.
8. *Ibid.*
9. Cross, 483.
10. *Ibid.*
11. *Ibid.*
12. *Ibid.*
13. *Ibid.*, 482.
14. Willey, 201.
15. Cf. Letters, V, 37.
16. Cf. *Ibid.*, VII, 390.
17. *Spectator*, June 6, 1868.
18. Cross, 514.
19. Cf. Letters, IV, 95.
20. Cross, 489.
21. *Ibid.*

22. Cf. Letters, IV, 96.
23. *Ibid.*, 348.
24. Cross, 496.
25. Letters, IV, 386.
26. Cross, 508.
27. *Ibid.*, 511.
28. *Ibid.*, 510.
29. *Ibid.*, 523.
30. Cross, II, 1.
31. *Ibid.*

CHAPTER 17:

1. F. R. Leavis, *The Great Tradition*, Garden City: Doubleday, 1954, p. 80.
2. Cf. Virginia Woolf, *The Common Reader*, New York: Harcourt Brace, 1925, p. 237.
3. Cf. Henry James, "The Novel in *The Ring & the Book*," *Notes on Novelists*, New York: Scribners, 1914, p. 385.
4. Cross, II, 13.
5. *Ibid.*, 27.
6. *Ibid.*, 1.
7. *Ibid.*, 4.
8. Cf. Letters, V, 51.
9. *Ibid.*, 56.
10. *Ibid.*, 57.
11. Cross, II, 14.
12. Letters, V, 81.
13. Cf. *Ibid.*, 83.
14. Cross, II, 18.
15. Letters, V, 101.
16. Cross, II, 20.
17. Letters, V, 118.
18. Cross, II, 29.
19. Letters, V, 168.
20. Cross, II, 29.
21. *Ibid.*, 48.
22. Letters, V, 282.
23. Cf. *Ibid.*, 239.
24. *Ibid.*, 169.
25. Cross, II, 58.

CHAPTER 18:

1. Letters, V, 388.
2. *Ibid.*, VI, 199.

3. *Ibid.*, 388.
4. *Ibid.*, 359.
5. *Ibid.*, 425.
6. Cross, II, 83.
7. *Ibid.*, 85–86.
8. Letters, VI, 11.
9. Cross, II, 109.
10. *Ibid.*, 125.
11. Cf. Letters, VI, 162.
12. Cross, II, 55.
13. *Ibid.*, 143.
14. *Ibid.*, 151.
15. Letters, VII, 84.
16. Cross, II, 153.

CHAPTER 19:

1. Cross, II, 154.
2. *Ibid.*, 157.
3. *Ibid.*, 160.
4. *Ibid.*
5. *Ibid.*, 12.
6. Letters, VII, 211.
7. Cross, II, 179.
8. Letters, VII, 258.
9. Cross, II, 177.
10. *Ibid.*, 189.
11. Letters, VII, 28.
12. Cross, II, 182.
13. *Ibid.*, 203.
14. *Ibid.*, I, 511.
15. *Ibid.*, II, 198.

BIBLIOGRAPHY

MAIN SOURCES

Cross, John Walter: *George Eliot's Life, as Related in Her Letters and Journals*. New York: Crowell, n.d. 2 volumes in 1.

The George Eliot Letters, edited by Gordon S. Haight. New Haven: Yale University Press, 1954–1955. (Letters)

Haight, Gordon S.: *George Eliot and John Chapman*. New Haven: Yale University Press, 1940.

Kitchel, Anna T.: *George Lewes and George Eliot*. New York: John Day, 1933.

Early Essays of George Eliot, Westminster Press, 1919. (privately printed)

SECONDARY SOURCES

Allen, Walter Ernest: *George Eliot*. New York: Macmillan, 1964.

Blind, Mathilde: *George Eliot*. Boston: Roberts Brothers, 1883.

Deakin, Mary H.: *The Early Life of George Eliot*. Manchester: University Press, 1913.

INDEX

333

ROSEMARY SPRAGUE, whose highly acclaimed *Red Lion and Gold Dragon: A Novel of the Norman Conquest* was published in 1966 by Chilton Book Company, was born in New York. She moved to Cleveland when she was about a year old. She admits that she was not overly fond of school. Her parents were aware of this, although they never let her know that they knew until she was in college. She learned to read before she entered the first grade, a discovery which surprised her father and mother as greatly as it annoyed the teacher!

With Cornelia Otis Skinner, she feels she shares the honor of being the most innocent freshman ever to enter Bryn Mawr College. There, she majored in English, took all the languages and history she could, and was an active member of the Dramatic Society, choir, and glee club.

Following her graduation from Bryn Mawr, she spent a year in New York studying acting with the late Frances Robinson-Duff. Then she entered graduate school at Western Reserve University, where she took her M.A., and was a Fellow-in-English during her last two years' work on her Ph.D. Since receiving her doctorate, she studied at the Shakespeare Institute at Stratford-on-Avon, England, and the University of London. She has been a delegate to the Conference on English Literature at Oxford University in England and to the Conférence sur des Auteurs Français at Brussels. She was also a member of the first School of Letters (New Criticism) at Kenyon College.

In 1962 she attended the Shakespeare Seminar at Stratford, Ontario, and delivered a lecture there on "The Men Who Were Not Shakespeare." She has also lectured extensively on children's literature; on Robert Browning; and on Queen Elizabeth I at the Thomas More Institute of the University of Montreal.

She has taught at Western Reserve University; Fenn College, Cleveland, Ohio; The Cleveland Institute of Art; and was director of dramatics at Notre Dame College, South Euclid, Ohio, where she staged the North American premiere of Paul Claudel's *The Satin Slipper*. She is now professor of English at Longwood College, Farmville, Virginia, the oldest women's college in the United States, where she teaches her two specialities, the Victorians and Chaucer. In her spare time, she plays the piano, experiments with gourmet cooking, continues to read incessantly, and goes to the theater.

Miss Sprague has carved a distinguished career for herself as the author of many historical novels for young adults. *Northward to Albion* was the first and was followed by *A Kingdom to Win,* and *Heroes of the White Shield. Heir of Kiloran* grew out of her love of the theater and the *commedia del' arte,* in addition to her fascination with the outcome of the intrigues surrounding Mary Stuart. It was named one of the 100 Best Books of 1956 by *The New York Times Book Review.* This was followed by such books as *Conquerors of Time, Dance for a Diamond Star*—concerning Maria de Camargo, the eighteenth-century ballerina—and *The Jade Pagoda,* set in Salem, Massachusetts, in the days of the China trade. In 1965, Chilton published her biography of Browning: *Forever in Joy: The Life of Robert Browning.*

Rosemary Sprague has recently edited *Poems of Robert Browning.*

Date Due